Game Warden

Centurion

1879 - 1979 +

Game Wardens break trail for future protectors of the outdoors, encouraging them to; as Ernie Swift would say "float their own stick".

Jim Chizek

Flambeau River
Publishing

Front Cover

This picture appeared on the cover of "THIS WEEK" magazine and in many newspapers around the country in 1938. It was used as the cover of the "WISCONSIN NATURAL RESOURCES" magazine to commemorate 100 years of warden service in 1979.

Painter J.F. KERNAN of New York used as his model Charles Lawrence stationed at Phillips, Wisconsin. Chuck later became chief of the U.S. Fish and Wildlife Service.

Copyright © 1992
Flambeau River Publishing
W10298 Wells Road
Lodi, Wisconsin 53555

First Printing — December 1992
Second Printing — April 1993
Third Printing — October 1994
Fourth Printing — June 1998

Library of Congress Catalog
Card Number 92-90583

International Standard
Book Number 0-9633353-5-9 $12.95

Printed by: Country Press
W9878 Highway 60
Lodi, Wisconsin 53555

Printed in the United States of America.

Dedication

This book is dedicated to my family who supported me through the good times and bad and to those of the Wisconsin warden service who were injured and to the memory of those killed in service.

Jim Chizek

Game Warden Centurion

About the Author

Jim Chizek, raised on a dairy farm near Fifield in Price County, became a Special Conservation Warden for the Wisconsin Conservation Department in the fall of 1955 after serving two years in the Marine Corps during the Korean War. Urged on by Warden Leonard Urquhart and Forest Ranger Frank Palenik of Park Falls, he reported to the Northwest Area Supervisor William (Bill) Waggoner stationed at Spooner. Bill assigned him to work for hard charging warden Edward Manthei of Ladysmith. A very productive period was spent during October, November, December and January rounding up violators, mostly deer hunters in Rusk County. Jim always commented his success as a warden was directly related to the sage advice and valuable experience gained that first fall with Ed. Ed taught by example with hard dedicated work but also showed compassion to those on the other side. "Humbility" a word coined by the warden force through the years best explains Ed's attitude.

Having quit a full-time job with the railroad Jim was thrilled after the Ladysmith experience to immediately be hired by Art Doll, the District Game Manager at Park Falls. Surveying winter deer yarding areas on snow shoes and drawing deer timber browse maps was valuable experience for the future. He saw his first starved deer and learned how to take bone marrow samples from the multitude of dead in the yards. Even though the department was feeding deer at the time, hundreds were found dead. This unforgettable experience helped him support controversial deer game management practices of the era. Gaining experience, Jim waited for another opportunity in law enforcement. His patience was rewarded when as spring approached he was ordered to report to the Northeast Area Warden Supervisor, I.C. (Izzie) Rheame at Woodruff. Izzie sent the anxious 25 year old man to Shawano to work with Ortis K. (OK) Johnson, a legendary warden of the time. Working the spring fish run on the Wolf River in that era was experienced by most trainee wardens. It was felt if you could make it there you would qualify for permanency. Valuable experience was gained, as he became acquainted with the wardens in the region forming life-long friendships working with fellow Specials Patrick (Pat) Burhans and Owen Anderson. All were to become permanent wardens and complete careers in the warden service.

As Harold Hettrick at Clintonville had charge of the Wolf River work group that spring, Jim was fortunate to work with a fully dedicated warden who would later become the first warden training officer and later Deputy Chief Warden.

The following fall found Jim working as a trainee warden with Bill Leasch and Royce (Smokey) Dallman in Jefferson and Rock counties. Obviously the Conservation Department moved their trainee wardens around the

i

state to give them as broad an experience as possible.

An interesting deer season followed with Jim reporting to Warden Omar Thorpe at Darlington to work the first deer season LaFayette County had experienced. Deer hunters being difficult to find, they went hunting, killing two nice bucks the first day — two of the sixteen killed in the nine day season that year in the county.

Reporting to Southern Area Warden Louis (Pat) Oshesky in January of 1957, Jim was stationed permanently at Portage as his probation period came to an end.

In September 1966, after working ten years in Columbia County, he accepted a promotional appointment as the District Supervisory Warden at Park Falls replacing Robert (Bob) Markle who had been killed that spring in a high speed chase of fish spearers near Bass Lake in Price County.

In the fall of 1968, Jim was seriously injured along with his Special Warden James (Jim) Golomb of Park Falls. The auto mishap took place while working deer shiners on the Lincoln, Price County line.

After nearly two years of rehabilitation, he reported to Chief Warden Walter J. Zelinski at Madison who assigned him to work in the Bureau of Law Enforcement doing law enforcement budgeting and planning and engaging in special investigations.

In 1986, after 30 years of law enforcement service Jim retired at his Lodi home to attempt writing a book about game wardens. He feels wardens lead unique lives different even than other law enforcement officers. He believes so varied and rich are their experiences they should be shared with others.

A warden career is unique in that their contacts with the varied public brings unexpected experiences. The job while not monetarily rewarding, is perhaps more personally gratifying than many positions, producing a true valuable public service in protecting our natural resources.

The author has attempted to base all stories on actual happenings that span and depict happenings in the last 100 plus years. The tales are as authentic as possible. Necessarily the author had to add his own interpretation to parts of the stories when he had to imagine what was said or felt under trying conditions. These conditions may have been serious or funny. None are routine in an endeavor to depict the unusual and/or dramatic circumstances wardens have and may find themselves in.

While this book is generally about Wisconsin wardens, their struggles and frailties, it could very well relate to events in other states during their formulative years and federal wardens during this period of history.

The names of many persons have been changed to protect them, their relatives and friends from any discredit that could be leveled against them.

As the author finishes this book, he realizes the many changes wardens experienced in law enforcement through the last century, probably the greatest change there ever will be in conservation and natural resource protection as an infant state and nation struggled to settle a wilderness and develop a conservation consciousness. A sameness runs throughout this period requiring wardens to have the same dedication and adaptability today as in the eighthteenth century.

Jim Chizek author and Cal Clark

Chapter 1

Axed

Enthusiasm filled the air early on the day before Christmas in 1922 as three wardens left Antigo knowing the corn crackers would be out looking for trout for Christmas. A soft new snow fell adding to the several inches already present as they drove slowly east toward the White Lake area. Their plan was to check several spring ponds where they expected Kentucks to take trout. Langlade County is gifted with many spring-fed ponds where trout gather in December. The talk was quiet and humourous as the old Model T Ford made its way through the narrow rutted snow covered roads of that era. Humourous and serious tales were exchanged of adventures with the local Kentucks Mac was accustomed to dealing with. Snatches of hill-accented speech seasoned the discussion with the words corn crackers often entering the discussion. Corn crackers was a common name for the transplanted Kentuckians who made moonshine whiskey during these years of prohibition.

W.H. MacKenzie, a tall, strong, solidly built man of 35 years, was the veteran of the group. Having worked on a temporary basis in the fall of 1910 under Jack Foster in the Wausau area, he had also worked near Tomah and Mather. The following spring, a talented athlete with a zest for baseball, he returned to his home in Poynette to play for Jake Beihl's Giants of Lodi, the Milwaukee Tigers (professional team) and the local Portage team.

In 1917, he started his second conservation career as a game warden serving with Johnny Mason at Janesville and later was finally stationed permanently at Antigo. Warned that the area had a bad reputation, he began his job full of enthusiasm to make his mark as a warden.

Langlade County during that time in history was a large wilderness area largely populated by people from Kentucky and Tennessee. Hill people, locally known as Kantucks, because of their highly accented speech revealing their mountain ancestry. When speaking of themselves, Kentucky came out Kantuck or Kaintuck.

Mac soon found their reputation for being quick tempered and handy with a gun or knife to be true. Violating conservation laws lended itself well to the illegal making and drinking of moonshine both occurring in rural areas. Predicaments a warden could find himself in under the circumstances were endless.

In five years, Mac had become accustomed to the hill people's ways and he'd found ways to deal with them. Deliberately accenting his speech to sound like them, he conversed as an equal with them. A humourous man, he often mimicked the hill country speech and became proficient at using it for this purpose. Even as an older man when joking, the Kantuck inflection easily slipped into his speech, tickling one's funny bone.

Accompanied by newly appointed Deputy Wardens Mader and Al Robinson (later to become Chief Warden) Mac laid out a plan of attack. After dropping Mac off at Evergreen Spring (Town Line Lake), Robinson and Mader proceeded with their plan to check several spring ponds in the area and return to pick up Mac at a specified time.

Mac walked cautiously through the silent wilderness made extra still by the soft new snow still drifting lazily down. Careful not to let his presence known, ever watchful, he scanned the area for signs of people walking into the spring. Although the whiteness told a story of small animals and deer feeding and even the large dog-like tracks of two timber wolves following a deer, it divulged no message of the men he would soon encounter.

Crossing a small swamp area forested with white cedars, Mac, a great lover of all types of trees, stopped to examine and smell the pungent thickly growing trees. Wondering momentarily why they rarely grow around his home at Poynette and whether a program could be started to introduce them further south. The trees became more sparse as he approached the partly open east side of the spring. While most water areas were frozen over, many springs stayed open through the winter months due to the 50 degree water seeping up from the bowels of Mother Earth. These warm water areas created an ideal gathering place for trout to spawn.

Leaving the cedar grove, Mac slowed his pace scanning the partially frozen three acre spring area. His thoughts were of Al Robinson's arrest of John Bekins for taking trout a year ago this spring. The arrest had been made inspite of John pulling a gun. Al had been lucky that no shots were fired when he tussled with Bekins for the gun. After being disarmed Bekins had submitted to arrest.

His thoughts snapped to the present as he rounded the last little clump of cedars and saw three people on the ice near the west shore of the spring.

Sneaking silently through the soft snow, raising his binoculars, he carefully scanned the three who were all dressed in wool stag trousers and plaid Macinaws, intent on their activity they did not see him.

Immediately recognizing Pete and John Bekins, he was thankful he carried the 30-30 Winchester carbine as he often did these hectic days in Langlade County, not trusting solely to the Luger nestled snuggly under his arm in the shoulder holster. He had arrested Pete once for running deer with dogs on the oxbow. Pete, after being disarmed, had grabbed to regain possession of the rifle. After a tussle, Mac had affected the arrest. On a later occasion he had arrested him for possession of trout during the closed season and possession of a deer hide in the red coat (showing it had been taken in the spring). Pete who had a notorious reputation around Elton where he lived, had fled the state rather than appear in court and face the charges. A warrant for his arrest had been issued.

The binoculars held steady revealed that as usual the Bekins were armed. A rifle draped nonchalantly across his arms, Pete was dangling a handline into the open water while John stood gazing around on guard for anyone approaching. The third, a young boy, walked around carrying a single barrel shotgun.

Mac's thoughts were of how he could approach the three. If he crossed the ice, they would undoubtedly scatter and escape into the surrounding pine forest. Still pondering, Mac's decision was made for him when John pulled up his line, rolled it up, bent for the double bitted ax and led the three off the ice tracking north along the spring's edge.

Entering the pines, Mac set a shortcut course to intercept near the north end of the lake. Mac, stepping unexpectedly from a clump of under-brush several feet in front of Pete, startled the three and they stopped staring wide-eyed at him.

"Well boys, you know who I am. I'll tell you anyway. I'm a State Conservation Warden and Pete you know I've got an arrest warrant for you." Slipping into his Kantuck dialect Mac stepped close to Pete, reached into the gunny sack, Pete had dropped at his feet, and produced a large trout. "Jus come home huh? Trying to get yourself some trout fish huh?"

Mac reached for the single barreled shotgun Pete carried, barrel forward, over his shoulder, he continued, "You're under arrest Pete. Give me the gun." Without a word or any warning, Pete twisted sharply to his right maintaining his grip on the gun. With both men gripping the firearm, they wrestled for its possession kicking up clouds of snow. Mac, fearfully aware of his unprotected back swinging toward John, was unable to stop the swing. Glancing apprehensively over his shoulder, he saw too late the gleaming arc of light reflecting off the double bitted ax as John swung for the homerun. Striking Mac against the side of the head , the ax did not bite in but glanced off with a tremendous thunk that brought immediate darkness to Mac as he fell prostrate in the snow.

The snow biting his face brought him to a half conscious state as he partially realized what was happening. Trying to sort out his thoughts, his dazed mind cried out to clear the fog. *He chopped me with the axe. Got to get up. They will kill me.* Realizing he still gripped the rifle, he used it as a means of partially parrying a second swing of the ax as John attempted to finish the job. The ax struck the side of his head a second time, again failing to bite through his skull, glancing off. Lights flashed at the contact and again Mac felt blackness temporarily envelop him. Shaking his head, throwing torrents of blood into the snow, he gazed through a bloody haze as John approached, the ax held high for the fatal blow. Still desperately gripping the rifle, he again used it to fend off the impending blow only to have Pete grasp the rifle in an iron grip and attempt to wrestle it away. Sensing that losing the rifle meant the ax would descend unimpeded and death would be but seconds away, Mac cleared his mind briefly and fumbled for the hammer of the rifle.   Finally, feeling the click that locked the hammer in a cocked position he pulled the trigger. The roar of the rifle reverberated through the silent snow covered wilderness with devastating effect. The slug entered Pete's mouth and tore a large chunk of meat out. As it exited through his heavily bearded cheek, Pete catapulted backward where he landed heavily on his back. Pete's blood spurted and joined Mac's blood to further stain the white surface with the crimson of life.

The rifle's kick on discharge and Pete's backward movement jarred the rifle from Mac's grasp. It flew tumbling through the air to disappear in the soft snow some ten feet away. At the discharge, John's face, which had been close to the muzzle, took part of the concussion and noise and he dropped to his knees losing the shotgun. Scooping snow with his hands, he frantically looked for and found it. Arising, the two Bekins and the boy walked swiftly away from the scene leaving Mac scrambling vainly to rise. Blood cascading down his face, he dragged himself painfully to a nearby tree, grasping it, be boosted himself to a half standing position. As he wiped the blood from his eyes, his fog-filled mind attempted to fathom what had happened to him. Turning through a bloody haze his mind focused on the unbelievable specter of John raising the shotgun and aiming it directly at him. Sudden realization that it was real required action. Desperately, he allowed himself to drop in the snow as the shotgun blast sent a charge of buckshot dangerously close to his falling body.

Realizing the Bekins still posed a threat, he fumbled inside his jacket and freed the Luger. Seeing the Luger surprised and frightened the Bekins who scuttled off into the pines with John directing his attention to the young boy. "Ya'all got any more shotgun shalls?"

Too scared to answer because of what he had experienced, the boy remained silent and hurried away.

Blackness enveloped Mac.

Awakening with the Luger still held firmly in his hand, Mac found himself alone in the blood spattered snow. Weak and blood soaked, he tried to rise to no avail. It seemed his mind could not order his legs to respond. Dragging himself heavily to the nearby open water, he bathed his gory head and face waiting for his thoughts and vision to clear. Slowly his mind wiped away the blackness and allowed him to take stock of his condition.

Several hundred yards away, the Bekins met well out of gunshot range of Mac's Luger.

John, still boiling mad, insisted they return and finish him off. "Pete, he maght live," he drawled. "Iffen he does we're juss outa luck. He'll be after us 'ens. Iffen I'da had another shell ited be over naw." Looking at the boy, he said, "Give me the rafle, ah'll go back and take care o Mac."

Pete, however, bleeding profusely, had concerns of his own. Inspite of efforts to control the bleeding torrents of blood continued to stream through his fingers covering the gaping hole in his cheek. Having no stomach for more of the matter, he muttered through the blood oozing from his mouth. "Les's jus get out o here John. A'hm sicker na pizened pup. Ma jaw aches. Lez go home. Jus got to leave the country. Hide out someres. Come on lez go."

Contritely, John agreed. "Kay Pete, but az's going to Kantuck then, cause I jus knows Mac'll be on our trail. Maybe he's bad nough off anyway and mighten dia,"

The decision made, the three tracked swiftly toward their hidden vehicle. As their battered Model T Ford rounded a corner on the old woods road they met another Ford. The three pulled up short as the road was too

4   *Axed*

narrow for the cars to pass. Getting out to consider how to navigate past the other car the Bekins were confronted by Wardens Robinson and Mader. Choking back their fear, they carried on a conversation to cover their day's deeds.

Not knowing of Mac's encounter, the wardens did not closely question them. Robinson asked about the rag held over John's cheek and his blood soaked beard. Pete's reply intimated he had run into a barbed wire fence severely tearing his face. They explained they were on their way to Antigo to have the injury treated. The conversation ended as the cars delicately passed each other, and the wardens proceeded to meet Mac.

After resting Mac tried vainly to rise. Finding he could not, he lay face down his mind raced considering further what was necessary to get out of his fix. *Got to get help. Got to get out of the woods. Wonder if the others can find me? I know where I'm at. Should be able to get out even if I can't walk. Can't stay here too long. I'll freeze if I don't do something,* Noticing the numbing cold entering his body made him realize he had been unconscious a considerable time. *Better to move, anything to stay warm.*

Mac's great stamina now stood him in stead as he began the tiring tedious task of dragging himself from the woods. Knowing the ice over the spring to be thin in spots and dangerous at this time of the year, he still choose the most direct route. Time was running out for him. Dragging himself to the spring edge, he found the ice much easier to navigate then the bushy timber. Pulling himself forward with his arms, crossing the spring brought relief as he no longer could go through the ice and had saved precious time. Tired but determined he began making his way through the thick cedar lowland. The decidious forest beyond the cedars being more sparse made crossing much easier even though the snow was somewhat deeper.

After hours of determined crawling and now on his "old trail' made earlier on the way in, he let out a sigh of relief at a glimpse of his old Model T. Movement near by it had to be the other wardens since he was well beyond the time they had set to meet.

"Hey, hey guys," His squeaking voice made him realize how dead tired he was.

The answering reply was sweet in his ears, "Yeah, that you Mac?"

"I'm hurt – come help me."

Tired but elated that he had made it, Mac welcomed the helping hands that carried him to the vehicle.

Quickly transported to Antigo, he was treated by the same doctor that was to treat him nineteen times for violent injuries received during his tenure in Langlade County.

Soon Mac was relating his story for the record to Sheriff Edward Buchen and the local police with Wardens Robinson and Mader listening intently.

Proceeding to the scene of the encounter, Sheriff Buchen and the district attorney inspected, photographed, measured and recorded the evidence painted vividly in the snow. Recovering Mac's rifle, they found the empty cartridge and the blood from Pete when the bullet exploded in his mouth. They reconstructed the grisly picture in the blood soaked snow where Mac had fought for his life. They measured the distance as seventy feet from where John had stood and fired the deadly shotgun blast to where Mac had dropped to save his life. They made the conclusion that had Mac not dropped he would have received the deadly buckshot charge waist high.

After questioning the young man now identified as the brother of John and Pete and releasing him, Sheriff Buchen with Robinson and Mader descended on John Bekin's home in Elton. The house search showed no signs of John or Pete being there.

During the several days that passed with Mac convalescing in his home, the Antigo Game and Gun Club offered a reward of $200.00 for the capture of the Bekin brothers. Rumors began to circulate that Pete, still bleeding, was spotted in the Three Lakes area heading north to escape. Later, word arrived he was holed up in a tarpaper shack near the Buchanan logging camp about two miles north of the Wisconsin line in Michigan.

On December 28, Wardens Henry Oberholtzer of Eagle River, Gwit of Rhinelander and Michigan Warden Woodward (Woody) Grey and Sheriff Morrison of Watersmeet, Michigan held a conference at Watersmeet to develop a plan of capture.

Arriving at the logging camp, the party split into two groups to prevent the fugitive from escaping. As they approached the tarpaper shack from two sides, Pete spotted them. Grabbing a 32 special Winchester rifle from behind his door he sprinted through the waist deep snow working the rifle's lever frantically to jack a shell into the chamber. Still fumbling with the rifle, he stopped, turned and pointed the rifle at the approaching party of wardens Robinson and Grey being led by Oberholtzer. When the rifle failed to go off, he turned and ran helter skelter, the snow tiring him as he continued to work the lever and dig in the chamber to free the lodged shell. Although physically strong and fleet of foot, his gallant attempt was cut short as Oberholtzer steadily gained. The pace slowed to not much more than a walk and breaths wheezed as they forced themselves to the utmost through the waist deep snow. Realizing he was no match for the giant compact man gaining in pursuit, Pete pulled up at Oberholtzer's shouted command and raised the rifle in both hands – a sign of surrender. Arms held high, eyes wide staring at the cocked hammer of the steadily held carbine directed at his belly he turned. Unnerved by the sight he stumbled several steps to the rear. "A-ah gives up. A-ahm done. Don't shoot."

Oberholtzer's calm stern voice boomed, "Drop the gun Bekins."

Tossing the rifle quickly to the side, his arms remaining high, he jabbered, "Ah's through. Don't shoot me. Ah gives up."

"Okay, Bekins, turn around and put your hands behind your back. I'm going to cuff you."

"Jus d, don't hurt mae," was the subdued reply. Turning to comply he dropped his arms and placed them obediently behind his back, to hear the double click, ending his flight and freedom.

The three wardens joined the other group with their prisoner. The Michigan officials escorted them across the line to an area well within the State of Wisconsin and left.

Lodged in the Langdale County jail, Pete listened to court testimony

6

the following morning of Mac and Oberholtzer and publicly admitted his part in the affair. Bound over to the upper branch of Municipal Court, he was remanded to jail without bond until after the arraignment. In May 1923, he was found guilty and sentenced to one year in the state prison at Waupun.

Meanwhile, the search for John Bekins continued with word from the community being he had returned to Kentucky. Uneventful months passed without a word and then in July Kentucky officials took him into custody while raiding a moonshine still. He was returned to Wisconsin.

While free on a $5,000.00 bail bond John was charged with cutting a man with a knife. The fray was between him and a still operator who hit him with a revolver in an argument over payment of a debt for moonshine whiskey. Bekins retaliated with a knife cutting a gash in the other's head. His bondsmen fearing complications withdrew their surety, and he was again incarcerated. On combined charges he was sentenced to one year in the state prison in Janurary 1924.

Though able to walk soon after the encounter, Mac continued to have medical problems as a result of the head injuries. Periods of dizziness and excruciating headaches continued with little help from the medical profession. Extensive medical treatments were administered at Rochester and Chicago. Finally, taking a leave of absence, he went to California to relax for several months.

Eventually returned to good health, Mac returned to work to set a shining example for the wardens of Wisconsin and all other states. Mac served as chief warden from 1925 through 1934 when he became the Director of the Conservation Department. His illustrious career brought many beneficial changes to conservation law enforcement and to conservation in general.

Known as a hard taskmaster he expected a lot from his men as chief warden and later as the department director. Wardens idolized him because of his straight forward ways and the way he backed them in times of trouble. They were proud to be known as Mac's Boys. The inscription on the Winchester rifle given him at his retirement in 1942 reads "To Mac from your boys."

After becoming chief warden, Mac lived in his home town of Poynette near the Poynette Game farm, which he proudly established while director of the Conservation Department. A part of the old game farm is now called the MacKenzie Environmental Center in his honor. He has been installed in the Wisconsin Conservation Hall of Fame.

Mac died in September of 1979 when he was honored as uniformed warden pall bearers carried him to his final resting place.

Chapter 2

Bullet Holes

Bernie Palis, stationed at Oconto with his new special warden, explained his problem to the Circuit Judge. The stopping of deer shiners had become very difficult. As soon as a red light and siren were activated, the violators knowing they could not be arrested unless found with a firearm would run until they hit a dusty dirt road—of which there were plenty in the early 1940's in Oconto County. The dust swirling around the pursuers allowed them to pitch their firearms without the wardens seeing.

The judge thought deeply about the problem, and then allowed that when pursuing such a violator one could perhaps fire a warning shot or two or even shoot the tires off the vehicle if confident of hitting them.

Meeting Carl Miersch, the warden at Antigo, later that day, Bernie laughingly told him of the discussion. "Can't you imagine what the Kentucks would say if we started shooting warning shots?"

"Yeah, I just can't imagine a circuit judge telling you such a dumb thing. Oh, well, guess we'll just continue as before. Should we work tonight?

"Yeah, I've got to go back and pick up my new special."

"How's he working out?"

"He's pretty green, but willing, so I think he'll be okay after a time. See you at 8 o'clock at that old abandoned road we sat on two weeks ago."

"The one with the tumble down shack on it?"

"Yeah, see you there."

"I suppose you're going back to Oconto to practice your shooting so you can pick off those tires in the dust, ha ha."

"Yea, it'll take a little work for that. See you tonight." Later that evening with Carl in the passenger seat, Bernie had his special sit in the back seat of the sedan hoping to give him some experience. The special warden seemed to take particular interest in the judge's statment to Palis. Setting up just south of the paved road to avoid the problems of dust they parked on the old abandoned road where they could observe the field known to have deer feeding on it.

After sitting a short time whiling away the time mulling over the judge's comments and telling stories of past adventures for the benefit of the new special warden, a car approached, passed them and stopped at the field. A bright light swung eerily across the field and stopped momentarily on a large buck about 500 yards away near the back edge of the field.

Already moving in without lights, Bernie was close when the car moved on.

"Must have been too far for them. Let's take them right here on the paved road."

Switching on the spotlight, headlights, red light and siren brought the usual response. The car shot forward with Bernie close behind. After going about one half mile, the old beat up Ford swung onto the first available dirt road they came to. Dust and gravel flew as they slewed in the gravel as they accelerated. Gravel pelted Bernie's windshield as he followed in a dense pall of swirling dust and pebbles. Concentrating on controlling the speeding auto, Bernie began to slowly creep up on the fleeing vehicle. Knowing if he could get close enough, although dangerous, the dust from the vehicle would pass under and around his car. In the vortex of the dust storm immediately behind such a vehicle one had some slight visability.

Concentrating closely on the speeding vehicle, Carl instructed the special, "Keep your eyes peeled for anything flying from the car."

With everyone tensely concentrating on the car the two deafening shots that rang out made Carl and Bernie visably jump.

"What the He-l-l-l-l!" shouted Carl as he turned to the rear. The young man grasping a revolver had his arm extended through the open rear window. "Hey, cut that out. Don't shoot anymore." Turning to Bernie who looked grim, his face drained of blood, Carl reported what Bernie already knew, "He shot at the car, Bernie."

Concentrating on the slowing car before him, Bernie had no chance to answer. At the sound of the shots, the car ahead swerved sharply from side to side as it braked to a slewing stop. Desperately braking, Bernie slid up tight behind them, luckily not hitting the car.

Carl slammed from the car and ran to the passenger side of the car where a man wrestled with a rifle as he attempted to stuff it in an uncooperative cloth gun case.

"We're conservation wardens," his deep voice boomed. "It's too late for the case. You're all under arrest. Now, give me the rifle."

Opening the door and taking the rifle his voice firmly commanded, "All right everybody out."

Bernie arrived at the driver's side of the car as the driver, a hulking six foot six man of Kentucky heritage, laboriously unfolded his broad shouldered form from behind the wheel. The Kentucks, so-called because many had immigrated from Kentucky to this part of the state during the thirties, were known to be quick to fight and quick to use a gun or knife. The huge man faced Bernie

"Do you have a deer?", asked Bernie.

"Nawa," drawled the rawboned man as two more men got out of the car.

"Well, we'd like to look in your trunk anyway."

"Go ahad, weones ain't got naathen."

As the two wardens approached the rear of the car they immediately saw a spot on the trunk — very obviously a bullet hole. Nervously exchanging knowing glances, neither spoke of it. Standing blocking the view of the hole, Bernie stalled for time to think as he grasped and turned the handle, raising the lid high.

The trunk being empty the group stood talking with the rawboned man leading off, "yaa guys shot at usens or I wouldn't aave stopped."

Uncomfortably Bernie replied, "Yeah, we shot."

"Hit maa tare. Had to staap."

"Okay we hit your tire, now get some identification out."

Busy writing up citations, the wardens left the trunk open. The problem of the bullet hole was left for later. Expecting a confrontation at the discovery, when finished, having no choice Bernie slammed the trunk unceremoniously closed.

As it closed the very large Kentuck stared unbelievably at the bullet hole. Both wardens stood poised ready for the flair up.

Shaking his head in disbelief, the big man bent over studying the hole carefully. "Thaat, theers a bullet hole. Who did done thaat?"

Silence reigned as the wardens uncomfortably sidled from one foot to another.

Suddenly from the darkness the silence was broken by the voice of the special who had stayed in the background until now. "I did it."

Turning on his heel the large Kentuck faced the special and extended his hugh paw, drawling, "put er thaar pal – good shooten, hit er dead canter."

With that the wardens left – the special sticking his chest out in pride.

The three men plead guilty to shining deer while in possession of a firearm. No one mentioned the shooting incident in court. The wardens were mightily relieved to have the case end thusly.

The special, inspite of being told he should not have shot, walked like a peacock for some time.

The next several years were strangely quiet. The Kentucks still shined and shot deer, but rarely ran for a dusty road.

Chapter 3

Venison For Sale

A light snow was falling as the three conservation warden under-cover agents entered the Bing Bong Tavern. The bartender looked up as the small bells jingled on the slamming door.

"Howdy fellows. Long time no see. Up for the deer season?"

"Yep," replied Joe. "Hunted all day just west of here."

"Any luck?"

"Nope. Didn't even get a doe."

"You got a party deer tag?"

"Sure, but couldn't fill it."

The three men maneuvered into the center of the bar between two groups dresssed in the reds, oranges and yellows of deer hunters.

Following along, the bartender grunted, "What'll you have?"

Jim Chizek author and Harry Borner as special investigators and venison and hawks.

Drinks were swiftly delivered to the investigators who nonchalantly eyed the assemblage. They started their own conversation loud enough so others could hear. The bartender joined in, "Say did you fellows scout that area on Brill Road that I told you about?"

"Sure did. Looked it over when we were up last month. Looked good then, but didn't see much today."

From the end of the bar came a shout, "Hey how about a drink down here?"

Leaving the investigators to their own devices, the bartender left to serve the rowdy group of hunters.

Glancing both ways, the veteran chief of special investigations, Joe Rubesch, quickly spoke to the other investigators, Jim Chizek and Harry Borner. "What do you think? Anybody here we're looking for?"

Blue eyes flicking over the group, Harry mused, "Could be. There's a couple about the right age."

Winking at Harry, Jim chuckled, "Looks like they have the right attitude. They're wearing their backtags upside down."

"At least two fit the description of Rudy and Nick Mossman," said Joe. "Let's give them a try." Harry moved slightly toward the group, raising his voice for all to hear, "Joe, you said there would be nothing to getting a deer up here."

"You're too damn hungry Harry."

"Darn right. I like to eat. I like venison. I've got the build to prove it." Harry, a barrel chested heavy set man in his early fifties swiftly moved about the bar, his swift flowing walk belying his build.

The bartender joined them, taking notice of their glasses. "Want another?"

"Yeah. Fill em up Hank."

"You guys really didn't see any deer? That's damn good country you were in."

Jim shrugged. "Saw a few tails." Snickering and motioning with his eyes toward Harry, he continued. "Some of us missed."

"You'll probably end up buying a deer." Joe piped up. Turning to the bartender, he continued, "We don't hunt that hard. We're here to have a good time. Are there any deer available in the area?"

Hank snorted. "No deer for sale around here. Even the DNR don't have 'em for sale."

Joe continued, "Got to be careful buying a deer. You know you can really get taken." Motioning with a sweep of his hand to the bartender to serve another drink, Joe continued, "Up at Hayward a couple of years ago a guy had a mule deer spoil. You know transporting it in the rain, way from Wyoming. Threw it away. Some Indians found it. Brought it into town. Sold it to some flatlanders in a bar. Hell, got $75. He thought he had a white tail."

Listening intently, Hank quickly returned, served the drink and grinningly took in the story. "Bet they were surprised when they skinned the deer."

The group at the end of the bar had quieted, obviously listening. Hank busily served the group another drink and joined their conversation — now considerably restrained.

Again the wardens caucused. Joe momentarily glanced at the group. "Well what do you think Jim?"

"The bartender was sure listening to you."

"He's interested", agreed Harry. Their conversation broke off as one of the group strode toward them and sidled up to Harry.

Voice barely a whisper, he said, "You fellows interested in buying a deer?"

"We might be. Price has to be right. You got one?"

"Yeah. Nice buck. Come with me. Don't want everyone to hear." Nodding his head, he directed Harry to a vacant corner of the barroom. "I've got to get $100 for it."

"That's an awful price."

"Don't care. I'm taking an awful chance. You know selling, it's against the law. You could be a game warden."

"Yep. Could be. But so could you. Where would that leave me?"

"Guess we're in the same boat. Still got to have $100. Nice six point buck. Not shot up."

"Seems like a lot of money. But, if it's a nice one, I'll take it."

"Come with me. I'll show it to you. I live just a few miles from here."

"What about my buddies?"

"Leave them here. We'll only be gone a little while."

"I'll talk to them. See what they say." Motioning for him to wait, he left and returned to the investigators.

"He wants to sell me a deer. Wants me to go with him."

Joe showed his concern by pushing his hat back, quick thoughts crossing his mind. "Not a good idea. These people have a bad reputation."

Jim's brow wrinkled remembering how Rudy Mossman shot at Warden Don Bjork during an arrest several years ago. "Who is this guy?"

"Told me his name is Nick."

Thoughtfully, Joe remarked, "That's got to be Mossman. Fits his description. He's a good one. It's up to you Harry."

"I'm not worried. If I don't show in a short time come looking for me. We're going to his house. The location is in our notes."

With a wave, he rejoined the pacing Nick near the door. "Let's get going."

Leading the way outside Nick motioned Harry to get in his car, slammed the door, and ground the starter. "Damn thing starts hard." It finally started with a sputter that slowly built to a roar. Amused at the startled look on Harry's face, he continued, "Don't worry about the loud pipes . It'll get there Harry."

"Why do you want to sell the buck. Don't you like venison?"

"Christ, I'm sick of it." snorted Nick. "We live on it year round. Sold a buck earlier today." After traveling several miles, with a flourish he swung the truck into a snowy driveway. "Here's my place. Come on into the garage. Got it hung up."

Entering the garage, Harry's eyes were immediately caught by the beautiful sleek buck hanging from a ceiling joist.

"See. Just like I said. He's a dandy. Nice neck shot too."

"Still think $100 is too high."

Angry now, Nick blurted, "Okay. If you don't want him, the hell with it. Take it or leave it. That's my price. I'll tell you something though, I got a hundred dollar bill for a smaller one this morning."

"Don't get mad. I really would like to take a buck home. Cut him down."

Re-entering the Bing Bong Tavern, Nick lead the way to his newfound friends. "Your buddy got a nice buck. Right Harry?"

"Yeah. He's really nice." Nodding toward Jim, Harry continued, "Nick, this is Jim. You know the guy I told you about. He's got a party deer tag."

Jim courteously extended his hand. "Howdy Nick."

Shaking vigoriously, Nick blurted, "You interested in a doe? My brother has one."

"Well I do have a party tag. The way this crew hunts I'll never fill it. I might be interested if it don't cost too much."

A smile crossing his face, Nick yelled at his cronies, "Dave, come over here." A slim tousled haired young blond man approached. Drawing him aside, Nick held a hurried, hushed conversation with many hand and arm gestures. Striding swiftly back to Jim, he bluntly stated. "I'll go get my brother and the deer." He eyed Jim quizzically. "How much are you willing to pay for the deer?"

"Oh, I'd give you $40 for a nice doe."

Nick's face reddened. "What! You've got to be kidding. He wouldn't take less than $75. It costs money to kill these deer. We're running quite a risk."

"Well, might pay more. Got to be a good one though. Got to see it first."

"Okay, we'll go get it." With that the two left the bar.

Left alone, the three lowered their voices. Joe took command. "Got to get those backtag numbers. Awful hard to read upside down. See if you can get them to play pool where I can get a better look."

Harry blurted out, "Jim and I will challenge any two of you to a game of pool."

A short chunky man stepped forward and replied, "What are we playing for?"

"A round for the house."

"Come on Jack before they change their minds," chuckled the middle-aged hunter. "It isn't every day we get a crack at a couple of rubes like this."

The balls were racked amid the laughter and jests as they put their best two players forward. After two games their jubilance had disappeared as they paid for the two rounds. The second drink was being served when Nick and Dave returned.

Approaching his new friends, Nick's voice was subdued. "He sold the deer. You're out of luck." He gave Jim a distainful glance. "He sold it for $80. Do you really want a deer?"

"Sure. I want to fill my party tag. I can't walk much. Can't really get into the woods."

Glancing at the cane Jim carried, Nick replied, "Yeah. Noticed your limp. Listen if you want a deer, be here tomorrow night."

"What time?"

"Seven."

"We'll be here", said Joe. Come let's get to the motel before we spend all your money. I'm tired."

Entering the tavern about 7:15 the next evening, the three were cheerfully greeted by Hank. "Hi guys. Nick and Dave haven't showed yet. They'll be here soon."

Jim sighed tiredly. "I'll have a shot of brandy. That beer'll kill me."

Joe snorted, "Drink beer Jimmie. Shortys. They're cheaper." The

14   *Venison For Sale*

conversation was interrupted by the jingle of bells as the door swung wide admitting Nick and Dave.

"Hi boys, see you're on time. Give these fellows a drink." As the drink was served, Nick brazenly pushed his proposition. "I've got a deer for you outside. But not for no $40."

Jim shrugged his shoulders. "Okay. Let's look at it."

Nick immediately motioned toward the door and let them outside and lead them to a pickup truck. Opening the topper, Nick played the flashlight on a large doe.

Eying it and rolling it over, Jim pulled on his mustache. "It's a nice deer."

Dave, blood rising in his cheeks, blurted, "You God damn better believe it, and I'll have to get $75 for it."

"Okay. Is this your deer? Thought it was Nick's"

"Yeah. It's mine and $75 is my low price."

Digging for his wallet, Jim appeared thoughtful. "Guess it's worth it."

Accepting the money, Dave whispered, "I'll cut the tag off." The whisper broke uncontrollably into a chuckle and finally a loud laugh. "It's last year's tag anyway."

Noticeably shivering, Nick edged for the bar. "I'm cold. Took off my longjohns."

Alone with Dave, the wardens had a little more liberty. As he bent over to cut the tag, Joe gently lifted his parka and backtag to read and memorize the number. Dave's knife slit swiftly through the metal band.

"Quick, put your tag on now before someone sees what we're doing."

Jim stepped forward tag in hand the crisp snap sounding unusually loud eased the tension somewhat.

Harry intently repeated the pickup truck license number over and over in his mind. Tenseness will impair one's memory. Quickly he went to his truck, jotted the number down, and backed the truck tailgate to tailgate with the other pickup. Dave gave a mighty heave and the deer slid into Harry's truck. Harry slammed the rear door.

"You live around here Dave?"

"Yeah. Just a few miles from here. A few miles east of Nick's turnoff."

"Oh, you're neighbors?"

"Worse than that, we're relatives." The tension broke as the conversation became more personal.

Dave asked, "You fellows interested in some more meat? We maybe could fix you up after the season."

Harry grabbed the opportunity. "We sure would. I have a lot of friends that like venison. Especially made into sausage."

"Sausage is good. I get awfully sick of eating plain venison all the time. We could make you a better offer if you would take them in lots — say five at a time."

"What kind of price are you talking?"

"Oh. Fifty dollars a piece if you take them pit run — does, you know, fawns, and everything."

Joe joined the conversation. "Sounds reasonable. When could you take care of us?"

"Right after the season closes. Give us ten days?"

Harry queried, "How would we contact you? We don't even know your name."

"I'm Dave Jones." Fishing in his pocket he continued, "Here I'll write down my name and address. Phone number too." Jotting down the information, he handed the frayed piece of paper to Harry, who in turn handed Dave his card, saying "Better yet, you can call me."

Holding the card up to catch the glow from the red tavern light, Dave read, "ITT – from Minneapolis. I've heard of it. That's a big outfit. You'll hear from me. Give us a few days though, We've got another order like this that we got to fill first. You know, first come, first serve."

"You must hunt steady", quipped Jim.

"We do hunt quite a lot. Doggone deer are getting scarce. Violators are getting them all. Ha. Ha. Wish that no good DNR would knock off that party permit. Let them rest for a few years." All laughed heartily at his reasoning.

"I'm serious though. It costs us plenty to get these deer. We drive about 100 miles a night hunting. Not only that—a person could get pinched. They got me once. Got to be careful. If they get me again, I'll be sitting in jail."

Joe broke in, "Really must get going – need our beauty sleep."

Harry reminded Dave, "You'll call me then in Bloomington, Minnesota?"

"Yeah, as soon as we get the order together."

A month later Harry received a telephone call from Minneapolis advising him to return a call to Dave.

The phone was answered on the first ring. "Dave this is Harry." "Harry Oh yeah glad you called. Got your order together."

"Is that right, how many?"

"We've got eight."

"Eight, that's more than we ordered. What's your price?"

"Told you. $50. My word's good. $400 for the eight."

"That is a good deal. When can we pick them up?"

"How about tomorrow?"

"Where do we meet?"

"Nick's house. You know where that is – you've been there."

"Yep. Noon. Okay?"

"Sure, that's fine. I'm hanging up now. You know – party line. See you tomorrow."

That afternoon was hectic. By telephone Art Schroder, the warden at Eau Claire worked with Deputy Chief Warden Harold Hettrick and the Special Investigations Section in Madison to formulate a plan for the next day. Art realizing he would need more manpower called in wardens close to Eau Claire. Coming in were Area Wardens Joe Pelikan from Menominee, John Goberville from Eau Claire and Roland Lee from Black River Falls. Field Wardens Omar Stavlo from Black River Falls, Bart Halverson from Menominee and Ken Larkin of Chippewa Falls were also called.

16   *Venison For Sale*

That evening, Harry and Jim drove their truck and utility trailer over dangerously icy roads the 225 miles from Lodi to Eau Claire. They arrived in time to meet with the many wardens gathering to participate in the next day's operation. The local warden, Art Schroeder who was in charge, laid out the plan for the bust assisted by District Warden Bill Barton and Deputy Chief Warden Harold Hettrick. They pointed out that communication and timing were vital. All during the investigation complete notes were kept involving others beside the Mossmens and Jones. Many local people were to be arrested who were all on the same party line. Wardens would approach the various places to be searched at a set time so little evidence could be destroyed or hidden. Warden cars were not to be seen in the area until the arrests began. The Bing Bong Tavern monitored warden radios during all operating hours. To counter this, an alternative radio system obtained from the State Justice Department was to be used. To assure no leaks all the search warrents needed were to be issued after taking down the main actors of the Mossmans and Jones.

Four wardens were to walk two miles across country to situate themselves across the road from the Nick Mossman home. They would be the eyes and the ears of the whole operation. Should things come off as planned, they would also be first on the scene when the first arrests were made.

Alternate plans were necessary should the sale not take place at Nick's house. The Eau Claire sheriff's department was to assist to assure enough manpower was available. Don Spindler and several other deputies responded.

Signals were worked out so the observers across the road could communicate with all cars and report progress or changes in plans via portable radio.

At approximately twelve noon as planned, Jim and Harry stopped their unit in front of the Mossman home to eye the snow-filled driveway. To their surprise a flashy new white Chrysler that was following them pulled alongside and stopped. The passenger was Dave Jones. Rolling his window down, he greeted them in a loud voice. "You're right on time. The deer are in that old shed behind Nick's house. Nick ain't here. You'll have to back your trailer up to the shed."

Harry looked the driveway over apprehensively. "Don't think I can get in there with all this snow. I'll drive up the road, turn around and come in from the other side."

Agreeing, Dave motioned to Jim, "Come on, I'll show you the deer."

Feeling his way with his cane, Jim followed Dave and the unidentified man through the deep snow to the tarpaper shed.

"God, must be 50 yards. Think Harry can back through all this?"

"He'll make it. It's really not so bad."

Opening the squeaky door, Dave motioned Jim in.

Entering, Jim was taken aback by what greeted him. The shed was completely full of skinned deer. Some were split lengthwise and some were quartered. All were hanging by meat hooks suspended from the rafters. "Oh, they are all skinned and ready to go."

"Of course, we treat our customers right."

Pushing hanging meat aside so he could get through, Jim counted. "Looks like you have about ten deer here, Dave."

"Yeah. There are ten, but we will sell them all for $400 like I told Harry on the phone."

With a sigh, Jim worked his way out of the hanging pieces. Glancing up he noticed what appeared to be a rough legged hawk jammed up under the rafters.

"What do you have here Dave?"

"That's Rudy's. He shot it during the deer season."

His heart missing a beat Jim turned to the unidentified man. Rudy was the ringleader — the one they really wanted and up till now had not been contacted. "Oh, are you Rudy?"

"Yeah. I'm Nick's brother." The name hit like a hammer in Jim's consciousness — "God, we've got a gusher here. He's the one who shot at Bjork."

Rudy's words brought Jim out of his reverie. "That's just a damned old chicken hawk. Here comes the truck. Let's direct him in."

The three struggled back through the snow to the driveway entrance, where Harry's truck wheels were whining and spinning in the deep snow in an attempt to back the truck and trailer to the shed.

Looking intently at the truck, Jim circled his way out in front of the truck where the view was clear to the wardens hiding across the road. "Whew. Really worked up a sweat walking through that stuff." Struggling with his zipper he removed his outside blue jacket, exposing the bright red under jacket, the predetermined signal — the deer are here—the transaction will take place here. Across the road, the tense wardens immediately radioed the information to all waiting ears.

With excessive huffing and puffing by the men, the trailer was unhooked and pushed by hand to the shed. The truck was then backed to the trailer and rehooked.

Reaching unobtrusively into his pocket Harry turned on the tape recorder. "How many deer Jim?"

"Looks like about ten."

Pushing the door open, Harry said, "Really been working hard, Dave."

"Scarce as hell. Had a hell of a time getting them."

Chuckling, Harry jabbed, "Ain't got any goats or dogs mixed in here? A guy told me to look for that. All deer huh?"

"Nope," replied Dave with a grin. All laughed heartily.

Jim interjected, "Harry, this is Rudy, Nick's brother."

Shaking hands, Rudy queried, "Do you fellows know a good place to sell hides? We have a hell of a bunch of 'em. Say fifty or sixty?" Pointing to a large pile of hides in the corner, he continued, "We have these plus Roger has a pile."

"Who is Roger?" asked Harry.

"That's my other brother."

"Oh, three brothers, sounds like a hunting family."

Unhooking some of the deer Jim and Rudy began handing them out to

Dave and Harry who were stacking them on the trailer.

Lifting a half above his head, Jim grunted, "What are you going to do with that chicken hawk, Rudy?"

Harry interjected, "Is that a chicken hawk?"

"Wasn't that what you called it, Rudy?"

"Just a damned old chicken hawk. Pretty though. I was going to get it mounted. Do you want it Jim?"

"Sure. I'd also be interested in getting it mounted."

"How much would you give me for it?"

"How much do you want? It's your hawk?"

"You are pretty good guys. It's yours. I can always get more. They're migrating at this time of the year."

Dave grunted as he threw half a deer on the trailer. "I've got one just like it at home. Mine ain't so shot up. Rudy killed his with a 30-30. I killed mine with a 22."

Harry took advantage of the moment. "I would be interested in getting the one you have Dave."

"It's at my house. I'll run home and get it for you as soon as we finish loading."

One of the hooks fell narrowly missing Rudy's head. Jim remarked, "Oops. Careful. You'll get brained. Sure some nice hooks."

"Yeah. Made them ourselves. We've got a nice little butcher shop here."

Dave joined in, "Next year, we will have a walk in freezer at my place. Then we'll have some bucks hanging for you before the season. We could start hunting a lot earlier if we could keep them from spoiling. Warm weather you know."

"Did you get any before the season this year?" Harry asked.

"Yeah. Fifteen bucks."

Jim's face showed surprise. "Wow! Look at the hole through this one."

Dave responded, "I shot a few of them through the shoulders. That's why we are only charging for 8. Some were long range shots."

Harry asked, "Did you shoot all of these?"

"Yup. I'm the rifleman. I've got a 300 Winchester Magnum. When you hit them with that, it knocks a hole in them the size of a pie plate."

"My God, Harry", said Jim, "We're going to have a trailer load."

"Told you so. That's why you need big equipment. Hope we can get out that driveway now. Pile most of the deer on the front of the trailer. Put more weight on the rear wheels of the truck for traction."

Finally the truck was fully loaded. The four began tying the canvas over the trailer. Harry showed concern, "Tie it down good and tight. Don't want that canvas whipping around so people can see what we have."

"Yeah," said Rudy. "Make sure you don't slip off the road. It's awfully slippery. That would be the time someone might see what's under here. You will be okay once you reach the interstate."

Dave threw the rope unceremoniously over the trailer. "While you are finishing tying down I'll go get that hawk for Harry. Give me the keys to my car Rudy." Walking over to the new Chrylser New Yorker, he spun his wheels all the way to the road.

Jim commented, "Nice car Dave has. What does he do for a living?"

"Cuts pulp."

"What kind of work do you do Rudy?", asked Harry.

"Packerland at Chippewa Falls. It's a meat packaging plant."

"Hell you're right in the business then."

"Yeah. Ha Ha. Let's get back to those hides. Do you know of anyone who would be interested in buying them."

"Not off hand. We will look around for you though. How much do you want for them?"

"Well damn. We got $5 last year. If we could get $4 we'll sell the whole damn lot."

"How did you do this year on buck hunting during the season?" Jim asked.

"Didn't do nothing. Got lost the first day. It was so damn foggy and I forgot my compass. Good thing I didn't shoot anything. Couldn't have found my way back to it anyway. Don't care much about just hunting bucks anyway. A deer is a deer."

Harry chuckled, "I suppose that's all you eat for meat?"

"Hell yes. I believe meat is selling for about a buck a pound. Been so long since we bought any I don't even know the prices anymore." He stared at Jim thoughtfully. "You guys want more deer"

"Sure. How many more could you provide?"

"Probably another load like this. Take a while though." At that point, Harry entered the truck cab to change tapes on his recorder. Jim kept up a light conversation to keep Rudy from wondering what Harry was doing.

Tying a corner of canvas fast, Rudy changed the topic. "You know that rifle of Dave's really lays them down, but the damn thing sure makes a loud bang. Wardens can hear it for miles. Do you know of any place where we could get a silencer?"

"I think I know of a place over in the Twin Cities. I will inquire there for you when we get back and let you know."

Harry rejoined them as Dave returned carrying the hawk. "See you got it. What do you want for it?"

"Nothing. You take it. I was just messing around with my little rifle when he landed in a tree by me."

Digging in his pocket, Harry pulled out a roll of bills. "Are you guys in partnership in this?"

Rudy answered, "Yeah along with Nick and Roger."

Counting out $200 to each, Harry stated, "You said you would get us another batch like this. When can we expect to hear from you?"

Dave thought briefly, "It will take a while. We don't have any for ourselves yet. We'll each need a couple. Depends on how soon they yard up. The way it looks now there are no damn deer left. I think the poachers and coyotes are getting them all."

"We should be able to get them in about two weeks." volunteered Rudy, "With this snow, they will be well yarded by then. Easier hunting."

"Well you have my number so I'll be expecting a call from you." Harry got in the truck which now had good traction and drove out to the road while the other three men struggled through the snow. Harry nonchalantly got out of the truck and walked in front of it. Out of sight he tipped his blaze orange cap to the wardens in the woods across the road — the signal which meant NOW. Rejoining the group, he said, "We'll be expecting to hear from you then Dave."

"Yeah. What's the matter Rudy?"

"Don't know. There are some guys all dressed in white clothing running out of the woods. What's going on?"

Both Harry and Jim produced credentials from their coat sleeves. "We are conservation wardens. You are under arrest."

Warden Bart Halverson and Omar Stavlo on a dead run slide to a stop in the snow. Waving their badges, they shouted, "We are conservation wardens. You're both under arrest."

The mouths of both Dave and Rudy fell open. Rudy stared blankly. "I don't believe it. I just don't believe it."

The two field wardens spread-eagled them for the search.

Digging in his pocket, Jim produced a small card. "I'm going to read the Miranda warning to you." His voice droned out the required warning as the search was completed. "Do you understand?"

"Yeah."

"How about you Mossman?"

"Yeah. I understand."

Cars began arriving hurriedly in the yard. Art Schroeder took over the case. More warden's cars drove into the driveway until the yard was full. Art immediately took the money back from their pockets and checked the bills for serial numbers which had previously been recorded. Two Eau Claire county policemen arrived on the scene to provide transport to the county jail.

Harry, Jim, Art Schroeder, and Ken Larkin proceeded to the Eau Claire County Courthouse to testify for issuance of additional search warrants. As fast as the warrants were issued, they were served. Venison was picked up all over the township. While waiting for warrants to be issued, watches were put on the many places to be searched. The word spread like wildfire. Wardens watched as chimneys spouted smoke that smelled of burning hair and meat. Because meat burns slowly, some who attempted to burn their venison were apprehended when the warrants were finally served. The searches were very thorough, turning up forgotten hides thrown on shed roofs or small pieces of venison in the extra refrigerator or other out-of-the-way places. The searches continued all afternoon. Finally, about 11:00 p.m., the last warrant was served.

Jim and Harry had returned to the Nick Mossman residence where all the deer parts were marked, photographed and turned over to Art Schroeder along with the hawks. Dave Jones' new Chrysler New Yorker was seized for evidence because he had transported the illegal hawk in it. His 300 Winchester Magnum rifle was picked up with a search warrant and seized subject to the court. Fifty-three hides were picked up in the searches in spite of the fact that some had been burned. Later Harold Hettrick and Art Schroeder working with and utilizing the expertise of Coila Jo Wegner of the State Crime Laboratory examined all the deer hides. Jo recognized as an expert wild game forensics analyst around the United States concluded what the wardens suspected. The deer had been taken through practically every month of the year.

The wardens, excitedly tired, met about midnight for supper. Because of the exceptional work done, an impromtu party developed at the Chicken Chasers, a local bar, resulting in hangovers for most the next day.

The main actors in this episode received long prison sentences and large fines, plus revocation of all hunting, fishing and trapping licenses for three years. They were Rudy, Nick and Roger Mossmen and Dave Jones. Jones also lost the 300 Magnum rifle. Eight more people were charged with lesser offenses. They all paid fines and lost hunting, fishing and trapping privileges.

Chapter 4

Ambush

The night of August 6, 1949 was deeply dark in the vast desolate swamp area along State Highway 70 where two young wardens worked. The wilderness area was familiar to them only because they had worked countless hours attempting to curb the illegal taking of deer. Deer concentrations had been attracted to the lush green growth along the newly reconstructed highway. Sparsely inhabited, the 25 mile span between Fifield in Price County east to the Pike Lake Chain of Lakes had been an area of concern. In spite of numerous arrests for shining deer, complaints continued. Deer kills were authenticated by drag trails and flocks of crows and ravens feeding on their entrails.

At this juncture in history, local citizens condoned and encouraged the illegal taking of deer. Some of the reasons were obscure while others more obvious. The north was still affected by the Depression of the 1930s. Even the citizens that were doing well could remember when the taking of a deer meant their children would be fed. Being sympathetic toward the poacher brought forward macho feelings in many people. Supporting your family at any cost as long as you don't steal from me seemed the code. Stealing from the state was widely considered proper as the state is an invisible entity. A sly wink and grin were usually the response to people illegally killing deer. Terms like jump meat, mouth organ sandwiches, government sheep and just take one to eat were common. Add to these attitudes a considerable number of people recently discharged from the Armed Services, who were at loose ends because of high unemployment. Many of these wanting to make up for lost time completed the picture. The war is over, spread your wings, let's have fun. Reflecting local peer pressure with jobs not readily available the cheapest entertainment was hunting.

To fully complete the scene the state appointed, warden Ken Beghin to Park Falls, a person short in stature but large in imagination and expectations. He utilized his outspoken, insistent and persistent manner to overcome his lack of height in a land of giant lumberjacks. His manner was thought cocky by many. A hard driving persistent worker his reputation grew as an individual who never slept and gave no quarter.

So in the twilight of this August day, as Ken drove east on the lonely stretch of Highway 70 he visited with his newly appointed neighboring warden to the south, Harris Jones. Their discussion of finding a home for Harris Jones in Phillips was interrupted as Ken glanced quickly into his rear view mirror. The mirror had picked up a car light far in the distance. "Wow. Look at that guy come." Ken accelerated as the car approached at a rate of speed inviting collision. At the very last moment, the car, squealing tires, swerved into the passing lane.

Jerking his automobile suddenly to the right, by instinct Ken alertly noted the car was a Blue 1948 Plymouth. A flash of annoyance crossing his face, he breathed, "Write down this number, Harris, 20783. Those guys know who we are and they're looking for trouble." Slowing and falling back until out of sight of the Plymouth, he hit the switches turning off the headlights, tail lights and brake lights. "Let's see what they are up too." Topping the slow rise in the road, they observed the car swing left into Memorial Grove, a park maintaining a large stand of virgin timber.

Immediately a light began probing, swinging back and forth illuminating small openings in the large timber where deer often fed. In spite of running black Ken swung his car expertly onto the same road. "Looks like they're shining deer all right." Open windows seemed to draw and magnify the eerie whine of the cars tires as they neared the auto. The left angle the road took slowly completed the loop back to a second entrance at the main highway. Slowing slightly fearing discovery left Ken about 100 yards behind when the car ahead turned east completing the half mile circle. Suddenly the car lights went out. The passenger door flew open discharging a man as the car slowed almost to a stop. The short burly man hit the road; running and stumbling up the right road bank, he stopped in a challenging manner as though to tempt one.

Surprised, Ken braked to a silent halt. "Harris there's something wrong here. Why'd he stop? He has no gun. He acts like he wants us to chase him. Saay, I know him. That's Fred Hemrick. I arrested him last spring, fish trapping walleyes. Wait here, I'll check this out." Quickly slipping out, flashlight in hand, not slamming the door, Ken sprinted to where Fred stood.

"What's going on here, Fred?"

Not surprised, Fred shrugged and scowled, "You'll find out soon enough. You're not the only one that can run black."

While trying to digest what the words meant the whine of tires behind his car jerked him into reality. *My God. They're making the loop again behind me. Can't see them coming in the black.* Eyes alight with suspicision, he centered his attention up the back road. *What's going on here. No game violations. I may be in trouble.*

The slamming of the car door in the blackness behind his car jerked him into reality as two large weatherbeaten men approached swiftly like wraiths in the blackness. Squinting to penetrate the darkness, Ken suddenly recognized Fred's brother John, whose reputation was widely known as a drinker and fighter. Then they were running for Ken's car. Seeing this, Fred also began to run for Ken's car. Surprised and startled by the happenings, Ken bolted toward his car.

Sudden fear hit him like a sledge hammer as a cry rang out. Don't let him get to their two way radio. Speeding up, Ken sprinted toward the open passenger door. Too late, Fred, a step ahead of him, savagely kicked the door closed with such force a tinkling of broken glass issued forth as the broken window cascaded to the pavement.

Ken turned to face the three men now approaching menancingly out of the murky darkness their fists upraised in the fighting stance of boxers. "What are you guys up too? Now just a minute. You'll be sorry for this."

There was no answer as the men stalked closer and closer like a wolf pack fencing with their prey at bay.

Backing down the road, Ken tried again, "Listen fellows, you're all going to be in a lot of trouble if." His sentence was never finished as his attention swiftly focused on the unknown man who broke off from the others and circled to Ken's left, darting furtively behind him. All were close now as Ken keenly aware of the danger from behind, hesitated. The forboding was more than Ken could stand. Glancing worriedly to his left and rear, he never saw John's smashing blow coming. The giant fist catching him above the right eye, completely dazed and immediately blinded him as torrents of blood gushed down his face. The road came up to smash him solidly, further blurring his fuzzy thoughts. Getting unsteadily to his feet, his legs limber and barely holding him up, he backed unsteadily away.

John, seeing Ken's dazed state, again like a wolf immediately took advantage and closed on him bellowing like a crazed bull. "I'll kill you, you little S.O.B." Ken reacted late because of his confusion. The five cell flashlight was wrenched savagely from his grasp. Mind fuzzy, he never saw and hardly felt the savage blow delivered with the light above the right ear. Somehow he maintained his feet and flopped around bent over with his arms held defensively in front of him to ward off further blows and clear his mind. To no avail. The next blow took him across the back of the head and slammed him to the ground. Stunned and dazed, he tried to gather his thoughts. Got to stop this. *Got to get up. Get the gun out.* Another blow with the light opened a large gash below his chin, allowing more blood to gush.

Ken was scrambling for his life now - half up, half down, crawling away. John followed hurriedly, the smell of death strong in his nostrils. Bending over the beaten man, he pounded and chopped with the flashlight. Oaths poured from him, "I'll kill you. I'll kill you."

Suddenly thoughts began to return to Ken as he realized the blows did not carry as much force. Forcing his eyes to focus, Ken spotted John as he momentarily hesitated, focusing stupidly, unbelievingly at the demolished light in his hand. With an oath he discarded it disgustedly, and again came toward Ken. The hesitation gave Ken enough time to gather his thoughts. Reeling down the road falling one last time, he struggled mightly with his revolver which seemed too heavy to lift free of the holster. Then, as if in a slow motion dream, the revolver cleared leather. Still reeling and backing away, he managed to point it at John, who hesitated.

He was surprised to hear his voice croak through the torn bloody lips. "Stop, or I'll kill you."

John hesitated, again giving Ken more time for his mind to clear. Heaving heavily and staring at Ken, his hesitation was only momentary as he lowered his head bellowed and charged forward again.

Ken's mind was clear enough now to concentrate. *Got to stop him. I can't take anymore of this. He'll kill me.* Finger tightening on the trigger, he was surprised when out of nowhere a blurred figure rammed John, bowling him aside.

It was Fred, who grabbed John by the arm and jerked him away screaming at the top of his voice. "Don't John. He means it. He'll shoot you. That's enough." John swearing and eyeing Ken allowed the blood lust to subside and let himself be held until reason returned.

Fred continued talking to him, "It's not worth getting shot. I can tell by looking at him, he'll kill you. Come on. Leave it go."

Holding the gun much steadier now, aimed directly at the glaring John, Ken looked around for Harris and shouted, "Bring the car down here. Swiftly the car approached and stopped beside the bloody warden. Ken swiftly slipped into the car. "Get me out of here. I need help. Get me to the hospital. " The 25 mile trip to Park Falls was swift. Within two miles of leaving the scene, Ken's eyes were completely closed.

Reacting to the radio call, hospital personnel hastily admitted Ken, removed the blood soaked clothing and put him to bed. A waiting doctor examined and treated him by stitching the many cuts and stopping the blood. A brain concussion required hospitalization and kept him off the job for a month.

Within several days, the sheriff's department served warrants on all three people involved. They were prosecuted for assault and battery. Even the court reflected the attitude of the citizenry during that period. Penalties were lenient. Assault of a warden also seemed part of the unwritten code of behavior. Harris Jones resigned his position shortly after the incident.

Untagged Trap

Chapter 5

Execution

In September 1986, John Buss, serving his first year as a State Conservation Warden at Sauk City, enjoyed a leisurely day off.

A young man of 26, John at six foot two inches was well-proportioned and strong. Quiet of nature, he thought things through and acted in a calm, calculating manner which reflected his grasp of the job gained during a year of intensive law enforcement recruit training.

With a few odd jobs to take care of and with his beautiful Labrador Retriever, Maggie, for company he drove leisurely to the Sauk Prairie Police Department, enjoying the comfortable lazy September day.

Entering, he greeted Betty Neumeyer, the radio dispatcher, "Hi Betty, sure a beautiful day. Can I use your copy machine? Got correspondence to move."

"Are you working today John? Really too nice a day for work."

"No, but you know one can't let the paperwork pile up."

As John stood copying some documents a middle-aged man entered. Approaching Betty, he said,

"Hi, my name is Bill Rush. I just came in from Plain. Thought you'd like to know, I saw a man hauling marijuana."

"Where did you see this?"

"On County B, but the guy is at August Derleth Park right now. I followed him in."

"Oh, do you have a vehicle description?"

"Yeah, I even have the license number."

"Good, give it to me."

"Y over U 8986."

A questioning look on her face, Betty wrote it down. "That can't be a Wisconsin plate. Are you sure you have it right?"

"No, it's not a Wisconsin plate, it's a Texas plate. I'm sure I have it right."

Betty quickly keyed the mike, "Car 63," When there was no answer, she continued, "what kind of vehicle was he driving?"

"A white pickup, a Ford."

Again jotting the information down, she again keyed the mike, "Car 63 - Car 63." Still no response. "Are you sure the man was hauling marijuana?"

"I was right behind him. The wind blew the stuff up every once in a while. You know over the tailgate. Dark green leafy plants. I'm not positive but I think its pot."

"Car 63 - Car 63." Betty repeated urgently. "Can't seem to raise Pete."

Pushing through the door to leave, Rush turned to Betty, "The guy's wearing a white ten gallon cowboy hat."

Overhearing the conversation, John volunteered, "Betty, do you want me to go over to the park and standby till you get Pete over there? It's only about five minutes from here."

"I'd sure appreciate it John."

Cooperating with local authorities is normal for all conservation wardens. So John proceeded to August Derleth Park between the small twin cities of Sauk City and Prairie du Sac on Highway 12. Swinging his truck into the park, he noticed the white pickup truck parked several hundred yards away in the parking lot. Letting his truck drift slowly down the inclining drive, he recognized Bill Rush's small dark Omni coming out. As they met both vehicles stopped.

Rolling his window down, John said, "I see the vehicle is still here."

"Yeah. It's parked down there but the marijuana is gone."

Looking ahead John saw the white pickup approaching. "He's coming out now." His thought to stop the vehicle was dropped as he realized he had no credentials or hand gun. The vehicle, driven by a middle aged man wearing the very visible large white hat, slowly continued its approach and passed the two parked vehicles. Checking his scribbled note, John ascertained that the Texas license number matched. Switching his police radio to the municipal frequency, he breathed into the mike. "Sauk City - C113"

"Go ahead C113," answered Betty.

"The suspect vehicle just left the park heading south on Water Street. I'm following him."

"10-4 - C113, Car 63 is now in service. I gave him the THC complaint. You can contact him direct."

Gaining speed John pulled in closely behind the pickup looking for evidence of the marijuana. With the tailgate down, small green leaves were occasionally whipped off the truck. With his previous information John was convinced it was marijuana.

"Car 63, this is C113. I'm following the suspect truck. It just turned off 12 heading west on Washington. I'll advise where he goes."

Siren wailing, Pete responded "10-4 - C113. I'm trying to intercept you."

Continuing to follow, John informed Pete of each turn made. His concentration at the time prevented him from recognizing several unusual things. Later, a recorded tape of the radio transmission would show that Pete's breathing had noticably increased and become louder and more audible, his apprehension growing far in excess of the occasion. Secondly during several transmissions his siren was running; on others it was not, indicating he was turning it on and off.

The suspect, becoming more anxious at the pursuing vehicle, glanced more often to the rear, his large white hat accentuating the nervous movements.

After several turns the vehicle turned into an apartment building driveway at the intersection of Oak and Ash Streets.

As the vehicle stopped a short distance down the driveway from the street John continued past turning his head to the right noticing the man slouch quickly down in the seat to avoid being recognized. Not wanting to lose sight of the suspect he turned into a driveway about one hundred yards beyond. Backing up into the street and turning around, he parked facing the pickup waiting for Pete.

Having told Pete the location, he sat and watched the immobile man sitting in the truck transfixedly staring straight ahead.

Peter Johnson stopped his squad at the intersection of Ash and Oak Streets, glancing from side to side in anticipation of spotting the suspect.

John's voice came calmly over the radio. "Look to your left Pete. That white pickup parked in the apartment building drive kiddy corner across the street is your man. He's still sitting in it, wearing a large white hat. I'm off duty and not armed, but I'll stand by. Okay?"

"I'm with you," came the curt reply. Red and blue lights continuing to flash, Pete's squad shot quickly through the intersection blocking the driveway behind the pickup. Stepping smartly from the squad, he marched very erect and straight toward the pickup. Peter Johnson, an experienced law enforcement officer, had worked with several enforcement agencies before taking a job at Sauk Prairie. A striking figure because of the way he carried himself and his immaculate uniform, the slender six footer strode forward in a rigid stance as though marching in review.

When Pete arrived John drove up nearer and parked. Hurrying he met Pete on the street behind the white pickup.

Curtly, Pete inquired, "what's going on John?"

"Well, as Betty told you, a Bill Rush came into the station saying this guy is hauling some pot. I picked him up at the park. I saw leaves that looked like pot fly off his truck. There's one thing though. I don't have my credentials or handgun along. I'll stay and back you up though. Okay?"

Coming in strikingly rigid radio code language Pete's answer surprised John. "10-4. I'm with ya. We'll do this by the book." Marching alongside the truck his rigid stance more noticable than usual he jerked the driver's door open and demanded, "Let me see your driver's license."

"What for?" the man objected.

Sternly Pete repeated, "Let me see your driver's license."

Without further objection, the man reached into his hip pocket and withdrew a wallet and began to fumble through it.

Without waiting a second stiff command came from Pete. "Get out of the car."

Stress and irritation showing on his reddening face, the man swiveled, dropped his feet hooking them on the bottom of the open door and sat facing Pete. "This is as far as I'm going."

John, alternately watching the pair and picking up marijuana seeds and leaves from the pickup, was startled as Pete uncermoniously yelled, "You're under arrest," grabbed the man's right arm and savagely wrenched him out of the truck, the large white hat sailing like a frisbee into the street. Desperately Pete struggled, attempting to throw him down, the man trying to jerk away.

John rushed to Pete's side and grasped the man's wildly swinging left arm. With the man now securely held, Pete slammed him belly down solidly

30

to the unyielding concrete. Going down with the man, John thought, *boy he sure put him down hard.* The small resistance offered by the man quickly turned to panicky questioning, "what's going on? Why are you doing this? What's this all about?"

Silently Pete slipped his handcuffs out and snapped one onto the man's left wrist, held firmly by John, and the other on the right wrist he held.

Incapacitated the man lay stiffly unresisting face down on the concrete drive in shocked silence.

John bent over, "Do you have any weapons on you?"

A subdued, croaking voice replied, "Y-yeah, j-just a pocket knife."

"Where?"

"In - In my right pocket."

"Front or back?"

"F-Front - R-right."

Bending lower John removed a folding buck knife and laid it well out of reach on the concrete. Continuing the search, he handed eyeglasses in a case to Pete, and he tossed other oddities into a pile with the knife. The search completed he stood to see the man roll on his side trying to get up. "Get down on your belly. I'm a State Conservation Warden." He had forgotten he carried Sauk County Sheriff's credentials in his pocket. Reaching down, he turned the man back to his stomach. "Just stay on your belly."

Suddenly a feeling of compassion for the man flooded his consciousness at the rough manner he had been thrown. Bending over, his calm voice gave the man encouragement. "Just hang on a few minutes. This will be over soon." Little did he realize how prophetic his words were to be. Arising he walked behind the truck meeting Pete who was returning from the squad. Gathering up pieces of marijuana leaves and seeds, he asked " Pete, do you have evidence bags? I'll package some of this stuff."

"Don't worry about it. It's resisting a Federal Agent."

Turning, puzzled at the strange answer, John looked intently at Pete who stared blankly into the pickup box as though looking completely through it.

Wondering at Pete's behavior his mind worked overtime to decipher the meaning of Pete's words. *Is Pete somehow working with the Feds? He doesn't make sense otherwise. Could be I suppose. I'll be glad when this is over.*

Continuing to gather marijuana John moved behind the truck to better reach in the box. He again glanced at Pete who suddenly shook his head as though to clear his mind of some strange vision. As though a decision had been made Pete's face appeared blank yet determined. He strode purposefully toward the cuffed man who lay quietly facedown on the concrete.

John jerked visibly at the crashing roar of a shot that reverberating up and down the sleepy Sauk City streets. Swiftly turning, his gaze fastened unbelievingly on Pete, arms outstretched, grasping the downward aimed silver .357 Magnum in the typical two handed police firing position. Frozen, his frenzied mind unable to comprehend the truth the split second allowed him to see the muscles in Pete's upper arms jerk as the handgun roared a second time directing the second lethel load into the already bloody man's head. Blood spurted like an artesian well gathering in a widening pool on the concrete.

With the muzzle blast and flash still vivid in his befuddled mind, John attempted to gather his thoughts and grasp the significance of what had happened. *My God! He shot the guy. Killed him. What's going to happen now. I'm a witness to murder.* Consciously wresting his mind from the macabre thought, he realized his actions in the next few seconds may mean life or death. Watching Pete walk stiffly toward him, his eyes strangely vacant the gun pointing in his direction caused spasms of fear to flood his being. His mind raced to provide a way out. *I better get down, maybe I can hide behind the truck, or just run. No, too close for that. Too late to do much. Pete's already too close.* John's snap decision was to face him as best he could. Hardening himself not to show fear, his step toward Pete appeared firm and sure, his outward appearance calm. "Pete, you're not going to shoot me are you?"

With little emotion except for his furious gum chewing, Pete answered, "Don't worry about it. He's resisting a Federal Agent." Turning on his heel, he holstered the firearm, walked stiffly to the squad, got in, sat down and stared fixedly straight ahead.

Blessed relief flooding through him, John, with a final glance at Pete and the grisly sight of the man lying in an everwidening pool of blood, legs jerking convulsively in the final throes of death, ran for his life. Jumping into his truck, he threw it frantically in reverse, motor roaring, wheels squealing as they propelled it down the street. While racing backward, somehow extremely calm now, he jotted down on his warden log. **Shot him in the head. Said resisting Federal - resisting Federal Agent - Shot twice.** Safely out of effective hand gun range, he stopped. Watching Pete intently, he keyed the mike, keeping in mind the fact that Pete could hear his every word, "Sauk City, C113, I have 10-33 (emergency) traffic." At this Pete opened the door, stepped out of the squad and walked deliberately toward him. John's thoughts again raced. *He's coming down here to shoot me.* Intent on Pete, he considered what might happen. Quickly he considered running between the buildings to escape. *He could hunt me down and kill me, and claim I killed that man. He could claim a struggle took place and I killed with his gun.* As he backed further away, he remembered the loaded shotgun at his feet. Grasping it, he began pulling it from its case. *I'm not letting him do anything to me. When he gets down here I'm going to shoot him.*

Glancing back at Pete he again felt relief flood through him as Pete turned back to the prostrate form, kneel and remove the handcuffs, return to the squad and get in as though sleepwalking. John made one last notation on his log, **took handcuffs off.**

John transmitted again, "Sauk County, C113, I have 10-33 traffic." His transmission partially covered by Pete's heavy breathing as Pete very slowly and deliberately spoke. "Oak and Ash, subject was resisting arrest. It was necessary to 10-42 (End tour of duty)."

John persisted "C113 - Sauk County. Get some help down here."

"I'll get you someone."

"Get one and two down here. (Sheriff Al Shanks and Chief Deputy Butch Steinhorst)."

"10-4, C113 will do."

"Sauk City, get your chief down here and whoever else is available."

"10-4, C113 will do."

"Sauk County to Car 63, do you need an ambulance?"

Again Pete's slow, deliberate voice responded, "Necessary for an ambulance at this time."

The radio went wild with calls interrupting and covering each other. John finally got back in, "Sauk City, C113."

"Go ahead C113"

"Do you have these transmissions recorded."

The sheriff's department answered, "They should be. Car one and two are enroute."

Feeling more sure Pete would not come hunting him John moved his vehicle closer to observe better. He continued to answer radio calls.

"Sauk County to C113 are things down there still 10-33?"

"No, I guess not. The emergency seems over." His answer was given in spite of his wanting someone to show up fast - reasoning, *no sense in injuring someone getting here.*

Pete sat staring vacantly into space as though alone in the world.

The wait seemed unending as John stared at the fallen dead man. His ,eyes were transfixed by the blood running slowly in a stream, stopping and starting as lava flows, slowly cooling. The blood had almost reached the street when a small group of people began to gather.

Astounded, John watched as Pete got calmly out of his squad, pushed through the crowd and began to direct nonexistent traffic. With jerky movements like a mechanical toy, he stopped and started the imaginary traffic indifferent to the transfixed crowd watching the exhibition.

Red and blue lights flashing the ambulance arrived with Sauk Prairie Chief Rentmeister immediately behind.

Disturbed that Pete still had his gun, John turned to his dog Maggie, "Stay," he commanded. He opened the door moving swiftly to the ambulance. Still afraid of what Pete might do, he used the ambulance as cover between himself and Pete in his approach. As John drew near, Chief Rentmeister strode calmly over to Pete. "You know Pete department policy requires you to make a report of incidents like this. It also requires me to take your gun." Without further dispatch,he reached unobstrusively over and removed the firearm from Pete's holster, without resistance. "Pete, go sit in your squad."

Without response Pete calmly obeyed. Sitting in the squad he again stared blankly at the activity around him.

Still concerned John siddled up to Chief Rentmeister, "Bob, are there any guns in Pete's squad?"

"Why yes, there's a shotgun in the trunk. He won't be able to get it though. John, I don't want you to talk to anyone about this. Why don't you sit in my squad. I'll take your statement in a few minutes."

When Bob entered the squad, John, relieved to be able to talk with someone, let the calm he had maintained crumble. His words tumbled forth while his mind still wrestled to comprehend what had happened. "God Bob, I don't know what's wrong with Pete. He - He just shot the guy, f - for n -no reason. An execution. With the handcuffs on yet."

"What? He shot the man with the handcuffs on?"

"Y-Yeah he, Pete took them o -off afterward. Th -the man was laying down when it happened."

Wiping his brow Rentmeister continued, "Laying down with the cuffs on, My God."

"Thought he was going to kill me too." Letting his bottled up thoughts escape in a torrent of words, he disjointedly told the whole of it as Chief Rentmeister took notes.

Suddenly John's stomach rolled. "I've got to get out, I'm going to be sick. Got to get some air." Stepping from the squad he began gagging. The sickness slowly ebbed with the fresh air. Wandering aimlessly among his friends who were measuring, photgraphing making notes and sketches of the grisly scene, John was unknowingly looking for solace.

Noticing this, Al Shanks asked, "How you doing John?"

Unable to resist, he glanced at the prostrate body where the large pool and long river of blood were congealing into a Jello like substance. "Not so good," a sob tore from his throat. "I feel sick, think I'm gonna puke." Suddenly tears began again as he felt the urge to talk of the happening. "God, he just killed the g -guy. Y -you know-shot him, in the head -in the head, twice- deliberately -can't believe this is happening. h -hope I'm not blamed for this. T -thought he was going to kill me too."

"Don't worry about it," comforted Al. "There's no question as to what happened here. There was a witness. The whole story is out. It will be okay, John."

Activity increased as others arrived including Bill Richards an off-duty Sauk Prairie officer and Denny Jameson, the warden from Baraboo. Relieved to see Denny, John joined him in his vehicle.

"Come John, we don't have to stay here." Denny's calm comforting voice brought some relief to John as he listened to his practical advice. Suddenly John felt the need to talk about his experience again. Crying softly letting the tears unashamably run down his cheeks, he again related the unbelievable tale of a warden caught in a paradox. He had unwittingly assisted a law enforcement officer who had done the unthinkable. Something everyone knows cannot happen. A thing a fellow officer just cannot do. Yet, John knew it to be a reality.

Denny continued to comfort John as they arrived at the Sauk Prairie Police Department. "It'll be okay John. Let's set out here a while, until they call for you. Give you a chance to get away from everyone and gather your thoughts. None of this is your fault. It seems you did everything properly. Pete just went off the deep end. Now, I'm sure they will take a detailed statement from you. Just tell it like it happened." He continued with some of his life crisis and how he had dealt with them. "There's only one way to get over something like this. That's to face it and have it over with."

Al Shanks suddenly appeared at the window. "John would you please

34   *Execution*

come with me."

Leaving the vehicle, John was confronted by Sheriff Shanks, Chief Deputy Butch Steinhorst and Detective Kevin Fults. Al explained, "John, we'd like you to walk through this whole thing with us. Starting from here we'll get in a squad and go through all the motions. We want a complete picture from start to finish. This will be to your benefit as we want every piece of evidence available linked."

"Okay, let's go." He sighed relieved at the chance for physical activity to free his troubled mind.

Suddenly John thought of his loyal Labarador Retriever back in his vehicle. "Denny will you go back to my vehicle and pick up Maggie? I forgot all about her. I bet she's gone. I left the door open. Told her to stay. But that's a long time ago. Be lucky if she's still there. I've got a thousand dollars invested in her. Sure hate to lose her. She's a dandy. I left the truck running too." Assured the dog and truck would be taken care of, he went with the group.

At August Derleth Park, curious as to how the marijuana had disappeared in such a short time the investigating party searched the area. Seventeen large leafy marijuana plants were found stashed under some overhanging brush about one hundred feet from where the pickup had been parked.

After the rerun of events, Kevin Fults asked John if he could take a statement.

Entering the station John saw Denny sitting in the rear. "Did you find my dog?"

"Sure did, she was still sitting in the truck. You must have her well trained.

Relieved, John turned to Kevin. "Let's get this over with."

John's uncomprending statement was a sixty-two page tortuous tale of disbelief. A nightmare come true.

A search of Pete's flat revealed a person obsessed with politics and self-improvement. Found in the apartment were an American flag folded military style, assorted books, and political material. The books had such titles as "Write Better, Speak Better," " The Miracle of Speech," "Power and Professionals at Their Best." Also found were eighty-four political letters he had received, a notebook listing letters to President Ronald Reagan, Vice-President George Bush and other politicians, a ledger logging political contributions, and ten Jim Beam collector decanter bottles and a bottle of anti-psychotic pills in a wastebasket. Represented by attorneys John Cates and Scott Hassett of the prestigious law firm of Lawton and Cates of Madison, Pete's mental problems of more than a decade were brought to light.

Pete was first institutionalized in England in 1970 while working for the National Security Council, a super secret organization set up by President Truman. Of this agency, he would not speak as laws still exist prohibiting such disclosures. It was reasoned he may still feel a part of this agency.

Obsessed with self discipline, he logged his daily activities and set and followed a self-imposed curfew. He looked for and copied inspirational phrases from the Bible. Very particular about his physical appearance he consistently looked like a fashion plate. He always acted the perfect gentleman toward women and especially to his fiancee. He was to be married on January 4, 1987.

He suffered through the loss of his three year old son in 1975 and a separation from his wife in 1981 culminating in a difficult divorce in 1985. At times he had sleepless periods lasting a week or longer. He saw things that didn't exist, often claiming to see blood. These things occurred after failing to take his prescribed drugs or when the medication was changed.

On September 14, 1986, President Reagan and his wife Nancy appeared on television asking the American people to aid in eradication of drugs. So on September 16, 1987, two things obsessed him: the President's war on drugs and his love for his wife to be.

He insisted he killed in the line of duty carrying out President Reagan's orders. A paranoid schizophrenic, he was sent to the Mendota State Home for the Insane where he continued to claim he rightfully killed a man resisting a Federal Agent, until his death in June of 1988.

The night following the killing shortly after midnight, unable to sleep, John welcomed Chuck Schreiber a Sauk County Deputy Sheriff and friend. Knowing John would not be sleeping Chuck stopped to help him talk things out.

The two sat drinking coffee going over the incident time and again. Still without an answer as to why Pete committed the terrible act John was nonetheless thankful for the opportunity Chuck had given him to ease his mind. Keeping Chuck until 4 a.m. John fell into bed exhausted. Drifting into a deep sleep he awoke screaming. His bizarre dream, was of Pete sneaking from John's deck into his bedroom to kill.

Arising the next morning he walked outside into a beautiful golden sunlit day. Gazing across the prairie at the many shades of green in the distant hills he was suddenly struck with a new awareness of the beauty around him. Things were sharper, clearer and more pungent than he remembered: The sweet smell of the sun drying the dew off the grass, the sweeter tones of the chirping birds, the beauty of nature all around him. This contrasted sharply with the sickening fear, the spectre of the gun roaring, blood spurting and the repulsive thrashing of a human body dying in handcuffs. Wiping the tears that ran so freely, he realized suddenly he was facing his own mortality. He would live with both extemes the rest of his life. He would forever feel more, enjoy more and care more and therefore live his life to the fullest as every person does who faces death squarely in the face and survives.

The dreams were to persist for some time especially when reminded of the episode by unkind people who delight in haressing law enforcement people. Later that month the dreams were to become vividly real after viewing a television news report of a protest against police brutality held at the State Capitol. Signs were posted around Madison and surrounding counties depicting a policeman shooting a handcuffed prone person. Printed in bold print were the words PROTEST PIG MURDER.

The dreams became fewer and less vivid as time passed. The tremendous out pouring of comfort and understanding from his peers and his department helped. Training Officer Larry Miller spent considerable time with him trying to relieve some of the trauma. Warden Joe Davidowski's wife Jan called and invited John and his wife Vicki to visit Superior. While working and hunting along Lake Superior, Joe shared some of his life crisis with him and how he solved them. Such concern was expressed by many wardens' families across the state.

While not completely over the shock, the vivid memories of that fateful night are slowly fading. Realizing they will never completely go away John and Vicki are constructively going forward to live the good life.

Chapter 6

Gutter Talk

Jim grumbled unintelligibly as he pushed back his supper plate. With a tired sigh he strode swiftly to the phone as if to quickly strangle the bothersome noise. It had been a hectic day. He had gotten up at 4 a.m. to check waterfowl hunters, and the dozens of complaints followed up without any results had rankled him. Unceremoniously he jerked the phone off the hook and spoke irritably into the receiver.

"Chizeks"

"This is John Graf."

"Yes John. What do you want?" Jim asked.

"I wanna collect deer damage on my corn. Those damn deer are eating me out of house and home. Come out and I'll show you."

"Look John, I'm eating supper. I've talked to you about deer damage before. Ya know the state can't pay on posted lands."

"I remember what ya said. That don't make it right."

"Look, I know your lands are posted. The law doesn't allow me to pay you."

"That don't make it right, and damn it, you're just like the rest of the conservation department. No good. The wardens are the worst of the bunch. Quick to arrest a poor farmer if he kills one of your sacred cows, but when we need help, you're no where to be found! I think you're just damn good and lazy!"

Fighting to control his anger, Jim spoke calmly into the phone. "I know you have a problem out there. There are a lot of deer in your area. There is no doubt they are doing damage to your crops. But I've explained my limitations to you a dozen times. I've already had a full day, and I'm not coming out. I saw the trespass signs on your lands just yesterday."

Bellowing like a bull, John shouted, "I'm a citizen. I have certain rights, and damn it you work for me. I'm demanding you come out."

"Okay. I'll come out and talk to you even though it's a waste of time. Be out soon as I finish supper."

Driving into the cold fall night, Jim mused. *What am I going to say to him? Don't want to start a fight. That's just what he'd like. He's too damn good at it, too. Remember how he swung with that monkey wrench the time he had the illegal deer? Tough as hell.* As Jim turned off the car in Graf's driveway, he thought, *Be careful.* Jim could hear the chug-chug of the milking machine. He knew John was in the barn milking.

Entering the barn Jim shielded his eyes from the glow of the gas lantern and jumped back as John rushed passed him with a milker bucket in his hand. As the farmer dumped the milk into the strainer, Jim said, "Hi John. I'll wait till you're done milking."

Stooping swiftly and swinging the teat cups up rhythmically, John replied, "No go ahead. I can talk while I milk."

"Well, as I told ya on the phone, there's no way I can pay you deer damage. I know you've got damage. But because of the way the law is written, I can't authorize payment. The legislature has decided it's better to have hunters kill the deer off where they are doing damage."

"The legislature is not always right."

"I'm not in a position to comment on that. I carry out their orders. Your land is posted. I can't pay and that is that."

"Like hell it is. I'm entitled to collect and you're just trying to bamboozle me out of it."

In desperation, Jim said, "I've got the statute book right here. Like to see the law."

"Don't want to see no damn law. Ya should do what's right. Those deer are ruining me. Just okay payment," he spat.

Face reddening, he jerked the milker violently from a nearby cow, and moving like a cat in spite of the weight as he passed near Jim, leaned over enough to allow the bucket to bump him. Catching his balance, Jim thought, *"He's looking for trouble, and damn it, I'm almost at the point to let him have his way. - Whoops can't do that. I'm a public servant. Got to keep the cap on. But just how much of this crap can I take? That big son of a gun might kill me. He's whipped half the people in this neighborhood. He enjoys it."* He was shaken from his reverie by John's shout.

"Damn you. Can't you hear? I asked if you're going to pay?"

"Look," Jim said pointing his finger and feeling the heat rise in his face. "I'm getting a little tired of your screaming. I've told you over and over I can't pay damages. And I meant it." Waving the statute book he'd carried with him into the barn, Jim said, "I will explain the law to you completely and be on my way."

Charging between two wildly balking cows, John swiftly ran across the barn alley and reached down to a shelf on the wall. Startled, Jim saw the tire iron swiftly rise. Backpeddling, he slipped in the gutter and stumbled into the cows, ducking just in time as the tire iron whistled dangerously close to his ear. In the same twisting motion, he reached desperately and grabbed the weapon with his left hand. John jerked to loosen it, but Jim's was a death grip.

"My God man, are you crazy?"

The warden's question was obliterated by the curses bursting from John. "I'll kill you!" the farmer screamed. His wild charge carried both men to the slick concrete floor where they sprawled in the manure filled gutter.

Caught in a headlock, Jim's head was jammed down into the disgusting, strangling manure and urine. His breath completely cut off, Jim felt himself weakening from the loss of air. *My God,* he thought, *he's drowning me.* Struggling desperately, he rolled clear. Relief flooded him as he blew manure out of his mouth and nose. Reason began to return with the oxygen. *Take it easy. Don't panic. It can't last long. Get your licks in when you can. The cool one will win.*

The two men were locked in a desperate battle fighting for the iron. Blows fell mercilessly on each man as they rolled crazily under the bucking cows and through the gutter a second time. The whole barn was a bedlam of kicking, jumping, bellowing cattle. The kicking and stomping cows brought grunts from the men as the hooves landed on them. The milker buckets flew off the cow's teats and spewed milk on them. The full gutter became a whitish brown as the milk mixed creating a digusting quagmire. John's cursing ceased. Out of breath, they fought silently now. Rolling under and toward the heads of the cattle, Jim suddenly felt the tiredness hit John. Now. Giving a mighty heave he rolled him off. Lurching tiredly forward he slid on top. The fight had carried the men into the manger under the cows' heads. The cows, more terrified than ever, lurched crazily to get away from this madness, the stanchions holding them solidly in place.

Looking at John, Jim could see and feel further strength drain from him. Placing one knee on the farmer's chest and the other on his throat, Jim brought his weight down heavily. Using both hands the warden gave a tremendous twisting jerk, wrenching the tire iron from Graf's grasping hand.

Now anger took over. Sneering an obscenity, Jim bellowed, "Now I'm going to ram this damn thing up your _____!" With a mighty effort he stopped his downward swing, thinking *don't do it. You'll kill him. So what that's what he was trying to do to me. No, I'll be in trouble. He's not worth it.* Looking into John's pleading eyes, Jim realized the vanquished man understood his unspoken thoughts as though they had been shouts. Moving his knee to allow breathing, Jim asked, "You done?"

"Yep."

"Okay, Get up. One wrong move and I'll brain you." Holding the tire iron in a threatening position he let John stumble to his feet. "Now move - out there." Pushing and nudging with the iron he directed Graf to the open barn alley.

"Sit on that stool. I came out here to explain the deer damage law. Damn it you're going to hear it. Word for word!" Brandishing the iron, Jim backed to where he could retrieve the statute book from the gutter. Brushing manure from his hands and face, he approached the beaten man, opened the statute book. Holding the iron high, he said, "Now listen." Still breathing hard, he read the deer damage law from start to finish.

"Now do you understand the law?"

Gasping, John nodded. "Yeah, yeah."

His anger cooling, Jim said simply, "John, don't you ever call me about deer damage again!"

Chapter 7

Beaver Shootout

Beaver were abundant before settlement in Wisconsin. Due to extensive logging and fur trapping they became scarce by the turn of the century. Factory production provided an abundant supply of economical, efficient steel traps, making the beaver more vulnerable. By 1903, there were only three known live beaver colonies left in Wisconsin.

Trapper Norman Thompson and Warden Harvey Mau

A number of steps were taken to repopulate the state with beaver. None were successful. Laws were enacted to more closely regulate methods of taking. Closed seasons were established and strictly enforced. The first closed season extended from 1893 through 1898. Again in 1903 the season was closed until 1917. From 1917 until 1923 very limited trapping was permitted. Because populations did not respond, the season was again closed from 1924 through 1933.

Slowly small numbers of beaver colonies began to be evident in the northern tier of counties. Beaver pelts, highly regarded during the era for use in making clothing, brought good prices. Because of the demand, a bootleg market began. With trapping seasons closed, trappers could not legally possess or sell pelts. Bootleggers were able to create a prosperous market and buy these illegal pelts at perhaps one quarter to one half the real value. An average prime legal pelt was worth $45. Twenty dollars for a beaver hide looked good to a hardworking farmer at a time when a loaf of bread or a ring of baloney could be purchased for 10¢.

This was the era of prohibition when it was illegal to buy and sell any intoxicating beverages in the United States. Often the people bootlegging illegal beaver pelts were also bootlegging moonshine whiskey, making both endeavors more profitable.

Game wardens during this era were putting forth a great deal of effort to protect the beaver with special emphasis on the bootlegger in an attempt to dry up the market. Without a market, the beaver would not be taken.

It is against this backdrop in history that this story takes place.

On Thursday, May 16, 1929, Einar Johnson and Alan Hanson, two young conservation wardens left Ladysmith heading north along Rusk county highway J to check for illegal beaver traps. Einar had received information that illegal trapping was taking place near the Bissell Lumber Company Camps in south central Sawyer County.

A newly fallen skiff of light snow covered the already icy, muddy, narrow dirt roads making driving extremely dangerous and slow. Maneuvering the Model T Ford carefully over the treacherous rutty roads, Einar told Alan of the complaints he had received, "John Heden says there are a number of beaver sets along the Thornapple river near the Bissel camps. He's given me good information before. I think the traps will be there."

Einar, stationed at Ladysmith for two and a half years, was a wiry man of five foot ten inches in his early thirties. An experienced warden who had worked around the state with a number of wardens, he had earned a reputation of being confident, earnest and steadfast. He had served overseas in the tank corp during the world war and had been discharged as a second lieutenant with an excellent military record.

While in the service of his country in 1918, he met and married Miss Evelyn Welsh of Eau Claire, their home town.

Alan Hanson at age 24, having recently worked in Bayfield County for several months as a warden had been assigned to work for Einar Johnson on May 8. Only slightly experienced, Alan had not acquired a handgun as yet. The last week had been spent working on the illegal taking of beaver. Einar and Alan talked for hours of the beaver bootlegging operation exisitng in their assigned areas. Alan, a well-built man slightly taller and heavier than Einar, sat contentedly absorbing the heat drifting up between his feet.

"Sounds good Einar. Where does this Heden live?"

"In a shack at the Bissel camps. We'll stop and see him on our way up."

"You know Einar I tried to buy that gun yesterday, you know the one I told you of, the 45. The guy wanted $15 for it. I just didn't have that much money." These prophetic words were to be remembered by Alan for many years.

"If you'd asked I would have loaned you the money. Dealing with some of these beaver trappers and buyers is dangerous. The state should really furnish guns for us."

Turning right at point where Highway J cut east toward Big Falls, Einar stared intently concentrating on a car slowly navigating the slippery road ahead of them. Still in the distance, he observed the car, "I believe that's the car we stopped last week at Ingram."

"You mean the one we suspected was buying beaver? The blue DeSoto with Minnesota plates?"

"Yeah, remember the guy. Grace. He's the guy that hangs around the Donaldson place. What was his first name? Lynn, Lynn Grace, that's his name.

42

He's definitely a beaver bootlegger. By the way, see this place on the left. That's Donaldson's. I know this Grace guy sort of headquarters out of here. They're in cahoots. I think they help him peddle some of the illegal beaver. He stays with them sometimes. They're good people otherwise, but be very careful of anything you say around them about the illegal beaver traffic. Look, see the tracks, that car came out of Donaldson's drive. That's got to be Grace."

Squinting, facing the brightness of the early rising sun, Einar continued, "He turned north on the Winter Road. Reports are that Grace buys beaver all over the north country. I know he bought beaver around here all winter. Maybe today is our day."

"You going to tail him?"

"No. He may have spotted us. He's great for stashing packets of beaver in the woods. With this new snow we should be able to see if they stop to hide anything."

Passing the Winter turnoff, Einar continued east toward Big Falls far enough so people in the other car could not see them turn around. Returning, they too turned north following the suspect car. Proceeding cautiously a short distance, Einar stopped just short of the crest of a large hill. "I'm going to take a quick peek."

Stepping quickly from the idling car, leaving the door open, he sprinted surreptitiously to the crest of the hill to study the road ahead with binoculars. Turning, he returned briskly and started the the Model T car with a lurch.

"Could see for a long ways and couldn't see anything ahead. Must have poured it on. Didn't think one could drive that fast on these slick roads. Maybe he suspects us?"

Lynn Price, alias Grace, had in fact noticed the black Ford on Highway J. "Damn it Neal," he spoke to his partner and brother-in-law. "There's a car behind us. It looks like the warden's car. We've got to get rid of these beaver. You got your gun loaded?"

"Yeah, I'm always ready for game wardens!"

Pushing the blue DeSoto to dangerous speeds, slewing from side to side, they continued north. Topping the large hill, Lynn had not anticipated its steepness. Unable to control the car, it slid from ditch to ditch and finally slid off the left side of the road where it mired in the half thawed gumbo. "Now we're in for it. Get rid of those hides fast."

"Neal Meister, alias, Pete Carlson, the name he used when buying illegal beaver, quickly grabbed the packsack of beaver pelts from the back seat and ran toward the nearby cedar and spruce swamp across the road.

Proceeding carefully down the hill, Einar commented, "Boy they sure slid around here. Look at those skid marks."

Shifting in his seat to better see ahead, Alan concentrated on a dark spot that attracted his attention to the left. "Hold it Einar. There it is. The car is in the ditch. No wonder you couldn't see it ahead."

Applying the brakes, Einar, unable to control the slow moving car, skidded from side to side slewing sideways to a stop about forty-five feet from the blue DeSoto.

Killing the motor, he said "That's the car all right, but it's got

California plates on it now. Something is screwy here. No one around. Wonder where he disappeared to so fast?"

Getting out they slowly approached the car. Looking through the windows, they quickly determined no one and no furs were in it.

Carefully scanning the whiteness of the new snow, the two saw plainly two sets of man tracks entering the swamp. The length of the strides indicated one was walking the other running.

Einar, gazing into the forested area, softly voiced his thoughts. "They're not far, didn't have time enough. They're stashing furs just as sure as God made little green hazelnuts."

Suddenly there was movement as a man pushed his way through the dense underbrush and evergreens moving swiftly toward them.

Recognizing the man immediately, Einar's suspicions were confirmed. "Well, Mr. Grace, what are you doing in this country today?"

"Oh, nothing, just passing through. You're always bothering me. What do you want?"

"Well now you wouldn't have a load of beaver hides stashed in the woods would you?"

"Naw, just walked out there to take a leak."

"Here in the middle of the wilderness you had to walk back in the woods to take a leak?"

"Yeah, what's it to you? Got to get a pull. I'm going down the road to Donaldson's to get a team of horses."

"Wait a minute Grace. How come this car has California plates on it? Last week it had Minnesota plates."

"Oh that, well, I'm moving to California. Those plates are mine and they're proper. Besides it's none of your damn business. I don't like you harrassing me like this all the time. I don't have to put up with it. You stopped me last week. I had no furs and now you're looking again. Why don't you leave me alone?"

"Well you don't have to get huffy. I don't believe your story. Plates are issued after you move from one state to another. I won't pull any punches, I think you're bootlegging beaver. I think you put those plates on your car to throw us off the track. I'm going to turn you over to the sheriff for using those plates on your car."

"Go on, you're so damn smart. But right now I'm leaving to get a pull."

"What is your partner doing out in the brush"

"What partner? I'm alone."

"Alone, you take us for fools."

"You're the one that said it and maybe I do."

Einar continued, "There are two tracks into the woods."

"Well, if you think there is someone out there, why don't you find him? Are you afraid of the woods? The big bad wolf may get you. I'm going."

"We don't have anything on you at this time, but we'll be looking up your partner and the beaver you stashed. You go ahead and get the horses. We'll be here when you return."

Returning his attention to the car, Johnson said, "Alan why don't you take the other track and see if you can shag the other guy out. I'm sure he has beaver hides."

"Okay. That guy was sure mad. Must be something going on here."

Entering the dense foliage, Hanson followed the distinct tracks in the snow a short distance to where they turned back toward the road.

As Alan disappeared, Einar noticed another movement at another spot in the swamp. That movement materialized into a man walking swiftly toward him stiff legged as though mad. "What's going on here?"

"We're conservation wardens and we're looking for illegal furs. What were you doing back in the swamp, may I ask?"

"You may ask, but it's none of your damn business."

"Well, it is my business. I think you've just hidden some beaver hides back in there."

"Naw. I was just taking a walk. Anything wrong with that?"

"Taking a walk with a bundle of furs no doubt."

"No furs, like I said, just getting a little excercise."

"What's your name?"

"What's it to you? We're not doing anything wrong."

"We'll see about that. I notice this car now has California plates on it. We stopped Grace in this car last week and at that time it had Minnesota plates on it. Can you explain that?"

"Oh it's Grace's car. Don't know anything about that. Why don't you ask him? It's none of my business. I'm just riding along."

Wondering about the change of plates, Einar lifted the hood. Bending he gazed intently at the motor. Pad in hand, he jotted down the motor number. "I'm giving this information to the sheriff." Satisfied he again returned to the passenger side glancing through the window and windshield to see if he had missed anything.

Meanwhile where the trail turned back toward the road, Hanson came upon a large leather packsack pushed back under some low hanging balsam trees. Squared off fully loaded, he was surprised at the weight as he dragged it from its hiding place. Glancing at a slit where the flaps did not quite reach his eyes picked up the glint of gunmetal and beaver fur. In a hurry to show Einar, he grunted as he threw the heavy load over one shoulder and hurried to the road.

Dropping the large packsack unceremoniously near the two between the road and car, he said, "Look what I found Einar."

"Just as I thought. Open it up. It has to be beaver hides."

As Alan struggled with the straps, he said, "I saw beaver hair before I came out."

Turning to the man who now stood slightly in front of the car, Einar barked, "I'm through monkeying with you, what's your name?"

"Pete Carlson."

"Well Pete, you're under arrest."

Still struggling with the taunt straps, Alan looked up with a start at the quick movement of the stranger as his right hand dipped into his mackinaw pocket. Two quick jerks and an upward glistening arc revealed a colt automatic pistol gleaming brightly in the strong morning sun. "Put 'em up you dirty..." The statement was never finished.

Seeing the gun brought a sudden lump to Einar's stomach. "Give him the stuff Alan. We're beat." Automatically reacting to the danger, he turned and leaped across the ditch landing in the road.

The roar of the .45 caliber pistol reverberated through the silent cut over area. The large slug slammed into Einar's back, the impact almost lifting him off his feet. The terrific shock spun him around to face his attacker. Another shot rang out as he fumbled desperately in his mackinaw pocket. Finally grasping the colt automatic, as if in a dream he raised it toward the blurred figure and pulled the trigger. The huge boom and recoil almost tore the large gun from his weakened grasp.

The bullet finding its mark pounded into the stranger's chest, the shock staggering him. Maintaining his balance only by supporting himself against the car, he continued to fire at his hated rival. The surging pain through his chest affected his aim and he swore silently as he attempted to draw down on the now unmoving target.

Intense pain and a great fatigue enveloped Einar as he directed the second shot at his adversary with no effect. Uncontrollably his arm dropped weakly to his side his numbed fingers letting the gun slip from his grasp. Gazing through a painful haze, he saw the man struggle to hold his gun steady for one last shot. *Here it comes,* he thought. *Can't move. He'll finish me now.* The subdued boom seemed as in a far off bad dream as he slowly realized the shot had missed. Thankfully, he saw the man lower his gun and sink to his knees.

Slowly realization of his situation returning, his mind raced as to what his next move would be. *It's over. I'm hit bad. Got to get help.* Centering his gaze on the now prostrate man, he thought, *don't have to worry about him. He's done.*

Alan had frozen at the sight of the gun. "Don't Shoot," he pled. The silence seemed unending even though it was only a split second that his breathing had stopped . Then he was moving, jumping to escape. In midair when the first booming shot roared from the stranger's gun, he was galvanized into further action. Fleeing for his life, he ran as fast as his trembling legs would carry him. Frantic thoughts tumbled through his benumbed mind. *He shot Einar. He's killing him. Don't have a gun. What can I do? Got to get out of here. He'll shoot me too.*

Turning as though impelled by some inner being, he wasted precious seconds as he took one desparate look to the rear. The sight would be engraved in his subconscious the rest of his life. Einar with gun in hand facing his antagonist was returning fire. The stranger was in turn leaning against the DeSoto firing at Einar, both firing at point blank range.

Though befuddled by the unbelievable happening he witnessed, he still had the forethought to zigzag several times to provide a difficult target before veering sharply to his left to plunge into the dense swamp. Desperate to escape he plunged on through thick cedar and spruce. While providing concealment, they tore at his clothing slowing his retreat. Breath wheezing, he swore at the impeding obstacles, twisting and turning to avoid their grasp. Mouth open, gasping for more air, he plunged on until he fell exhausted into the thick soft moss of the swamp. Laying still gasping for breath, he waited and rested, the deep softness of the moss and the coolness of the fresh snow encouraging him to stay.

Listening desperately for pursuit, he imagined branches breaking as he knew the gunman would pursue and kill him. He was a witness to a shooting. Slowly his breath returned and his heart slowed though it still hammered in his ears. He now could hear well enough to know there was no pursuit. Resting, he anticipated his next move. *Can't go back to the road. That guy is surely looking for me. Think I saw him wince once. Maybe he's hit. Got to get help. He'll be looking for me on this side of the road. I'll sneak across. Know there's a house up ahead of the cars. Maybe I can get help there.*

Putting his plan into action called for being far enough away from the cars to avoid detection. Assured no one at the cars could see him, he slunk across the narrow road like a scooting coyote. Turning north, keeping a comfortable distance from the road he worked slowly and quietly toward the house. Missing the driveway he wandered aimlessly looking for the house. Hurrying now realizing his wanderings had taken a lot of time he finally, hitting the driveway, and followed it to the house. His urgent pounding on the door brought no repsonse. No one was home. His decision to break in and use the phone was discarded when he saw there were no phone lines leading to the house.

Working slowly down the drive toward the road he sneaked a glance down the road. No one was in sight. Slowly he emerged from behind the foliage and cautiously approached the car. The De Soto was gone. Tracks revealed it went south after being pulled out by a team of horses.

Blood stains in the whiteness of new snow depicted the previous savage struggle that had taken place. Two blood trails starkly marked the direction the two wounded men had taken. Following the trails a short distance down the road, he was forced to a decision, where the two trails parted. The one showing the most bleeding and staggering entered the woods on his right. *Must be the stranger,* he wrongly concluded. *He's heading for Donaldsons. He knows the area well. I'll stay on Einar's trail and help him.* Continuing down the road a short distance, the snow revealed the blood trail going into the brushy roadside on his left. *Could this be Einar?* A groan in the woods made him hasten to the area where Meister lay bleeding on a bed of boughs. Approaching hesitantly he saw it was the stranger whose breath wheezed hoarsely with blood oozing through the large bullet hole in his breast.

"I - Im need help. C -c - can you help m - me?"

"Don't know. What happened to Einar?"

"I - I shot - t him."

"Where is he?"

"D - Don't k - know. He - He walked away."

"I'm going for the sheriff." Without another word he returned to the road to continue his trek toward Donaldsons.

Barely able to stand after the shooting, Einar called out for Alan. His voice barely audible, he called out several more times. The enormity of the situation struck him sharply. Gazing at the blood blood spurting from his stomach, he instinctively placed his hand over it to slow the rapid loss. Staggering around, shock further weakening him he again called Alan's name. No response. *I'm alone. Hit bad. Can't last long. Got to get help.* Finally through the fuzz of pain and weakness, he thought of the car. I"ll drive to Donaldsons. Weaving his way to the car he reeled and spun along it catching the door handle in time to keep from falling. Bracing himself, he slowly opened the door, felt for and found the crank under the front seat. Clumsily setting the controls of spark and gas, he clung to the car working his way along it to the front. Fumbling the crank into the hole behind and through the bumper, he heaved mightily on it to no avail. His weakness was now so compelling he could not turn the motor over. Leaning against the car his dazed mind attempted to grasp the enormity of his situation. *Now what? I'll have to walk.* With one last look at the man lying in the blood soaked snow, he began his tedious tortured trek down the road. *Got to make Donaldsons.* He left a trail soaked with bright red blood, reeling from one side of the road to the other. His experience in the war made him face the cruel reality that he was mortally wounded. *Only a miracle will save me now. Got to conserve my strength and still get help fast.* A short distance down the road a quick decision was made to cut through the woods to the Donaldson farm. *It's a chance, I must take. If I pass out along the way, I may die before I'm found. It's much closer through the woods though Got to get help fast.*

Staggering from tree to tree using them as aids to support himself, he began what seemed to be a never ending journey. The instinct of a woodsman guided him ever forward in a southwesterly direction. Finally staggering into the farm yard at Donaldsons, he let himself drop to the ground. as Arthur Donaldson approached him, he let unconsciousness overtake him mercifully ending the searing pain in his middle.

The Donaldson brothers, Arthur and Erwin, were cutting firewood along the edge of their field about one fourth of a mile north of their home.

Suddenly Lynn Price appeared on the woods road walking swiftly toward them. "Hey boys, I need a pull. Ran off the road about a mile from here. Can one of you hitch up your team of horses for me? Got to hurry. The wardens are there."

Ervin responded, "Did they find the furs?"

"They hadn't when I left. They probably will though with this fresh snow. Neal ran into the woods to hide the packsack."

"Where's the car?"

"Right below the big hill on the winter road."

"Okay, let's go."

Suddenly a loud volley of shots rang out. All quickly turned to the southwest to face them.

Ervin stared unbelieving at the sound, "Oh, Oh, what's that? Sounds like about where your car is. Too fast to be hunters."

"Yeah sounds like Neal might have got into a shoutout. He always said he would never be arrested as long as he had his forty-five."

"I know. He's said that as long as he's been coming down into this country. I always thought him to be exaggerating. But you never know."

"He's really a good shot," commented Price. "We've all seen him shoot. He practices the quick draw enough to beat Johnson. He may be okay. Let's get going. I've got to get out of this country."

Arriving back at the farmhouse Ervin hurriedly harnessed the large team of workhorses and drove them east with the dragging heel chains and the logging chains jingling a melody. Turning north, he spotted Meister staggering along holding his breast with his left hand. On nearing him he could see the blood oozing between his fingers.

Nervously, Lynn questioned him, "What happened Neal? Did they find the furs?"

"Yeah, that damn J - Johnson s - shot me. I - I shot h - him too."

"Is he dead?"

"No, I- I don't t - think so. He's hurt worse th -then me -me. though. He - he's b - bad h - hit. He's h - heading to - toward yo - your place. Erwin. He's b - bleeding a l - lot more than m- me."

Price said, "You don't look so hot yourself. Come, we'll lay you down in the woods. No sense in walking any further."

Hurrying, the two men lent support to Neal as he was led into the woods where the pair broke down spruce boughs and formed them into a bed of sorts.

Assisting him onto the boughs, Price said, "You can rest here until Ervin gets me out of the ditch. I'll be back to pick you up in a short while. We've got to get the hell out of this country."

Laying on the boughs, depression suddenly hit Neal. "You k - know this mean l - life i - imprisonment for me. H - hell might as w - well finish m - myself off. I - I could n - not stand s - sitting in p - prison the r - rest of my l - life Lynn."

"Don't worry about it. We'll have that car out soon. We'll be on the road. I'll get you help. I'll get you back to Finland."

"T - there's n - no way we're going t - to g - get away w - with this." He fumbled the gun from his pocket maneuervring toward his temple. "T - there's n - no use. G -got my g - gun, I - I'll think a-about it. I- Im -might b - be d - dead when you return."

Reaching down Ervin gently pulled the gun from Meister's hand. "You're talking crazy. You'll get away. We'll help you." Turning he pocketed the gun. "Come Lynn let's get that car out."

With the chain hooked to the bumper, Ervin yelled, "Get up." The large team leaned into their collars and the DeSoto creaked and groaned as it was hauled back onto the road as if it were a toy. In the middle of the road, Price motioned to Ervin that he should slide the car sideways and Ervin reined the horses around the car. The car slid sideways and stopped, heading south.

As Irvin unhooked the team and drove them off to the side Price, excitement showing in his drawn face, grabbed the packsack heaved it into the back seat, jumped hurriedly into the car and started the motor. Wheels spinning, mind racing, he drove at breakneck speed south, not once considering stopping to pick up Neal Meister. Brother-in-law or not, Price was taking no chances. He was saving himself from the sheriff he knew would be on the scene soon.

Skidding to a stop at Davidson's fur shop in Ladysmith, he ran around the car, removed the packsack and ran into his shop. Better not have any evidence in the car if stopped. Gasping for breath, he slung the packsack at Davidson's feet, "Hold on to these. I've got to leave the country."

Davidson, a long time fur buyer who had often purchased illegal fur from Price, was immediately apprehensive. "Now, wait a minute. What's going on here? Are you in trouble? I don't want trouble with Johnson. Where's Neal?"

"We got in a scrap with Johnson. Got to get out of here."

Davidson, remembering some of his unpleasant encounters with Warden Johnson over the handling of illegal furs, was not one to easily involve himself in situations as sticky as this sounded. He commanded, "You're not leaving those furs here. Johnson will be around looking for them."

"Johnson won't be around. Not for a while, anyway. Neal shot him."

"W - What! Neal shot Johnson, and you want me to take these furs? Oh no, not me. Where is Neal now?"

"He was hit too. I'm going to pick him up now and we're leaving."

With Davidson protesting, Lynn hurried to his idling vehicle. "Got to get out of here. No one will know you've got the furs. Just keep your mouth shut. I've got to get out of here." Without further conversation, he entered the vehicle and drove speedily away leaving Davidson scratching his head as he watched the car slew around the corner.

Afraid to return to his home in Wautoma, Wisconsin, he headed north to Finland, Minnesota, his home town where he felt more secure.

Laying in the woods, Neal's life's blood seeped from his chest and back coagulating in piles on the spruce bough bed where he lay. It seemed a long time since Ervin and Lynn had stopped. Suddenly the De Soto appeared speeding down the road toward him. Relief flooded his anguished mind. *Maybe we can still get out of this mess.* Incredously he watched the speeding auto careen past. *What's goin on? Why didn't Lynn stop for me?* Slowly realization hit him. *Lynn left me.*

An urge to wipe his mouth startled him as his hand came back bloody. Looking at it closely he saw it was whitish red. An experienced hunter and trapper he immediately knew the reason. *Dang it. I'm lung shot. Won't last long.* As the pain increased he began silently cursing Lynn. *Damn him anyhow. I do his dirty work for him and this is how he thanks me. He's left me here to die. The least he could have done was to finish me off. Not much to live for now. Wish I still had my gun. If I ever get out of this, I'm going to get back at Lynn. I'll get even. Hell, I'll get ahead.*

When Einar passed out at Arthur Donaldson's feet, Arthur ran to the house to get his mother, Chris. Between them, they loaded the unconscious Johnson into their Model T Ford. Arthur drove the old car at breakneck speeds the eight miles to St. Mary's hospital. Thinking Einar slouched in the front seat to be dead, he ran inside for help.

Doctor Woodruff Smith, on duty at the hospital, rushed to Einar's side, and examined his wound while he was still on the stretcher. "Einar, Einar can you hear me? This is Doctor Smith."

Eyes flickering open slightly he indicated recognition by a weak grunt, "y - yeah. H - how b - bad?"

"I won't fool you Einar it's bad. We need to do surgery right now. Do you understand."

"Y - yeah. o - okay - m - my wife - E - velyn."

"Yes, Einar we've someone out looking for her now."

"T- tell W - Wilson [Sheriff E. Wilson] t - to l - look f -f or blue D - DeSoto. C - California plates."

"Okay Einar. Do you know who shot you?"

Nodding his head in the affirmative, he gasped, "P - Pete Carlson. I - I shot h - him too."

Motioning to the litter bearer Doctor Smith said, "we've got to get you to surgery right now."

Einar nodded his head in the negative trying to talk further. Doctor Smith bending over with his ear near Einar's mouth detected the whisper.

"C - call M - mac."

"Mac? Who's Mac?"

"M - Mac, B - Boss."

"Does Evelyn know who to call Einar?"

He nodded his head up and down as blissful darkness closed over him.

Surgery was long and tedious with Dr. Smith working savagely to save Einar's life. The large bore bullet had done its job well. Entering just above the hip, barely missing the spine, expanding as it went, it had pushed pieces of his red and white wool mackinaw jacket halfway through his body. The soft nosed bullet had expanded ripping and tearing its way through Einar's intestines and bowel exiting in a gaping hole near his navel. Walking and the rough ride in Donaldson's car had made conditions worse pushing the contents out of the bowel and intestines where they mixed into a jelly like composition. Doctor Smith cleaned, cut and stitched for hours. Making a last minute inspection to ascertian all holes were sutured, he finally closed the belly. Shaking his head and wiping his brow he left with Einar still under anesthesia. "I don't know about him," was his comment. "He's young and strong and may make it. But he was an awful mess."

After dropping Einar at the hospital, Arthur Donaldson drove to the sheriff's office where he told the story.

Sheriff E. Wilson grasped the situation swiftly. "Where's Alan Hanson? I know he was with Einar this morning."

"I don't know. Einar is the only one I saw except for Lynn Price who came to our place to get a pull for his car."

"Do you think he's involved in this?" Sheriff Wilson thought he noticed a slight distraction as Arthur answered, "I don't know. The shooting came from the direction of his car."

"Oh you heard the shooting? How many shots were fired?"

"Don't know. They came awfully fast. Ran altogether. Maybe six or seven."

"You say there is another wounded man out there?"

"That's what Einar said at the hospital."

"Do you know who he is?"

"Yeah, it's Neal Meister."

"Do you know him?"

"Well, yeah, he stays at our place sometimes."

"Do you know what brought about the shooting?"

"Not really. Well maybe."

"Come out with it man, we don't have a lot of time to waste."

"It may have been over illegal beaver hides."

"Okay, you can tell me more on the way. We'll pick up Doctor Caldwell as Doctor Smith is busy with Einar."

Arriving at the Donaldson farmstead, they saw Alan Hanson wandering aimlessly around the yard. Apprehensively he sidled up to Wilson, a question on his lips he really didn't want to know the answer to, but could not resist asking, "How's Einar?"

"Not too good. Where were you when all this happened?"

"I was there. I was unarmed so I had to beat it."

"Who shot Einar?"

"A guy called Pete Carlson. A fur buyer. Einar shot him too."

"We know that. We're on our way to pick him up now."

Ervin Donaldson had joined the group. "I know where Neal is. I'll go with you. He's hurt bad. Come on let's get him."

Meister had lain cursing Price until finally peaceful unconsciousness overtook him. He awoke with a start as someone shook him from his deep stupor. "W - what? W - who are you?"

"I'm Sheriff Wilson. I'm here to take you to the hospital."

"I - I want that damn J - Johnson arrested."

"What for?"

"H - he - e s - shot me."

"He claims you shot him first."

"H - he's crazy. He s - shot me and I s - shot him in s - self - defense."

"Makes no difference right now. Roll on this stretcher. We've got to get you to the hospital."

Later that evening when Einar was reported as resting easy, District Attorney H.F. Duckart attempted to get a statement from him in case his injuries were to prove fatal. Although concious, Einar was unable to talk.

The following day, Chief Conservation Warden Harland MacKenzie (Mac) and Warden Barney Devine arrived in Lady smith. Both tried to talk with Einar. The only words Einar was able to whisper were "D - Don't think I - I'll make it M - Mac."

As noon approached they left him to rest. With several other wardens they went to local diner for lunch. Discussing the shooting over after dinner coffee, they were interrupted by a nurse who had hurried over from the hospital. She informed them that Einar had just died.

After delivering the wounded man to the hospital, Sheriff Wilson drove to the scene of the shooting. In his investigation he found a colt 45 caliber automatic pistol and four empty brass casings west of where the DeSoto had been ditched. He also found three empty cartridge cases where Einar had turned and fired. The snow revealed stark testimony as to what had occurred. Studying the tracks in the snow and where the blood had first begun he determined that Einar had turned and jumped the ditch. His blood first showed in the ditch. The other person had first dropped blood on the other side of the car. Both had fired at point blank range of from ten to fifteen feet. Sketching the area, completely he returned to Ladysmith. Alan Hanson's story jibbed completely with Wilson's conclusions at the scene.

The following day, Wison interviewed the man known as Pete Carlson in the hospital.

"Will you tell me in your own words what happened out there?"

"Sure why not. I didn't know that Johnson guy was a game warden. He pulled his gun and shot me, so I pulled mine and shot him in self defense."

"What happened to your partner? Grace isn't it, Lynn Grace?"

"Damn it, he left me in the woods to die. I'll tell you about him. His real name is Lynn Price."

"Where's he from?"

"Wautoma, Wisconsin. I hope you catch him."

"For what? Did he do something wrong?"

"Yeah, he was bootlegging beaver around this country."

"You were too? Right?"

"Yeah, he hired me to help him."

"What was your job?"

"Well to protect him from wardens."

"Okay, and your name is not Pete Carlson. Correct?"

"Naw, might as well tell you. I suppose you have my wallet anyway."

"Yes and I've talked to the Donaldsons."

"My real name is Neal Meister."

"Where you from Neal?"

"Finland, Minnesota."

"Are you a fur buyer?"

"No, I just ride along with Lynn and trap beaver. I just keep him company."

Wilson slapped his notebook closed and rose to leave, "You told the Wardens the DeSoto car belonged to Price, is that right?"

"Yeah."

"Where did the California plates come from?"

"Don't know. Lynn put them on."

"This was to fool the wardens, was it not?"

"Yeah."

"Okay, Neal, I'll be in to see you when you're feeling better."

Sunday afternoon funeral services were held for Einar Johnson in Eau Claire, Wisconsin, his home town. A huge crowd attended with a large contingent of conservation wardens in full uniform making up part of the cortege.

His wife Evelyn and their two young daughters, Patricia and Delores were left to face the gloomy future. They would pay the supreme penalty for many years to come. Their future had been reshaped by the roar of automatic pistols. It would take years before they were able to adjust to the terrible thing that had happened to them. Never would they be able to forget the kind considerate husband and father they had lost. But live on they must, and without an income for there was no money provided by goverment programs at that time in history to provide for a family who lost the bread earner. All that remained was Einar's badge which Evelyn asked Chief Warden MacKenzie for to remind them of their loss.

The Ladysmith News in an article about Johnson's funeral stated, "This brave young man had repeatedly shown his fitness and alertness as a warden. He held to the path of duty regardless of danger. His untimely death is not only a severe blow to his family and friends, but a loss to the cause of conservation in Wisconsin."

On May 31, the Ladysmith News was headlined, **"Hold Inquest in Johnson's Death - Coronor's Jury Hears Evidence of Shooting of Conservation Warden and Names Neal Meister as Assailant. - Hearing in County Court Next Tuesday - Neal Meister Accused of Murder, Refuses to Take Stand at Inquest, and Will Face Preliminary Hearing Next Week; Doctor, Warden and Sheriff Testify."**

The Neillsville Press of May 23 stated that the Price brothers were in Neillsville Tuesday morning, Lynn Price had tried to sell his car to an acquaintance there saying that game wardens were after him for transporting beaver skins and in all probability if captured his car would be confiscated. It continued, "the Price brothers have lived for some time in an isolated settlement called Finland in the wilderness of northern Minnesota, where they claimed to be starting a fox farm, but admitting to acquaintances here that rum running from Canada had been one of their industries."

Any lawman makes enemies. Einar was no exception. In this area, where many people trapped beaver illegally to sustain their families, public opinion favored the trapper and fur buyer. People worked hard to beat back the wilderness. To trap a few beaver seemed their privilege.

Personal attacks and rumors circulated about the dead warden. In the public's eye his attitude was bad. It was rumored he often pulled his gun while making arrests, and intiminated people . Though the majority of the residents realized the need for protection of the resources, in particular beaver, at this juncture, they were silent.

The Ladysmith News editoralized, "Enforcing Conservation Laws Seems a Most Hazardous Occupation. It apparently was a safer proposition, in point of percentage, at least, to face the enemy in the world war, than it is for a game warden in Wisconsin to try to enforce the law. The death of E. P. Johnson last Friday makes the second death in the ranks of wardens this spring, met while in performance of their duties.

Indirectly only, we have heard remarks that would condone the shooting of Warden Johnson. It must require a very warped idea of citizenship to inspire a remark like that.

The man who talks the most about personal liberty and his right to violate any law that doesn't please him, and his intense dislike of any officer who will stand in the way of such violation, is the very first one to run under the sheltering wing of the law when someone encroaches on his legal rights.

Meanwhile the investigation continued under District Attorney Duckhart, Sheriff Wilson and Chief Warden Harland MacKenzie. Neal Meister was kept under guard night and day in the hospital. His wife came to visit him from Finland, Minnesota.

Under further questioning Meister admitted he was a hired gun for Lynn Price and responsible for the killing of Warden Johnson. He also implicated a number of people in the area who under questioning admitted selling many illegal beaver to the large bootlegging enterprise. Warden Barnie Devine (later to become chief warden) placed charges against these people. All paid fines of $50 and costs.

The Ladysmith News of May 24 carried an item headlined **Charged with Having Beaver, Probe of Warden Shooting Discloses Evidence of Beaver Hide Traffic; Many Warrants Issued.**

Two warrants were issued for Lynn Price. One for trafficking in illegal beaver hides and the other for being an accessory before the fact in the first degree murder of Johnson.

Price was finally taken into custody on May 18 by the sheriff in Lake County, Minnesota. The same sheriff that was to later testify to the good character of Neal Meister now released Price on a promise he would surrender himself to the Sheriff of Rusk County the next day. He did come to Ladysmith, however instead of going to the sheriff, he contacted his attorney and left town.

In July, the conservation commission adopted a resolution at their Ladysmith meeting honoring conservation warden Einar P. Johnson who was shot on May 16 "while faithfully performing his duty." Chief warden H. J. MacKenzie stated, "He was one of the finest wardens we ever had."

By November the stage was set for a rowdy trial. Neal Meister, after spending nine days in the hospital had recovered. The remaining time had been spent in the Rusk County jail.

The Ladysmith News of November 8, 1929 was headlined, **"Meister on Trial Now for Murder, Circuit Court Opens, Case Against Neal Meister of Finland, Minnesota, Here Wednesday Afternoon. Attorneys Debate Death Bed Statement."**

Wednesday the trial began with the courtroom filled to overflowing. Rumors were rampant, with most people who had an interest favoring Meister. Many thought Einar Johnson guilty of a crime of some kind. Law enforcement people were generally looked down on. Game wardens considered the worst of the bunch. Many people thought the state should not stop them from taking beaver. These were settlers, hardworking people who didn't need the state interferring with their intent. Working marginal land cleared by logging and burning, farmers in the area barely eeked out a living. After all wasn't the fish, game and fur there for their taking? They used them to subsidize their living regardless of laws.

Thirty jurors were questioned before a panel of twelve were selected. All women were stricken by the defense because most did not hunt or fish and therefore, they may have favored protecting beaver. Nine farmers, two merchants and a cement contractor were finally selected. All trapped extensively or occasionally except one.

Representing the defendant was O.J. Falge of Ladysmith and former United States Congressman from Duluth Minnesota, O.J. Larson.

After district Attorney Durkart outlined his case, defense attorney

Falge questioned whether the D.A. had sufficient grounds to support a first degree murder charge. He stated no malice aforethough had been alleged.

Judge Wickam ruled that if Meister had shot Warden Johnson because he thought the furs in the packsack were to be taken from him, that would indicate sufficient malice.

The defense admitted Neal Meister had fired the fatal shot taking Johnson's life, but in defense of his person.

Falge advised the court Lynn Price would not attend court. He said he had received a telegram from Price's attorney saying Price would not appear because of the pending charges of being accessory to murder.

Testimony began with Doctor Woodruff Smith describing Einar Johnson's wound.

His attempt to relate Johnson's death bed statement brought forth a barrage of objections from the defense. Judge Wickam upheld the objections and instructed Doctor Smith to confine his comments to what he had seen and not to what Johnson had said.

Thursday morning Judge Wickam asked Doctor Smith several carefully worded questions as to whether Einar Johnson had in fact made a statement before his death.

Doctor Smith indicated Johnson had made a death bed statement.

"Objection," shouted attorney Larson. "Only when a man is convinced he is dying is a death bed statement admissable in court. There is no testimony on record that Johnson knew he was dying. In fact I intend to put a witness on the stand that will show that Johnson expected to recover and be out of the hospital in several weeks."

"Ojection sustained."

With the setback, Duckart called Chief Warden H.W. MacKenzie. "Mr. MacKenzie, did you talk to Mr. Johnson shortly before his death?"

"I did."

"When did you talk to him?"

"Between 10 and 12 a.m. on May 17."

"The day of Mr. Johnson's death?"

"Yes, he died about 1 p.m."

"You talked to him just several hours before he died then."

"Yes."

"And what was Mr. Johnson's physical and mental state?"

"Very weak, but his mind seemed sound."

"Did he make any statement about whether he would live or die?"

"Yes sir."

"And what was that statement?"

"He said he knew he was dying."

"No further questions."

Attorney Falge jumped to his feet. "I ask for a recess so I can look for my witness."

Judge Wickam inquired, "Was your witness to be here?"

"He was." His name is Muriel Jones. He will testify that Johnson had expected to recover and be up town within two weeks."

Wickam chided, "You should have made sure your witness was on hand to testify. I will not hold up this proceeding at this time. You may put Mr. Jones on the stand when and if he shows up." Muriel Jones was never to testify.

The prosecutor then called Doctor Woodruff Smith back to the stand. "Now Doctor Smith could you relate any conversation you had with the deceased Mr. Einar Johnson the day of his death."

"Mr. Johnson was very weak and I didn't encourage him to speak."

"But he did."

"He wanted to and he did."

"What did he say? Please repeat those words exactly for the court."

"He whispered, 'I know I can not live.' He said, 'I told Pete Carlson he was under arrest. Carlson pulled his gun and yelled put them up you S.O.B.'"

"Dr. Smith, on the day Mr. Johnson first was admitted May 16, did he make any statement?"

"He said he had been shot by Pete Carlson and he had also shot Carlson. He also said Carlson drew his gun and fired first."

Dukart then called Miss Elizabeth Sandbate, a special nurse at St. Mary's Hospital who was assigned to care for officer Johnson.

"Miss Sandbate, you just heard Doctor Smith testify. Did you hear any statement made by Mr. Johnson."

"Yes."

"And was it substantially the same as Doctor Smith's testimony?"

"Exactly the same. I was with Doctor Smith when the statement was made."

"You had the privilege to talk to Warden Johnson at an earlier date also?"

"Yes, when Mr. Johnson first came in."

"Were you alone with him at that time?"

"Yes, sir."

"What was his statment?"

"He told me he knew he would die."

"At a later time was there another conversation between you and the deceased?"

"Yes."

"And what was that conversation?"

"He said Pete Carlson fired two shots at him."

Late in the day the District Attorney called Miss Melcher, another nurse at St. Mary's hospital.

"Did you have a conversation with Warden Einar Johnson?"

"Yes."

"When was that conversation?"

"About 4 a.m. on May 17th."

"That was early the day Mr. Johnson died. Did Mr. Johnson inquire about anyone?"

"Yes sir. He asked about Mr. Meister?"

Did you answer his inquiry?"

"Yes, I told him Mr. Meister was in the hospital."

"What was Mr. Johnson's response?"

"He said, Meister had it coming, he shot first."

The defense had not objected once during the testimony of the four people.

The testimony did not go unnoticed by the jury. At least three of them were highly disturbed because they knew Einar Johnson was a mad man who went around jabbing guns in people's ribs. Here were people they knew testifying that Johnson had not pulled his gun first. Johnson must have lied to all of them.

A request from the defense to break into the state's case was made. A group of people had arrived from Finland, Minnesota, to testify to Meister's good behavior and reputation. The sheriff and former sheriff of Lake County testified they personally knew Meister to be of good character. They said they would trust him under any circumstances. When asked they both admitted they knew Meister always carried the 45 caliber pistol. They admitted they had told Meister he could carry his handgun into Wisconsin. They both knew he was trapping and buying illegal beaver in Wisconsin. Neither seemed bothered by it.

A former school teacher and two friends testified to Meister's good name in Finland. They said he was a peaceful citizen who often brought wolf hides to the county seat for bounty. He had held several prestigious public offices.

A wave of relief ran through the jury. They were more sure then ever that Meister was a good citizen. Einar Johnson had to be guilty of something. The sheriffs' testimony had completely eased their minds about Meister carrying a gun. "So what if it's illegal to carry a concealed weapon in Minnesota and Wisconsin. The sheriff knew it and gave him permission to carry it in Wisconsin."

Next Coronor O. B. Ellmboe displayed the blood soaked clothing of Johnson. He described where the bullet had entered in the back and gone through his body and exited through the front of his shirt and trousers.

Sheriff Wison testified and identified the pistol Ervin Donaldson had taken from Meister. He related there were three cartridges remaining in the 45 caliber colt automatic pistol which had a capacity for eight. He then identified Johnson's gun, also a colt 45 pistol. He said 4 cartridges remained in it. It also had a capacity for eight cartridges. He displayed a silencer found in the defendant's pocket. He explained that silencers were illegal under U.S. law to possess, and that this was made to fit a .22 caliber rifle. He said Meister may have used it to muffle the sound of the rifle when it was used to shoot beaver, thereby avoiding detection.

Wilson testified about his interviews of Meister while Meister was hospitalized. He related that Meister had told him he had been hired to protect Price and his fur runners from game wardens and to protect Price while carrying large sums of money carried to buy beaver and the illgotten proceeds. He related that Meister had bragged to him of his prowess with the 45 caliber pistol. His brag was that he was a crack shot and that was why Price had hired him. He also stated his mackinaw jacket pocket where he carried his pistol was leather lined so the gun would slip out easily. He said the leather had been badly worn and actually hooked the gun when he attempted to draw it, slowing his draw, forcing him to jerk twice to get the gun out.

Wilson related how mad Meister was at his brother-in-law Lynn Price for leaving him in the woods to die. The sheriff said that was the reason he had identified him as Price instead of Grace. He went on to say Meister told him they used phony names and false license plates to confuse the wardens who they knew were trying to catch them. The sheriff said Meister admitted making claims that the wardens would never take him as long as he had his 45 pistol.

Wilson identified the empty brass cartridges found at the shooting scene. He said there were 4 spent cartridges on the west side of the road. He continued that, where found, the cartridges had to be fired by Meister. The three spent cartridges found in the road had to be fired by Johnson. Asked if the cartridges had been submited to a microscopic examination, he said no.

Alan Hanson outlined the search of Lynn Grace's (Price's) car a week before the incident and the trip north of Ladysmith on May 16th. He told of the disagreement Johnson had with Price over the changed license plates, and of Price's leaving for Donaldson's to get a pull for his car.

He described how he searched for and found the packsack, delivered it to the road and told Johnson he had found the furs.

Attorney Larson objected, "There are no furs involved in this case your honor. The prosecution has not entered any furs in evidence."

"Objection sustained."

Dukart backed up. "Mr. Hanson you said you were looking for illegal furs?"

"Yes."

"Why were you looking for illegal furs?"

"Because Einar had information that Lynn Grace, I mean Price, had been buying large numbers of beaver pelts throughout the north country."

"And you had stopped and searched Mr. Price's car for beaver pelts prior to May 16th."

"Yes, just a week earlier."

"Did you find any beaver hides?"

"No sir."

"But on May 16th you did find something. Would you explain to the court what you found?"

"I followed a man's track from the ditched vehicle to a packsack."

"And did you look in the packsack?"

"I didn't open it."

"But did you look inside?"

"I looked through a slit that was open at the top."

"And what did you see or feel?"

"Blue metal that appeared to be a gun and beaver hair."

"Objection your honor, " shouted Larson, "we still have no beaver hides as evidence."

The Judge turned to Hanson. "Do you know for sure what you saw was beaver hair?"

"Well your honor, I've handled many beaver pelts. The hair looked and felt like beaver hair. Whatever was in the packsack felt stiff like dried beaver pelts. I believe they were beaver skins."

Several of the jury members heaved sighs of relief, reading the testimony the way they preferred to. Perhaps the packsack didn't contain beaver hides at all. Looks like Johnson was wrong again.

Satisfied, Judge Wicham instructed Duckart to continue.

Questions were asked about positioning of the auto and where Johnson and Meister were standing prior to the shooting. Pictures taken by the sheriff were produced with people posing in them depicting where the three men had stood. It was finally agreed after some dickering the pictures did correctly show where the participants had stood prior to the shooting. The district attorney continued, "Mr. Hanson, now that we understand the positioning of the car, Mr. Johnson and Mr. Mcister, is it safe to say they were facing each other across the hood of the car which was ditched off the west side of the road? The car pointing northwest?"

"Yes."

"They faced each other a a distance of perhaps 10 to 12 feet?"

"Yes sir."

"When you placed the packsack on the ground on the east side of the car, please tell me what happened."

"I began to loosen the straps holding it shut."

"Did you ever open it?"

"No, I got one strap loose."

"And what stopped you from loosening the other strap?"

"A sudden movement by Mr. Meister"

"Would you explain that movement?"

"He had his hand in his mackinaw pocket and gave two hard jerks to get his gun out."

"Did you know Meister had a gun?"

"No sir, but Einar and I talked about this earlier. He warned me about Lynn Grace or Price carrying a firearm."

"So you thought if Price carried a gun, Meister under these circumstances might also carry one?"

"Yes."

District Attorney Duckart continued.

"When Meister's hand came out of his pocket, did it in fact contain a gun?"

"Yes, a colt automatic pistol."

"And you recognized a colt pistol."

"Einar had one just like it. I've fired his pistol."

Producing the gun the sheriff had identified as Meister's, Dukart continued, "Is this the gun you saw Meister pull from his pocket?"

"It was one just like it."

"Let the record show the witness identified the gun taken from Meister as a gun like the one he saw Mr. Meister pull from his pocket."

"Mr. Hanson, what happened next?"

"Well, things happened very fast. Einar said, 'Give him the stuff Alan, we're beat.' Meister said "put them up you S.O.B.' Both Einar and I jumped

60

back across the ditch into the road. I yelled, don't shoot."

"Did Warden Johnson have a gun in his hand at that time?"

"Objection your honor," intoned attorney Larson. "The witness at that time was in no condition to observe whether Johnson had his gun out or not. He was too busy trying to save himself."

Turning to Hanson, the judge said, "We'll let Mr. Hanson decide if he was too scared to notice. You may answer the question."

"No, he had no gun in his hand."

"Okay, Mr. Hanson, what did you do?"

"I turned and ran."

"What happened next?"

"I heard two shots fired from Meister's gun."

Again Larson objected, "Your honor, how could he tell which gun the firing came from? It may have been Johnson shooting."

"Mr. Larson, he has testified he saw a gun in Meister's hand and certainly at that close proximity one can determine where a sound came from. You can go into this on cross examination. Go on Mr. Duckart."

"As you were running, did you turn and look back?"

"Yes."

"And, what, if anything, did you see?"

"Meister standing on the running board leaning against the DeSoto shooting at Einar. Einar now had his gun out and was returning the fire."

"Objection," yelled Larson. "He's testifying as though we've established that my client fired first. My client will testify that Mr. Johnson fired first."

"Objection is overruled. Mr. Hanson has testified that Mr. Meister did fire first. You can rebut that testimony on cross examination or with your witnesses. We're trying to get at the truth here. Continue Mr. Duckart."

"At this time, Mr. Hanson, did you see either man fall?"

"No."

"Did you see anything that would indicate anyone had been hit?"

"Yes."

"And what was that?"

"I saw Mr. Meister wince as though hit."

"He did not fall though?"

"No."

"So it was long after Mr. Meister had begun firing at Mr. Johnson that you preceived Mr. Meister was hit."

"Yes, sir."

"How many shots were fired by Mr. Meister before Mr. Johnson began firing?"

"Three."

There was no objection as questioning went into other areas of the incident. Several of the jurors were visibly disturbed at what the judge had allowed. They were sure Einar Johnson was gun happy. Hanson had to be lying and yet the judge had allowed him to testify that Meister had fired first.

That afternoon Alan Hanson was cross-examined by Attorney Falge.

Questions were asked about the pictures and if the positions of the men in them were similar to the positions of the participants in the event. The jury was showed the pictures a second time.

Then attorney Falge questioned Hanson's qualifications to be a warden. "Mr. Hanson you started as a warden just a week before this incident?"

"Well , I actually started ..."

"Just answer the question, Mr. Hanson."

"Okay. No."

"You are 24 years of age?"

"Yes sir."

"When did you work before as a warden?"

"I worked several months in Bayfield county."

"Were you allowed to work alone?"

"Some."

"But mostly you were supervised by other wardens?"

"Yes."

"So your experience was very limited?"

"Well I don't ..."

"Just answer the question sir."

"Yes, I..."

"Thank you, Mr. Hanson, and what did you do before you worked as a warden?"

"I was a bookkeeper for several lumber companies."

"I see. So your only experience in law enforcement was for several short months of part time work in Bayfield County?"

"Well I work..."

"Mr. Hanson, I've told you several times to just answer the question. If you continue to add things, I'll ask the judge to instruct you what is expected here."

"Yes, sir."

"The question was about your experience in law enforcement. You only worked part-time in Bayfield County. Is that correct?"

"No."

"But you just told me you had worked several months in Bayfield County."

"Yes, but you would not let me finish."

At this Duckart objected, "Your honor the prosecution is badgering the witness. He won't let him give a full answer then rebukes him for not answering correctly. I ask the judge to correct Mr. Falge."

Turning to Falge, Judge Wickam said, "Let him answer the questions fully."

"All right Hanson, what is all this experience you want to tell use of?"

"It's just that I did not work part time in Bayfield County. I worked full time."

"Okay, several months of experience. Did anyone ever instruct you on how and when to make an arrest?"

"Yes, sir."

"And how much instruction did you receive?"

"I received instruction from every warden I worked with."

"How many was that?"

"Five in the Bayfield County area."

"But you had only worked for Einar Johnson one week?"

"Yes."

"And did he instruct you?"

"Yes sir."

"Were you with Mr. Johnson when arrests were made?"

"Yes sir."

"Did Mr. Johnson pull his gun at those times?"

Duckart objected, "Your honor it appears the defense is trying to make Mr. Johnson look bad in the eyes of the jury. There has been no testimony that Mr. Johnson has ever pulled a gun in making an arrest."

"The objection is sustained. Mr. Falge you will confine your questions to facts already testified to."

"All right your honor."

"Mr. Hanson, you testified you assisted Mr. Johnson in searching Mr. Price's car a week before this incident?"

"Yes sir."

"And did you have a search warrant for that search?"

"No sir."

"Did you know a search warrant was required?"

"No sir, as far as I know it's not required."

"You have less than three month's experience and you don't know when a search warrant is required?"

Duckart objected, "Your honor the witness answered correctly. A search warrant is not required to search a vehicle because of its mobility. I would ask the defense be instructed to cease this type of questioning."

Judge Wickam instructed, "Mr. Falge you know a search warrant is not required under such circumstances. Drop this line of questioning." at this time the courtroom was a boisterous yelling mob.

Pounding his gavel to silence the bedlam of the overcrowded court, the judge ordered all the standing people removed from the room. At least a hundred people were escorted from the courthouse, where they waited anxiously on the street for word to be passed along to them of new revelations.

Falge continued, "Mr. Hanson, you were there when the shooting started?"

"Yes sir."

"You saw Mr. Johnson draw his pistol?"

"No sir."

"Isn't it a fact that Mr. Johnson drew his pistol and fired before Mr. Meister?"

"No sir."

"Things were happening fast, right?"

"Yes."

"So you are not really sure who drew their pistol first?"

"I am sure."

"In spite of the fact that you were running you still insist Mr. Meister fired first?"

"Yes sir."

"But you only heard the shots, you did not see anyone shoot?"

"I did see both shoot."

"But you don't know which fired first?"

"Yes, I know who fired first."

"Are you positive?"

"Yes sir."

"At the time the first shots were fired you did not see anyone shoot."

"Yes, but ..."

"Just answer the question Mr. Hanson, you did not see anyone shoot at that time?"

"No."

"You did not know anything of Mr. Meister of your own knowledge?"

"No I didn't. Einar told me of Mr. Price."

"And what did he tell you of him?"

"He said he had information that he was buying illegal beaver in this area."

"Okay, but he did not tell you anything about Mr. Meister?"

"No."

"Now on the day of the shooting you ran away, correct?"

"Yes sir."

"Do you think that proper?"

"I don't know."

"Well why did you run away?"

"I, I."

At that juncture, Judge Wickam interceded, "You did not want to get shot in the back did you?"

Relieved, Alan sighed, "No sir."

"Mr. Hanson, after the shooting on May 16 and after you ran away, you met Mr. Ervin Donaldson along the road. You did not inform him of the shooting. Why was this?"

"Because Einar told me the Donaldson family were not to be trusted as they harbored Mr. Price and assisted in the peddling of beaver hides."

Surprised by this information, Falge changed direction. After arriving at the Donaldson farm, you talked to Arthur Donaldson?"

"Yes."

"And you told him that Mr. Johnson had fired first at the shooting scene."

"No sir."

"I have it on good authority that you told Mr. Donaldson that Johnson fired first."

"No sir."

"Are you sure?" Falge obviously angered, snapped.

"Yes sir, I had no conversation with him about who had fired first."

Late in the day both Arthur and Ervin Donaldson were called as state's witnesses. They admitted being a part of the fur running business. They further stated how the business operated. They said Price and Meister often brought furs from the north and south and planted them in small parcels in the woods. They testified that when enough furs were collected to fill three large packsacks they were delivered to Greenwood where they were sold. They admitted that both Price and Meister often stayed with them during the times they were moving illegal beaver and that Meister was trapping beaver on their land. They said they had helped transport some of the beaver to market in Greenwood. The sale of illegal beaver to fur buyer Davidson in Ladysmith was never brought out. They stated 70 to 80 beaver made up the average shipment, and that Meister and Price were paying about $20 for the average beaver skin. They stated had the beaver been legal the price would have run about $45.

When pushed to answer, both brothers admitted they had witnessed Neal Meister practice with his handgun. He often shot at their place and practiced the quick draw. They said he was a crack shot and could draw very fast.

They related they had often heard him brag that he would never be taken by wardens as long as he had his gun. Further they had never seen him go unarmed. He always wore the same mackinaw jacket, the reason being he had lined the pocket with leather to allow the gun to slip out easily.

The jury and courtroom was abuzz as the state rested its case. Several jurors were noticeably distressed at the testimony of the Donaldsons. *How could they testify against their good friends as they had? They are practically saying Meister had prepared himself to kill Johnson. Maybe Meister knew of Johnson's reputation and therefore had to prepare to defend himself.*

They wondered if the state had made any promises not to prosecute the Donaldsons in exchange for their testimony.

Finally Ervin testified that he pulled Lynn Price's car from the ditch with his horses and was surprised to see him drive off to the south leaving his wounded partner. He also told how Meister had wanted to kill himself and he had taken Meister's gun to prevent it.

Mrs. Chris Donaldson was called as the first defense witness.

The three attorneys agreed to let Mrs. Donaldson tell what she knew of the May 16th incident. She began, "I've known Mr. Price and Mr. Meister for some years. They often stop and stay at our place. I would call them friends and good people. The morning of May 16th, they stopped and I fixed breakfast for them. They left right away saying they were going to the Pete Johnson place."

Prosecutor Duckart cut in, "Were they to pick up beaver hides from Johnson?"

"I don't know , they never mentioned fur that morning. Within a half hour after they left, Lynn er-Mr. Price returned saying his car was in the ditch, and Erv harnessed the horses to pull him out. Mr. Price and I were having coffee when Mr. Einar Johnson showed up badly wounded. I tended him until Art took him to the hospital.

"Shortly after that, Neal - er Mr. Meister was brought to our place by

Sheriff Wilson. He too was badly hurt. Doctor Caldwell was treating him when Mr. Hanson came looking for Mr. Johnson."

Defense attorney Larson asked, "At that time did you hear a conversation between Mr. Hanson and Mr. Price?"

"Yes, I did."

"Did that conversation center on who was the first to shoot when the incident began?"

"Yes, It did."

"Would you in your own words, Mrs. Donaldson, tell the court what you overheard?"

"Well Mr. Hanson and Mr. Price were talking about the shooting and while I didn't hear everything they said, I did hear Mr. Hanson tell Lynn Einar Johnson had shot first."

Duckart objected, "Mrs. Donaldson, that is not the same story you told other people. May I question Mrs. Donaldson on this issue your honor?"

"You can question her on cross examination."

Larson said, "He can question her now. I have no more questions."

"Mrs. Donaldson, may I remind you that Sheriff Wilson and chief warden MacKenzie questioned you immediately after the shooting. You did not mention such a conversation even when asked specifically about any conversations you engaged in or heard?"

"I must have been nervous and forgot about it."

"Madam, how could you forget such an important piece of evidence in this a murder trial?"

"Objection, your honor," shouted Falge. "Mrs. Donaldson has answered the questions."

Thoughtfully Judge Wicham cautioned the district attorney, "She has answered the question. Do you have other areas to cover?"

"Yes, Mrs. Donaldson you testifed at Municipal Court that Mr. Price had only one pair of trousers at your place and that you hardly knew him. Now, I find he has a whole wardrobe at your place. You just stated he is a friend that stays at your place often. Can you explain this difference in testimony?"

"I forgot some things at the other trial. Attorneys make me nervous."

"So both Meister and Price are personal friends that you may want to protect?"

"They do stay at our place, but I'm sworn to tell the truth and I have."

"That remains to be seen. Does Mr. Meister trap beaver on your land?"

"Yes."

"Have you ever seen Mr. Meister with beaver in possession?"

"Why - I guess - I did - yes - several times."

"You also knew these two along with your sons were trafficking in illegal beaver on a large scale?"

"I really don't know much about what they were doing. But whatever it was, it was to support our family."

"So you think it's okay to violate laws as long as the money is used to support your family. Does that also include robbing a bank or killing a game warden?"

Beaver Shootout

"Objection," shouted Falge. "The prosecutor is badgering the witness."

Judge Wickam intoned, "She did bring out what the illegal money received was used for on her own. I would caution the prosecutor to tone down your voice and continue. Answer the question, Mrs. Donaldson."

"No, there are limits as to how far a person should go."

"But you did know that Price and Meister went armed with handguns to protect their runners and illicit shipments from game wardens?"

"Guess I did know Neal - Mr. Meister carried a gun. I've never seen Mr. Price carry one."

"And you've heard Mr. Meister brag that he is a good shot and will never be taken by a warden?"

"No, I've never heard that."

Judge Wickam asked, "What did you think Meister had the gun for. Did you think it was for beaver or the game wardens?"

"I r - really don't know." Flustered she left the stand, her testimony thoroughly tested as to its truthfulness.

Several jury members squirmed uneasily in their seats not happy with the way the judge had allowed the district attorney to confuse the lady. "Maybe everyone should carry a gun to protect themselves from the wardens. After all wardens carried them too."

Next the defense called Kenneth Donaldson, age 7, the youngest witness and probably the strongest witness for the defense. He immediately when asked identified Alan Hanson and Neal Meister in the courtroom.

Attorney Falge patiently questioned the young lad. "Now Kenny do you remember Mr. Price talking with Mr. Hanson?"

"Yes sir."

"Was there a conversation on May 16th at your house about the shooting?"

"Yes sir."

"Where were you when you heard the conversation?"

"Just inside the door of our house."

"Very well, and did Mr. Hanson say who had shot first?"

"Yes sir."

"Who did he say shot first?"

"Einar Johnson."

A ripple of sound crossed the courtroom as a wind crosses a prairie. This testimony by a child had hurt the prosecution.

Judge Wickam rapped for order. "Quiet in the courtroom."

He rapped again when the din continued. "Quiet or I'll clear the courtroom." He lent emphasis to his command by rapping several more times. As the room settled and quieted, Falge triumphantly stated, "I have no more quesitons of this witness."

Duckart knew his case had been hurt, but to put the heat on such a young person would only alienate the jury and increase the damage. So it was with a heavy heart that he very carefully began his cross examination. In a fatherly manner, he asked, "Now Kenny, are you afraid of me?"

"No sir."

"Are you afraid of game wardens?"

"I don't like them. They are always bothering us."

"By us, who do you mean? Your family, Mr. Price or Mr. Meister?"

"All of them."

"Did you know Mr. Johnson before May 16th?"

"Yes sir."

"And you said you don't like him. Why?"

"He stops by and bothers us."

"Did you know Mr. Hanson before May 16th?"

"No sir."

"But you still don't like him. Why?"

"He's a game warden."

"Have you known Mr. Price and Mr. Meister a long time?"

"Yes."

"Do you like them?"

"Yes."

"Why do you like them?"

"They're good to me. They give me gifts."

"Oh, like pocket knives and such?"

Digging in his pocket Kenneth said, "Would you like to see the new knife Neal gave me?"

A roar of laughter rolled across the room with Judge Wickam pounding the gavel for order.

As the room quieted, district attorney Duckact continued, "Okay Kenny, you like Mr. Meister and Mr. Price. Would you do a favor for them?"

"Sure would, they're good guys."

"Would you tell a lie for them?"

"Maybe a little one."

"Okay are you sure you told all the truth about what you overheard Mr. Hanson say?"

"Yes sir."

"And what exactly did Mr. Hanson say?"

"That Johnson shot first at Neal."

Again bedlam broke out with Judge Wickam furious at the display of the partisan crowd. Hammering his heavy gavel, he laid down a reprimand. "Displays such as this will not be tolerated. Bailiff clear the aisles." As Kenneth's testimony had proceeded, people began to push in from the outside to hear. With the aisles cleared and silence regained, Judge Wickam told Duckart to continue.

Realizing he had lost considerable ground and not wanting to lose more he dismissed Kenneth.

The next witness was Doctor Caldwell who testified the wound to Meister was serious and life threatening. He stated a large caliber bullet consistent with a 45 caliber had passed through his chest puncturing the right lung.

Neal Meister then took the stand in his own defense. Attorney Falge started with statistics. Neal answered that he was 35 years old, had resided in Finland, Minnesota most of his life since 1904. He was married and had spent 13 months overseas in the world war. He held the office of town officer and school district treasurer. He said he met Lynn Price when he began a fox fur farm a few years ago at Finland.

At his attorney's urging, he told how Lynn Price had about two years ago talked to him and asked him to come to Wisconsin to assist in buying beaver. He said he knew the beaver season was closed In Wisconsin but because he was short of money had agreed. Since then, he continued Lynn had made many trips. He said on many he came to Wisconsin only to trap beaver which he sold to Price. He said he had only assisted in buying and selling on two of the trips.

Meister admitted he stayed at the Donaldson farm trapping beaver on their land. He said he had been there from May 1st until May 16th trapping beaver. He told how Price, while not a trapper, bought beaver throughout the northern tier of Wisconsin counties. He said on several occasions Price paid him to assist in moving illegal fur to Greenwood where they were sold.

Meister told of how Price liked to hide parcels of hides in the woods. These parcels were usually in gunny sacks or packsacks. Directly north of the Donaldson house, they stashed many parcels with Donaldson's approval. He told of how but not to whom the furs were sold in Greenwood. Arthur Donaldson was implicated in two selling trips. Price's DeSoto, he said, was always used to transport the illicit cargo.

Finally, Meister related the facts of the last trip made. They had delivered a load of beaver skins to Greenwood on May 15th where they were sold. He said they had returned to Donaldson's at 6 a.m. on the 16th.

After breakfast, Price had asked him to go to the Pete Johnson place nearby to see if he had any beaver. He put special emphasis on the fact Johnson had no fur and therefore the packsack that day only contained clothing and toilet articles. In the toilet articles, he pointed out Price had a blue steel razor that could be mistaken for a gun.

After leaving the Johnson place, Meister said they went east on the Big Falls road and turned north on the Winter Road. After about one half mile, he said they skidded into the ditch and became mired in the mud. He stated he had thrown the packsack in the woods for safety as they were going to walk back to the Donaldson place to get a pull.

Meister said he watched and listened to Price and another man argue over the changed license plates. Then he saw another man enter the brush as though looking for something. When Price left to get the horses, he had walked out to where the man stood by their car.

When asked by Falge what had happened next, he replied, "This stranger asked me my name. I told him Pete Carlson."

"Why did you use the name Pete Carlson?"

"I always do when I'm in Wisconsin."

Dukart objected; Meister did not answer the question. There had to be a reason for using an alias.

Judge Wickam agreed, "Why were you using an alias?"

"Because we were buying beaver in Wisconsin."

Falge proceeded, "Did Mr. Johnson at any time identify himself as a game warden?"

"No sir."

"So you thought him to be just another ordinary person asking a lot of foolish questions?"

"Yep."

Dukart jumped to his feet. "I object your honor. Mr. Meister has just testified he did not know Johnson was a game warden. Johnson's badge is still attached to his mackinaw jacket. That jacket has been entered as evidence."

Falge responded, "Your honor the prosecution can question my client on this issue during cross examination. May I proceed?"

"Proceed Mr. Falge."

"Mr. Meister while in the brush you saw these strange men search Price's car. Didn't that bother you?"

"I couldn't understand why they would do such a thing. It scared me."

"Now when you talked to the stranger, was there any quarrel with him?"

"None sir."

"Then Mr. Hanson came out of the woods carrying a packsack is that correct?"

"Yes, I wondered what he was doing with it. It wasn't my packsack though, it was Lynn's."

"Do you know what was in the packsack?"

"Lynn had his clothes in it."

"There were no beaver hides in it?"

"None."

"What if anything happened next?"

"The man with the packsack yelled as he approached, 'I've found the stuff.'"

"What happened next?"

"He threw the packsack down and began to open it."

"What if anything did Johnson do then?"

"He asked me my name again and put his notebook in his pocket."

"What did he do then?"

"He put his hands behind his back and told me I was under arrest. He also asked if I had a gun."

"And you told him yes?"

"Yes, and I put my hand in my pocket to give it to him."

"What in the chain of events happened then?"

"Hanson yelled, 'Give it to him.'"

"Then what happened?"

"Johnson drew and fired a shot right past my face."

"Then what?"

"Johnson fired again, the second shot hitting me in the chest."

"Did you then respond in kind?"

"Yes sir. I jerked my gun out and pointed it at Johnson."

"What is your next recollection?"

"Hanson was running down the road."

"Okay, did that scare you?"

"Yes, I thought Hanson would shoot from another angle, catch me in a crossfire."

"Did Johnson at this time speak to you?"

"Yes sir."

"And what did he say?"

"He yelled, 'Don't do it' and fired another shot."

"Did you then fire in self defense."

"Yes sir. I was between two fellows and I was afraid for my life."

"How many shots did you fire?"

"I don't know. More than once."

"How many shells did you have in your magazine?"

"I don't know."

"Did you hit Johnson when you fired in self defense?"

"Yes sir. I don't know which shot hit him."

"What did Mr. Johnson do at this time?"

"He started walking toward Donaldsons."

"What did you do?"

"I was badly hurt, when I finally could get up I started walking toward Donaldsons too."

"Then you met Mr. Price, correct?"

"Yes, he helped me into the woods beside the road, where I lay down on some boughs."

"You told him of the shooting?"

"Yes."

"Then he said he would be back to pick you up?"

"Yeah, but he drove off after Ervin pulled him from the ditch."

"He left you?"

"Yeah, he left me."

"What happened next?"

"Sheriff Wilson found me and took me to Donaldson's where Doctor Caldwell treated me and they took me to the hospital in Ladysmith."

On cross examination Meister was reluctant and cautious with his answers. Very few answers were forthcoming about where he spent his nights in Greenwood and to whom the illegal furs were sold.

When asked about the 45 caliber pistol he carried, he responded he used it in trapping. He reluctantly admitted he was protecting Price because of the large amounts of money carried during beaver buying and selling. He forgot he had told the district attorney that Price often carried up to $4,000 to buy beaver. He now thought it may be as much as $1,000.

"Now Mr. Meister, let's get back to that gun you carried. When did you start carrying the gun? Was it when you started coming to Wisconsin to buy beaver?"

"No, I've carried that gun since I was a child."

"I see, you always carried the gun, why?"

"I like it and it's harmless."

"Harmless, it killed Einar Johnson."

"Well I mean it's safe to carry."

"You don't consider a 45 caliber colt automatic pistol to be dangerous."

"No, about as dangerous as a pen knife."

"Why didn't you use a pen knife on Warden Johnson? Did you really have any other use for such a weapon except to shoot a game warden?"

"Yes."

"And what would you use it for?"

"To protect myself from dangerous animals."

"Have you ever used it to defend yourself against dangerous animals?"

"No sir."

"You've never used it to protect yourself from dangerous animals and yet you've spent most of your life in and around a wilderness as a hunter and trapper. Isn't it true that the 45 caliber automatic pistol was created for and more useful for killing people?"

"Yes."

"Why is this true?"

"It's a good gun at short range."

Judge Wickam interrupted, "Mr. Meister, did you carry the handgun in your car to protect yourself against wolves?"

"Well, in the car I just had it along."

Duckart continued, "Okay and you knew it was illegal to carry a concealed weapon in Wisconsin?"

"No sir."

"Well you knew it to be illegal to carry a concealed weapon in Minnesota?"

"But I went to the two sheriffs, there and they both told me it was okay."

"Did they also tell you it was okay to carry the handgun concealed in Wisconsin?"

"Yes sir."

"Do you really think a sheriff in one state can give a person permission to break the law in another?"

"I don't know."

"Okay, how many trips have you made with Price illegally buying and selling beaver in Wisconsin?"

"Three."

"Come now Mr. Meister. How long has this operation been going on?"

"I don't know how long it's been going on. I've been going with Lynn about two years."

"But you still insist you only made three buying and selling trips in Wisconsin. Did you hear the testimony of Arthur and Ervin Donaldson? They claim you spent a lot of time in Wisconsin."

"I don't care what they said. I was on three buying trips with Lynn."

"Do you consider yourself handy with a gun? Are you a good shot?"

"Yes sir."

"Now about the threats to game wardens, I've heard. Did you ever make statements to the effect you would never be taken by a game warden as long as you carried your handgun?"

"No sir."

"Did you hear the testimony of the Donaldson brothers and Sheriff Wilson?"

"Yeah, I was excited when I talked to Wilson, and I don't know where the Donaldson brothers got the idea that I threatened wardens."

"I wonder how such stories get started?"

"I don't know."

"You testified that Warden Johnson fired at you first. How then do you explain him being shot in the back?"

"Well he fired under his left arm as he jumped the ditch."

"But you said he fired three times at you. To do this he would have had to have turned, correct?"

"No sir."

"He fired three shots at you from under his arm?"

"Yes sir."

"Forgive me Mr. Meister but that story just does not wash."

Attorney Carlson objected, "Your honor I believe it improper for the prosecutor to make such a conclusion before the jury."

"Mr. Duckart, you will refrain from making conclusions before the jury. Mr. Duckart's statement will be striken from the record. I'm instructing the jury to disregard Mr. Duckart's statement."

Several smiles appeared among the jurors. "It's easy to believe the game warden shot from under his arm, the gun happy fool. It's no wonder he got himself shot."

"Okay," continued Duckart, "Johnson fired three shots from beneath his left arm as he jumped the ditch. Is that correct?"

"Yes."

"Why didn't you also fire at Warden Hanson? Was he not a threat to you?"

"No, he was not shooting at me."

"But you testified you were afraid of being between two wardens that could put you in a cross fire."

"Yes but he did not shoot."

"You told the sheriff while in jail you were hired by Mr. Price to protect him and his runners against game wardens, correct?"

"Well it's not true, I was badly hurt when the sheriff talked to me."

"But you made such a statement?"

"I don't remember, but the reason I was along was to trap beaver in Wisconsin."

"You were paid by Mr. Price to accompany him on his illegal buying and selling trips?"

"Yes, just to watch over his car."

"How much were you paid by Mr. Price for caring for his car?"

"About $80 a trip."

Judge Wickam indicated he had several questions, "Mr. Meister, did Mr. Johnson fire on you before you reached for your gun?"

"I think he did."

"Are you sure you didn't reach for your gun before Mr. Johnson shot?"

"W - Well I may have."

"Why instead of reaching for the gun to hand to Mr. Johnson, did you not raise your hands and tell him to come and get the gun?"

"G - Guess I just didn't think of it."

"While in the jail did you not tell the district attorney that you made a quick move to your pocket."

"No sir."

The defense then called Joe Speich, a janitor at the courthouse, who testified that Johnson had a reputation of poking a gun in people's ribs when making arrests. He admitted he knew no one to whom it had actually happened even though he had personally been stopped and searched by the warden. He admitted the incident had made him very mad.

Mr. H.W. True testified that Johnson had a reputation of pulling guns on people he arrested. He reluctantly admitted the warden had checked him several times without pulling a gun. He said he had no unfriendly feelings toward warden Johnson.

Several rebuttal witnesses were called. Alan Hanson stated that he and warden Harry Hosford were at the Donaldson place several weeks ago. Mrs. Donaldson at that time told them that Price had recently been there and told her Johnson had shot first. Hanson and Hosford both said that they had never told Mrs. Donaldson that Johnson had shot first.

Sheriff Wilson was recalled. His testimony was that, when questioning Mrs. Donaldson at the jail shortly after the shooting, she never mentioned she had overhead Hanson say Johnson had shot first. He also testified he had been present when Johnson made a number of arrests and Johnson had never pulled his gun. He said he too had heard rumors that Johnson had pulled his gun while arresting people.

Also testifying were Wardens K.C. Jaboubek of Phillips, Harry Hosford of Medford and Clifford Reed of Prentice, Harry Haugen of Loretta and Chief Warden MacKenzie. All testified they had worked with Einar Johnson a great deal and had never seen him pull a gun while making an arrest. All admitted they too had heard such rumors but felt them unfounded.

In summation district attorney Dukart pointed out that the defendant had come to Wisconsin to violate the law by trafficking in unlawful beaver furs. He had come constantly armed with a heavy pistol that was carried for only one reason to protect Mr. Price from game wardens. He continued, "The defendant and Mr. Price were out to get that fur through and woe and betide any who tried to stop them. They traveled under false names and deliberately changed license plates on their car to deceive wardens who they knew were trying to catch them." He emphasized the words of the dying warden that Meister had fired twice before he fired. "Wardens are not killers. They both tried to get away. As a result Johnson was shot in the back as he retreated. The testimony of Mr. Meister that Johnson fired three shots under his left arm while going away just doesn't wash. After all Mr. Johnson was not a trick shooter. I'm convinced Mr. Meister's inclination toward suicide when he realized his capture was imminent is an indication of a guilty mind."

The defense's summation was first given by attorney Falge. He stressed the good reputation of the defendant and his standing in his community. "I don't believe the wardens had any reason to search the auto which my client rode in. They found no illegal furs. The packsack continued only personal belongings which my client simply hid to protect. That's only reasonable since they were to leave the car unprotected. When Mr. Meister reached to hand his gun to the wardens, Johnson began to fire at him. Any reasonable person would have returned the fire. Hanson admitted Johnson fired first"

Attorney Larson took over at that time with an impassioned plea to find his client not guilty of all charges.

"My client did carry a gun but he is a trapper who uses it to dispatch animals and protect himself from wolves. He's never had any trouble with law officers. In fact, two sheriffs from Lake County, Minnesota, testified they knew him well and gave him permission to carry the firearm. His school teacher, a respected person in her community, knew Neal well and testified of his good character. Testimony reveals that Warden Johnson needlessly used a weapon in making arrests. Naturally the wardens would all testify for Johnson, that he did not intimidate people with his gun."

Discussing Johnson's dying statement, he said he had never heard of an officer who shot at someone who had not claimed the other person shot first. He also said Hanson's testimony did not jibe with Johnson's statements. "Why would a person shoot a lawman when he had no means of escape? Their car was stuck in the ditch."

In the closing plea, the district attorney pointed out the uncollaborated testimony of the defendant. "I'm appalled at the defense's new theory that self defense consists of shooting a man in the back. The location of the wounds of both parties confirm Alan Hanson's testimony. The conduct of the defendant in Minnesota should have no bearing on this case. When these two men came to Wisconsin, it was their intent to and they did carry out an extensive illicit operation buying and selling beaver at great profit."

"All this discussion about who fired first is immaterial. Meister reached for his gun first and I believe fired first. But even if he didn't fire first, the fact Meister carried a gun to Wisconsin to commit a crime must be considered. The gun carried to protect Price and his furs from game wardens was certainly used for that purpose."

"Gentlemen of the jury please do not let the grand and eloquent oratory of the defense sway your decision. We must protect law officers. You must keep your feet on the ground in Rusk County and find Mr. Meister guilty of murder in the first degree."

Early Saturday morning in instructing the jury, Judge Wickam discussed at length the rights of wardens in making an arrest. He pointed out they are entitled to use the amount of force necessary to effect the arrest, even to the extent of taking a life if threatened with the loss of theirs"

Meister, he stated, was not legally entitled to carry a concealed gun, while wardens are. He further stated that if Meister started to pull a gun indicating he was to shoot, it made no difference who fired first, the wardens could legally shoot to protect their person or the person of another.

Finally, he submitted they had four forms of findings they could reach: "Murder in the first degree, murder in the second degree, third degree manslaughter, or acquital."

Alone in the jury room the jury quickly chose a volunteer a farmer as foreman. Foreman George Hanson called for an immediate ballot to see where they stood. The result was four for second degree murder, five for manslaughter, and three for acquittal.

He advised them he was surprised at the count. "I personally don't see how anyone could vote for anything but acquital. I've heard about this Johnson. I'm convinced he is gun happy. Besides what's so wrong with selling a few beaver? I have a number of friends who sell them to keep the wolf from the door. "I'm sure glad there is no one here foolish enough to vote for first degree murder. Let's have another ballot and see if we can come closer together."

With his litany in their minds acquital gained a convert.

George Hanson began again, "Well we've made some progress but we've got to do better. I'm still for acquittal."

Finally a voice was heard for second degree murder.

Jim Bixby, a store owner said, "You know we're dealing with the taking of a life here. Regardless of what George thinks, Meister took a law officer's life while he was doing his job. A job we all pay him to do. You mentioned Johnson is gun happy. There was no evidence that was substantiated that he ever used his gun. All we heard were rumors. I think you're wrong, George."

"Well I've heard it and I believe it."

"We are not to use things we've heard or rumors. We also heard rumors that Meister bragged about not ever being taken by a warden."

Surprise showed on Hanson's face that someone would disagree with him so vehemently. "How many times have you heard people making brags like that? I've probably made statements like that myself. Well you know how I feel. Let's vote again."

The third ballot results were eight for manslaughter three for acquital and only one voting for second degree murder.

With Hanson leading, the vote slowly changed.

By the eighth ballot, ten were for manslaughter and one each for acquital and second degree murder.

Electing to stay through the lunch hour, sandwiches were brought in and they continued their deliberations.

It was obvious who was disagreeing as many of the jury sat passive as Hanson and Bixby argued.

Hanson, a simple talking person, was also very persuasive. "Now Jim, we don't want to stay here forever. We've already wasted a half day. Let's get on with it."

"I can't change my mind. In fact I believe Meister may be guilty of first degree murder."

"Come on Jim you never voted for first degree."

"No, but I think we're wrong if we let Meister off so easy. After all, he killed a law officer while committing a crime."

"What crime? You don't consider trapping and selling a few beaver a crime?"

76

"The judge said it is."

"But in this country everyone traps beaver and therefore someone has to buy the furs. Quite frankly, I think Meister just outdrew Johnson. He was just a little faster. He shot in self defense. Tell you what Jim, it's obvious the rest of the jury is for manslaughter. If you change your vote, I will change mine. I'm sure if we come up with manslaughter the judge will let Meister out on probation. He doesn't think Meister has committed a crime either."

Bixby, outnumbered, began to bend. "I don't know. I just feel bad about Johnson's death."

"But Jim, Meister did something that all of us have done. We've all broken the game laws. The way they're set up you can't help it. As far as a few beaver go I wish Meister would come out to my place. They're flooding my land. Maybe I shouldn't admit it, but, a couple of years ago, I shot a few."

"I've never broken a game law."

"But you don't hunt or fish or you would have. They even got after me for a little fire I started."

"But wasn't it awful dry? Didn't it burn a chunk of your neighbor's woods?"

"Oh that was just an old cutover area. Burning is good for it."

"But I still don't believe anyone has the right to take another's life."

"Right Jim, Johnson was trying to take Meister's life. Neal only shot in self defense. He had the gun along to shoot wolves. I shoot them too. They kill my livestock and dogs. Why don't you change your vote? I'll change mine and we'll get out of here. I've got chores to do."

Resignedly Jim threw up his hands. "Looks like everyone else has made up their minds."

As the jury returned the judge cleared the unruly mob. Only seated people were allowed to stay with the rest of the throng flooding the street. Money exchanged hands as people bet on the verdict.

As the foreman read the verdict a ripple of sound ran across the room bordering on a cheer. The ripple of sound continued outside to the crowded street.

Rapping his gavel, Judge Wickam demanded silence as he polled the jury. Only one person hesitated at his turn to agree with the finding.

Judge Wickam seeming a little suprised at the finding, said he would review the case and perform the sentencing next Tuesday.

Moonshine bottles passed from hand to hand that evening as the jubilant people celebrated long into the night. Their wishes had come true. Judge Wickam would certainly let Meister off easy. with a very short sentence and perhaps no jail time. Why lock up a good citizen? He had only killed a game warden - a bully that was gun happy to boot.

At Tuesday's session of court the crowd again showed up to more than fill the room, with many standing in the street.

Defense attorney Larson sensing the feel of the local community asked the jury's finding to be set aside. With feelings running so high he felt they could do even better in another trial. Judge Wicham summarily turned down the request and immediately went into sentencing. He asked for a recommendation from Duckart. Subdued at the outcome he gave none.

The court was deadly silent as Judge Wickam briefly reviewed Meister's good reputation in Minnesota and commended him on his fine service record in the world war.

He continued, "I believe this court is on the verge of committing a miscarriage of justice to the people of this state. While I commend the jury for their long consideration and I'm bound by their decision, I don't necessarily agree with it. After all, here we have a defendant who came to Wisconsin deliberately to engage in illegal trapping and the buying and selling of beaver skins. He knew the seasons were closed but was willing to gamble he not be caught because of the high profit motive. Further he came armed knowing there was a good chance he may take a human life. This is not the wild west. Disagreements cannot be settled by how fast one can draw or how straight one can shoot.

"Mr. Meister deliberately used tactics to hide his identity by using a false name and traveling in a car with changed registration."

"There was testimony about the reputation of conservation warden Einar Johnson. He was accused of being gun happy. Yet no one could produce a witness who would testify that he had pulled a gun on them. There was also testimony that Neal Meister threatened to kill game wardens to protect their illicit operation. I believe rumors on both sides should be disregarded. Innuendoes are not evidence. I have worked with Mr. Johnson and received no complaints as to how he enforced the law. Quite to the contrary, I found Mr. Johnson to be a reasonable well-grounded lawman.

"It seems to me the jury has granted Mr. Meister all the leniency the court can allow. Therefore I'm sentencing you Mr. Meister to the maximum sentence allowed for manslaughter in the second degree. You will serve not less than six nor more than seven years in the state prison at Waupun, Wisconsin."

Bedlam broke out as court was adjourned. People were baffled and dumbfounded at the judge's remarks and sentencing. Had he really listened during the trial. It was inevitable Johnson would one day be shot flaunting his authority and brandishing guns.

The Ladysmith News of November 15, 1929 carried bold headlines **Prison Term for Slaying Warden,** "Jury in trial of Neal Meister charged with killing warden Johnson returns manslaughter verdict" **Sentence is for six to seven years** "Judge declares jury had shown leniency, hence sentence is near maximum for second degree manslaughter; Four forms of verdict submitted."

Public opinion had played a large role in the outcome of Neal Meister's trial. Slowly opinion changes. Today public opinion in many areas supports protection of the natural resources. However, there still remains a visage of the frontier past in parts of this state and throughout the country that would let assailants of wardens off easy. A 1981 example is the Claude Dallas case. Dallas, also a trapper cold bloodedly gunned down Bill Pogue and Conley Elms, two Idaho game wardens. These cases are similar in that in both cases the murderers were only convicted of manslaughter, with many people pointing accusing fingers at the wardens, crying for acquital of the accused. In both cases, the fast draw was considered as a legitimate way to settle disputes by the jury.

Dallas took advantage of the jury system and people's attitudes toward game wardens and authority in general a second time. Charged after escaping an Idaho state prison, he was acquited. His counsel required sixty-three prospective jurors fill out a twelve page questionnaire resulting in a psychological profile for each. Thus, the defense was able to develop a defense needed for acquital. The court allowed this procedure. The $21,00 for the expense of this questionable procedure was raised by a lady friend of Dallas.

The jury agreed with the defense that it was necessary for Dallas to escape because he feared prison officials.

Neal Meister served five years in the state penitenary system. Returning to Finland, Minnesota after his release, he rejoined his wife where she lived on her parents' farm. Known as a good trapper, he spent much of his life trapping and hunting.

It is strange how the lives of violators and game wardens sometimes become intertwined. One day in 1946, seventeen years after the murder, Meister met Bill Richards the new warden at Finland. He told Richards he had killed a warden in Wisconsin. They talked and, as irony would have it, they became fast friends. Neal often rode with Richards on his patrol.

He told the entire story of the happenings that eventful day in Wisconsin to Bill just once, and never mentioned it again, except in fleeting instances when he seemed bothered, occasionally voicing concern with the way his brother-in-law Lynn Price had left him bleeding in the woods.

Lynn Price wandered around the country to avoid prosection. His attorney's promise that he would turn himself in was never fulfilled. Spending considerble time in Texas, he eventually returned to Finland, Minnesota where he lived out a long life. He is buried at Finland.

Warden Billy Richards arrested him twice, once each in 1947 and 1948. Charged with taking mink during the closed season and gill netting walleyes and northern pike, he plead guilty on all counts. Fines of $100 and costs on each count were administered in Lake County, Minnesota.

Billy says he had no idea Wisconsin held murder arrest warrants for Price. The record shows Charles Price, Lynn's brother of Finland, was convicted of possession of beaver during the closed season and transporting beaver skins during the closed season on August 14, 1929 in Wisconsin. He paid $100 on each count. Arresting wardens were Einar Johnson and Alan Hanson. Evidently these arrests were a part of the continuing investigation after Einar Johnson's death. So Einar got credit for an arrest after his death, and Lynn's brother was prosecuted while Lynn never was.

When Meister's wife died in the mid '60s, he moved to Washington state where he lived with a nephew until age 85. Every summer, he returned to Finland to visit his friend Bill Richards.

In 1978 Neal's remains were shipped to his best friend Bill Richards who made arrangements for his burial in Finland. Billy Richards, now retired says, "he was my very best friend."

Chapter 8

Tracers

Leonard Tomczyk, newly appointed state game warden, had received his first permanent station at Ashland, Wisconsin. The area because of several serious encounters between citizens and wardens had a reputation in 1948 as an area to tame. Resentment toward wardens ran high creating defiance and obstruction.

Len, a strongly built young man of five foot ten inches and 180 pounds, exuded a rock hard appearance. Possibly his appearance partly made up for his lack of experience and confidence in himself in his new job. He had been recently discharged from the Marine Corps after extensive combat duty against the Japanese. His competive nature and high ideals and expectations required he perform at a higher rate of excellence than the state required.

This November morning would try his competence and build a reputation and a style of unorthodox methods to obtain discernible results throughout his long career.

Len slipped in the new slushy snow as he picked up his pace in pursuit of the four fast moving deer hunters. *I've got to handle this in a professional manner,* he thought as he was quite aware of his inexperience. *They don't have to know I'm new on the job.* Beads of sweat broke out on his brow as he struggled through the last bunch of alders to burst out in front of the hunting group just as they were about to enter the second growth of maple.

"I'm a state game warden," Len announced for all to hear. "I would like to check your hunting licenses."

The tall rawboned leader with a touch of sarcasm in his voice snapped, "We're too busy to be monkeying around digging out hunting licenses. Hands are cold. Backtags are displayed; that's all you need."

There was a moment of silence. Len, trying to grasp what was going on, realized the battle lines were drawn. The man was deliberately inviting a confrontation.

"Come on fellows. Let's get on with our drive as planned before this young upstart interrupted." Flipping the rifle carelessly over his shoulder, he led the hunters in single file through a small opening in the trees.

Realizing he had to take command of the situation. Len bolted in front of the tall man, commanding, "Just a minute mister. I asked to see your licenses in an nice way. Now, I'm not asking anymore. I'm demanding. Get those licenses and tags out right now."

"Boy, you've sure got a sharp tongue for such a young pup. I'll bet you're one of those damn wardens that shoot at cars too."

80

Len was aware of an episode the previous spring. Wardens had shot at a vehicle fleeing from a fish spearing incident. *Got to get control of this situation now or I won't last long in the Ashland area,* Len thought. Stabbing a pointing finger at the man, he ordered, his voice firm and steadier than he felt, "You with the big mouth. Get over here!"

"Why?"

"I want to show you something. Here, right over here. See that pine stump?" His heavy hunting boot chunked into the decaying wood, sending rotting splinters flying into the stark whiteness of the unbroken snowy surface. His booted foot pushed a bunch of tinder dry debris into a pile. The unsnapping of his holster was startlingly loud in the stillness that had fallen. Deliberately drawing his revolver, Len chuckled to himself thinking as he changed the shells in the handgun, *Good way to use these old tracers, I brought home from the Corps.*

The man, his voice now showing a trace of fear, haltingly asked, "What, what are you going to do with the gun?"

"I'm going to show you something that may help all you fellows in the future."

Len surprised himself at how steady the gun was as he directed it at the pile. Everyone jumped as the sharp crack of the revolver broke the prevailing stillness of the deep forest. All eyes focused on the dry wood as a wisp of smoke rose, immediately followed by a flickering blue and yellow flame which briefly licked at the tinder and died.

Aghast, the man asked, "My God man, what kind of shells are you shooting?"

"Gas tank shells," Len calmly replied. "Now let's see some damn hunting licenses."

Chapter 9

The Saga
of Ernie Swift

Ernest (Ernie) Swift's pleasant patrol on a sunny spring morning in 1928 was shattered. The glint of light reflecting off the black Lincoln automobile nestled in the tight brush brought him up short. The large automobile brought instant recognition. It belonged to deadly Chicago mobsters infesting his area.

It was parked in a tag alder thicket near the twin forks of the Chippewa River, where the Winter Dam formed the mighty Chippewa flowage creating a virtual fisherman's paradise in the turbulent waters below the dam.

Swift correctly interpreted the situation to mean these desperados were again fishing below the dam in an area where walleye and muskelunge were so vulnerable a fish refuge had been established for their protection.

Letting his thoughts run wild, he thought back to when he had accepted his transfer from Crandon to his home at Hayward the previous year. He had considered that sooner or later he would be required or rather that his hard headed drive would require him to some day face these desperate men who openly defied law and order using their notorious reputation as killers to intimidate the community and local government.

His thoughts ran back to his days in Crandon where his mettle had been tested by the multitude of hill people from Kentucky who had migrated to the relatively unsettled Forest County area. Many of the -Kaintucks as they were called had fled one step ahead of a Kentucky hill country sheriff. Many admitted they had as they put it -Got ma self a man dawn there. They lived off the land taking wildlife at will, collecting ginseng and making moonshine.

Hard bitten they followed their own code of honor, showing admiration for the pint sized red head who faced them down many times under trying conditions and against tremendous odds. Chief Warden Harley MacKenzie who had also dealt with the Kentucks told Swift, -They are quick with a gun or a knife. Don't let them get behind you with a rifle.

Ernie soon came to honor their woodsmanship and strange preverted sense of honor. Tense situations arising during the three tumultuous years there were always resolved due to his steadiness under pressure. the Kentucks respecting size in a man soon came to respect Swift's inability to back down under any conditions in spite of his small stature.

Their desperate economic situation in the Forest County area and to some degree Swift's suffering through the Great Depression in northern Wisconsin made him humble. He knew what is was like to be poor and to live on the other side of the badge. Peeking at a few paragraphs of his story, "The Man with the Badge," is quite revealing, as he said, "I chuckle over an incident during this investigation. Boomer and I were driving on a back trail on the reservation looking for an Indian witness. Boomer remarked that he had worked in the Chippewa River country before the war. "Mostly up on the east fork," he replied. "I spent most of one summer, 1916, it was trying to catch a couple of outlaws reported to be fire hunting the river and bringing out deer."

"I know that country pretty well," I told him. "who were these two outlaws?"

"Well," Boomer replied, "One's name was Bill Hogue, and the other one was a little red-headed son-of-a-bitch, but I never found out his name."

I missed a chuck hole in the road, and there was a long minute of silence before I said, "Boomer, that little red headed son-of-a-bitch you are speaking of is driving this car."

These experiences affected his law enforcement activities thence forward. Possibly it inspired this fictional story that revealed his humanness.

An Officer's Duty
(by Ernest Swift)

Conway rapped sharply upon the cracked, unpainted door. The makeshift porch, crusted with the accumulated filth of pig swill and slop pails, complained as old Tom Brothers added his two hundred fifty pounds to its burden. Muffled noises came from within followed by silence.

"I hope we find the stuff, " whispered young Conway. "It's not in the house, though; weather is too hot to keep it there."

"It's me that's hopin' we find it," growled Old Tom, as he contemplated a row of pinched little faces that stared at them from behind a grimy window.

The door finally opened, and a stoop-shouldered man in dirty overalls and a ragged beard eyed him sourly.

"Here to look you over again, Lampher," stated Conway, flipping a paper from his pocket. "Search warrant." He commenced reading, the warrant stating that there was good reason to believe that illegal deer meat, venison, was concealed on the premises of one, Jake Lampher and against the peace and dignity of the State. When he was through, he turned to Warden Brothers and said, "If you'll watch the house, Tom, I'll take Lampher with me and look over the outbuildings."

A thin, barefoot woman was putting clothes to soak in a tub as old Tom went into the house. He looked rather formidable as he stood there, six foot two in height, in his high laced boots, frayed canvas hunting coat, and slouch hat. Peaked little faces and skinny legs faded into hiding.

"It's me that's botherin' you again, Mrs. Lampher. Didn't know you'd moved away over in this part of the country." Old Tom's eyes narrowed as he watched the woman's palsied hands stirring the clothes.

"It's your job, Mr. Brothers; your duty," she answered without looking up. The woman's voice sounded husky through tightly pinched lips.

Old Tom's professional eye took in the broken down stove, the pitiful little cupboard, and the two frowsy beds that stood across the room. In one corner a drygoods box cradled a wan-faced child who feebly fought a swarm of flies. He noticed a rifle hung from a nail, and crossed the uneven floor to inspect an old jacket on the wall. he turned to watch the woman again, drumming on the table with his thick, stubby fingers.

He spoke gently to her. "I'll have to be lookin' under that trap door, Mrs. Lampher, that you've got covered with your tub. He sighed deeply. "It's me that's always gettin' folks into trouble, ain't it?"

The woman backed away from the tub and sat down heavily in a chair. Her worn, knotted hands dropped into her soiled lap and her eyes stared tragically into space. Old Tom lifted the tub from the trap door, and producing a flashlight, lowered himself with much grunting, down a ladder and into the hole below. Fruit jars rattled as he disappeared from sight. A barrel toppled over, and after a time he could be heard scraping on the dirt floor with his foot. There was a long period of silence, followed by the rustle of paper as he pawed through a box, and finally he thrust his head through the hole and laboriously heaved himself up onto the floor.

"It's me that thought I'd be findin' meat down there, for sure I did," he rumbled in evident disappointment as he replaced the trap door.

The woman, with her head on the table, was sobbing in dry choking gasps, while a tow-headed tot patted her drab, unkempt hair.

Old Tom was trying to coax a little boy from under one of the beds when Conway came in followed by Lampher. Conway shook his head to indicate that he had found nothing.

"No luck-here," said old Tom, busy with his pipe. "Better check up again, son, I might have missed it. Cellar under that trap door."

Conway made a careful search of the room and then went through the trap door into the cellar. As he came up the ladder he heard the deep boom of Old Tom's mighty voice outside. "Don't be denyin' to me you haven't had meat. There's deer hair on your jacket, hangin' on the wall. Out violatin' laws and not even a garden or a milkin' cow for them kids of yourn. Jake, I'll get you, and when I do, it'll mean six months with your record." He turned to Conway as the latter came out of the house. "Let's be a goin' before I forget myself."

Lampher stood watching them as they got into their car, and an ugly grin twisted his bearded face. "Too smart for you this time-ya damned old skunk," he muttered.

The car crept out over the rock-strewn road, and as the Lampher place disappeared behind the bush line, Conway ground out savagely, "That was tough luck. It's hell to know they've had meat and you can't do anything about it. I found a stone jar buried in the sand down cellar. That's where they've been keeping it. We were too late."

"I discovered that jar, son," Old Tom pulled on his pipe. "If it's there we get it; if it ain't we don't. If I recollect, I had Jake Lampher in jail for killin' deer before you were born. That's when he lived in my part of the country. Well, better luck next time."

At the County Seat, Conway let Old Tom out at his home with the remark that he had to hurry back again on another complaint. "Thanks for the help, Tom," and he was gone.

Old Tom watched the disappearing car for a moment, and then in his vast, rolling gait walked to the rear of the house and on out to the garage. As he opened the door he was welcomed by a smiling setter, whose plumed tail gave double evidence of the welcome. Four half grown pups tumbled headlong to a place of honor.

"Well, Fanny," Old Tom's voice rumbled in kindness. "How are the brats?"

For a long time he petted the dog's sleek head, watching the clumsy pups as they rolled and chewed and fought.

"Conway's got the makin's of a good warden, Fran, " ruminated Old Tom, ruffling the dog's ears. It's me that can tell. He's smart and will go a long way. But, Fran, when he's seventy and been enforcin' the laws for forty years, maybe that high sense of duty of his will get warped, the same as mine. Forcin' people to do right won't worry him quite so much."

He reached into the depths of his faded hunting coat and pulled out a package wrapped in bloodstained newspaper. Slowly he unwrapped it to expose a scant pound of meat, dark with age. He carefully picked off stray bits of paper that stuck to it and a dozen tawny hairs, and with a low, warm chuckle, tossed the venison to the setter.

Ernie would now be tested to the ultimate by a different breed. Men who knew little about woodsmanship or the natural resources who would ruthlessly take all they could with no care for anyone or anything. They were to abuse the beautiful northern Wisconsin woods, lakes and resources as wantonly as they would plunder a rival gang's truck load of illegal beer. They used the area as a retreat when fleeing the heat in Chicago and as a safe playground or refuge and hideout.

The notorious Al Capone had a retreat north of Lac Court Orielles near Blue Berry Lake aptly named the Hideaway Resort. Other well-known mobsters habituating the area was the Moran and Touhy gang, the Joe Saltis gang of which Frank McErlane known as Machine Gun Frankie, inventor of the one-way ride, Stanley Novak and Tony Maloga were members, the deadly Barker Karpes gang, Potatoes Koffman, Lefty Koncel, Gus Winkler and many others.

Indiscriminately they fished below the Winter Dam where a 2,000 foot refuge had been established to protect the hordes of fish that gathered there. Their methods of bagging fish were far from orthodox and illegal under Wisconsin law. They blasted, speared and netted fish. They also loved casting and tangling with the trophy fish below the dam. They machine gunned deer mostly for the fun of it, openly challenging wardens to do something about it. Their brag was if interfered with a warden may end up at the bottom of the Chippewa wearing concrete boots as many had in the Chicago canal. Local people dubbed the area the place where the roads run to Hayward, Hurley and Hell. (Hurley during that era was noted for its houses of ill repute and gambling.)

Ernie sat further contemplating the controversy swirling over the unsavory presence of these characters infesting the north. A large share of the northern Wisconsin inhabitants had capitulated to them in one way or another. Some were intimated by their fearful reputations and swaggering attitudes, others by their free spending during the greatest depression the country had experienced. Many hoped a few of those scarce dollars would come their way. Disrespect reigned for all law and order. People felt the illegal taking of game and fish was acceptable while settling the wilderness area. Prohibition existing for the last nine years was so hated it became easy for the population to accept people who defied it. The mobsters inhabiting the area were engaged in the business of providing beer and liquor. Most people felt they should be entitled to drink in spite of the fact they had no money. A large segment of the population of the north looked at the mobsters as godly figures. Persons considering them assets included many local government officials including policemen and persons in the judicial system. They therefore had free reign in the north.

Yet there existed a minority element of the community that recognized these underworld characters for what they represented. It was up to this minority to rid themselves of this plague.

Ernie was brought out of his reverie by a loud mating whistle and a bright streak of color as a male cardinal belligerently raced after his duller unaroused companion. The booming crash of the mighty Chippewa tumbling over its recent impediment suddenly loud in his ears reminded him of the job at hand. *How do I do this: Certainly I will face guns down at the dam.* His mind again wandered to the reports of these dangerous men brazenly showing their firearms around the area.

Should I get help? No way to immediately communicate with other wardens. Don't trust local enforcement to go against these guys.

Letting his Model A Ford drift down the hill past the Lincoln where it ran out of momentum, he parked. Exiting carefully easing the door closed, he carefully walked to where the car was skillfully hidden. On the front seat lay a sub machine gun (Wisconsin did not ban machine guns until 1929.) Not surprised at seeing the gun did not quench his fear of the ominous symbol.

Could still leave, he thought, knowing his steel like quality would never allow it.

Sneaking to a high point, he let his binoculars scan the area. They hesitated on the signs in plain view. **"Fish Refuge Area, Spawning Grounds, Fishing Prohibited, Wis. Conservation Commission."**

His glasses moved steadily scanning until they riveted on three men busily casting into the roiling frothy water immediately below the dam. Shifting the glasses slightly he picked up a flash of white in the water, then another. Several walleyes were tied to the bank rising and falling with the smooth rolling waves near shore. Each man had a handgun protruding from what Ernie knew were leather lined pockets to provide a fast draw. A lever action rifle leaned against the wing wall of the dam.

Quietly Ernie observed giving way to further consider leaving. *No one will ever know. But I would, God hates a coward.* "Ah hell," he muttered stepping into the open letting his slow quiet muted pace be covered by the pounding of water hurtling heavily over the dam. *Ah, at least, I've taken them by surprise.*

As if by signal the three whirled to face him, guns in hand. So swift was their draw that Ernie stood transfixed. His mind unable to grasp the obvious. *My God, they were fishing with their guns in their hands. Well now I'm in it. Nothing I can do but play out the hand.*

"What in hell ya want?" bellowed the largest, a beefy man of about 45 years of age.

Staring unbelievingly at the muzzles of the three pistols pointing unwaveringly at him, he tried to think his way out of the situation.

Studying the beefy man, recognition slowly seeped into his benumbed mind. *My God, that's Frankie McErlane. Machine Gun Frankie. I'm in heaps of trouble here.*

With fear clutching his heart, his steeliness slowly returned.

His voice surprised him as it emerged unwavering unexpectedly steady and steely. "I'm a Game Warden and you're all under arrest. Now, let's see some fishing licenses."

"For christ's sake," muttered MacErlane. "A hick cop." Smiling at the gall of the miniature sized warden, MacErlane slid his gun into his pocket. "Put the guns away boys. We don't wanna hurt this little guy."

One of them later identified as Frank Novak, a burly killer was unmoved as he continued to belligerently stare at Swift. "I kill him, Frankie? Draw yer gat punk."

"No put your piece away, Frank." MacErlane ordered.

Concentrating on Novak as he hesitantly deposited the gun in his pocket, Swift was again startled as the third man behind him who was later identified as Joe Milaga breathed slowly, "Draw your gat wise guy. We'll settle this now. Good bye ya son a bitch."

Fear raced through Ernie, his back tingling at the expected bullet. *Well I made a decision looks like I'll have to live by it or die by it.*

"Shove it Joe," ordered MacErlane his voice now revealing irritation.

Ernie stood then for what seemed an eternity while they argued and swore back and forth as to whether they should kill him.

Trying to take command, his face not revealing his anxiety, he faced MacErlane. His steady voice demanded, "I asked for your licenses earlier. Now I mean it. Get your license out."

Flustered at the tenacity and nerve of this obviously mad steely eyed wraith facing them, MacErlane dug a license from his mackinaw pocket handing it to Ernie. "Here wise guy. I've got one."

Astonished that he'd received a license Ernie's clammy fingers let the license slide through them. As it fluttered to the ground, he bent over to pick it up. While bent over, Milaga snatched at Ernie's holstered gun. Reaching back Swift brushed the hand away and retrieved the license.

Turning to Novak he snapped, "Your license too." Reaching for the license, Milaga again attempted to snatch Ernie's gun. He savagely slapped the hand away and turned around. "Keep your damn hands off my gun and get your license out."

Milaga still in an arrogant state began, "The hell I!"

"Can it Tony," retorted MacErlane. "Give him the license."

Glancing at the licenses, Ernie finally knew exactly who he was dealing with. Retaining the licenses, he scurried around quickly picking up the large muskellunge and several sizable walleyes tied to the bank and dumped them unceremoniously into their gunnysack. "Ok, I'll keep these licenses," said Swift slipping them into his front pants pocket. "All three of you be at the courthouse in Hayward tomorrow at 10:00 o'clock."

Savagely Milaga jerked his gun from his pocket. "God damn Frankie. I kill him now." It was evident who was in charge as his gaze centered on Mac Earlane for approval.

"Leave em go, Tony. He's only a hayseed. We'll talk to Saltis on how ta deal with this damn knothead."

Relieved, Ernie grasped the bag of fish, turned on his heel and walked away with electric shocks running up and down his spine where the bullet might enter.

The three failed to appear in court. Ernie arrested Novak a month later and transported him to court where he paid his fine. It should be noted the District Attorney would not entertain charges against these three for assault or resisting arrest.

Swift never got to serve the other two arrest warrants, as soon after this encounter Milaga and Novak were fished from the Chicago Canal their bodies wrapped in wire, weighted down and riddled with bullets. The same fate came to MacErlane the following winter.

Meanwhile the indiscriminate violating by other desperados continued.

Shortly after noon on a bright day in July in 1928 Percy Button stationed in Sawyer County approached the Winter Dam refuge. He was aware of the presence of the Chicago mobsters in the area bragging of their exploits below the dam and the danger they presented. He was also aware of Swift's encounter with the three Chicago mobsters earlier that year. He knew of the multitude of walleyes and muskies that congregated in the turbulent waters of the stilling pond off the aprons of the dam.

Hiding himself carefully among the short brush that had sprouted from the ashes of the burned over forest area, he waited

About 4:30 p.m. four men meandered down the trail from the bluff area. All carried fishing rods and reels. They also carried hand guns that jutted prominently from leather lined jacket pockets.

Soon their baits were flying into the stilling basin.

Only minutes passed before one of them yelled mightily. "Got one!" Heaving heavily against the steel casting rod, he danced up and down the stream so as not to run out of line which peeled off his squealing reel as the large fish made mighty runs in the foaming water. Reeling furiously to maintain a tight line, he frantically thumbed the reel to avoid a pile up of the heavy line in one spot as the level wind reel was not yet available. Suddenly it happened. The reel stopped. "Hey, I can't reel any more. Help me."

Dropping their rods, the others ran to his assistance. One grabbed the heavy line and ran up the bank pulling a huge musky to the river's edge where it flopped and sloshed in the shallows. The others quickly gathered at the fish , grabbed it and carried it up the bank where they flung it into the grass. As the group gathered to admire the flopping giant, Button stepped from hiding and unnoticed walked up to them while they were distracted.

"Well fellows looks like you've got a dandy. It also looks like I've got you. I'm a game warden and you're all under arrest for fishing in a refuge." Without another word he walked past the stunned men, placed his hand in the fish's gills and hefted it with a grunt. "I'll take this."

Turning to face the largest of the four, a beefy chunk of a man, he was transfixed at what his eyes beheld. The big man directed a 45 Colt pistol at his midsection.

Fear gripping him, he suddenly realized who he faced. Machine Gun Frankie MacErlane.

"Drop that fish, punk or I'll dump ya."

As the fish thudded heavily to the ground. MacErlane barked, "Back off" warily directing Button with the gun. MacErlane shuffled forward, kicking the fish, moving it ever toward the water. With a splash, the fish finally entered the water, where it laid recovering from the ordeal. With a splash, it swam ahead melding into the turbulence that immediately swept it downstream.

"There now whatcha gonna do? Ya got no evidence."

"I don't need the fish. You be in court at Hayward on Thursday morning at 11 o'clock. I'm sure the judge will take my word for what happened here today."

Suddenly white-faced MacErlane stuttered, "Wa-Wait a min-minute. No sen-sense in ya getten so damn huffy. Hell, I'll make it right with ya." Glancing at the others for support, he shoved the gun into his pocket and dug feverishly in his rear pants pocket producing a wallet that popped open from the pressure of the huge stack of bills in it. Systematically counting out loud, he handed Button a handful of bills. "Here take this $55.00 That's more then ya make in a month."

"Look MacErlane, I'm not for sale. Just be in court on Thursday like I told you."

"Hell man be reasonable." Stopping to think he again dipped into the wallet counting off more bills. "Here's $200.00 and that's my last offer. take it. We can settle this right here."

"I told you I can't be bought. Now listen." Button's voice hardened. "I mean this. Put your money away and be in court like I told you. I mean all four of you."

"Wha the hell, your crazy man. Any Chicago Dick would jump at this chance."

"You're not in Chicago now. Just be in court." Turning on the ball of his foot, he retreated up the trail with baited breath waiting for the expected bullet that would end it all. It did not come and neither did MacErlane or the others on Thursday morning.

In October 1928, Swift received a copy of a letter of complaint received by the Railroad Commission

Railroad Commission of Wisconsin,
Madison, Wisconsin.

Gentlemen:-

Referring further to the complaint of Hayward Rod and Gun Club in
regard to conditions at the Chippewa Reservoir Dam in Sawyer County, will say
that we have just received a report from our caretaker that for several days there
have been eighteen men fishing at the dam.

They came in four automobiles bearing Illinois license plates, and
each automobile had a machine gun in the rear seat.

The spokesman for the party came up to the caretaker's house and
stated that they intended to fish at the dam, spearing fish if necessary to get them,
and probably do some hunting and get some venison. This man had four guns
on him, which he carried in leather lined pockets, and stated that all they wanted
of the caretaker was to be let alone.

They did not do any dynamiting at the dam but may have done some
work of this kind farther down river. They did considerable fishing off the wing
walls of the dam, and all our man dared to do was to let them alone, and sell them
a little milk when they came after it.

When conditions like this exist we feel that the proper officers should
take a hand in the matter, and that the Hayward Rod and Gun Club should not
attempt to hang all the blame on this Company when some dead fish are found
in the river channel.

Yours very truly,

Chippewa & Flambeau Improvement Co.
By Donald Boyd
Secretary

In September of 1929 another letter of complaint was routed to the
Railroad Commission.

Mr. A.R. Frahm, Eau Claire, Wis.   Sept. 10, 1929
Mr. G. E. LOUGHLAND, Hydraulic Engr. Minneapolis

Wisconsin Division
Electric - Hydro

Dear Mr. Loughland:

While at the Chippewa Reservoir on September 6th, I noticed that the
Conservation Commission has the river posted for one mile below the dam. This
notice prohibits fishing in this area for the purpose of protecting the fish for
propagation purposes.

Mr. Finley's log books shows that during the two weeks prior to the
above date, on six different occasions, Illinois people, principally Joe Saltis and
his gang, have been fishing off the wing walls on the stilling basin. They have been
taking fish by the sack full, principally pike, which Jim said will run from five to
eight pounds. Usually there are five or six men in the gang and no effort seems
to be made on the Conservation Commission's part to prevent this illegal fishing.

It would appear that, if the thought of installing the fish hatchery at the
reservoir dam is carried through, some pressure should be brought to bear on the
Conservation Commission so that the fish below the dam will not be molested.

Mr. Finley states that the people who live in this territory are very much
aroused over the action of the Conservation Commission in making a reserve on

that end of the river, preventing the natives from fishing there, and taking no steps to see that outsiders obey the law. Mr. Finley reports that there is much talk about the situation in Winter and that it has been rumored around that if the Conservation Commission does not take any action the natives will take action themselves and when their job is finished there won't be a place left for anyone to fish.

We would be very glad to hear of any action which might be taken in this matter.

Yours very truly,

General Superintendent
Wisconsin Division
A.R. Frahm

The following year in November of 1929, Swift again came into contact with one of the kingpins of the Chicago beer wars.

Joe Saltis, known as the Beer Baron, a huge muscular slab of a man at 260 pounds, with only a slight bulge showing above his belt, ruled his large organization by brute strength and murder when necessary. His hands hung like hams slung on the end of telephone pole like arms. Hands that had hammered his way to the top of his notorious gang. Hands that had more than once pulled a trigger taking life. It was known he had killed another gangster and a police officer. Seemingly untouchable because of his strength and control of the political apparatus and courts in Chicago, he had been tried for the two murders and many other crimes. In all but several, he had been cleared.

He flouted his status by openly admitting the murders and by the car he drove, a black bullet proof Lincoln touring car bearing a mounted machine gun and a red banner in the manner of a military staff car. Specifically his brags were that Ernie Swift would never take him. He'd fish the Winter Dam and the Devil be damned.

Ernie in November 1929 preparing carefully, was now ready to call Saltis threats as he and Fred Minor from Iron River waited in ambush along the road leading to the dam. Finding Saltis' large car parked below the bluff satisfied Swift his prize was fishing the refuge.

Positioning themselves so they could observe, they saw Saltis catch several large muskies.

Huffing and puffing, Saltis's beefy 260 pound form wheezed its way up the trail half carrying, half dragging the six large muskies he had tied together at the gills.

He stood frozen at the audacity of the pint-sized red head who stepped gingerly out of the roadside brush cover. Swinging his gaze to the other side of the road, he fastened his eyes on the tall slim figure of Fred Minor. Riveted in position he glared at the two hand guns directed steadily at his midsection. "Wha the hell, why the gats?"

Ernie replied, "Saltis you're under arrest."

"What fer? These few fish? G'wan punk, put the piece away. Hell I won't hurt ya."

Facing Ernie's stern expressionless countenance the forced smile seemingly stuck on his puffy face faded as he dropped the fish on the ground.

"Ok wise guy, ya want to tangle with Joe Saltis go ahead. Let's go. Y'all never pin a rap on me. It'll be a dark day in purgatory when ya arrest Joe Saltis."

"I just did Joe," intoned Ernie. "Now carefully slip that gun out of your pocket and hand it to Fred.

In court later Saltis swore, pleaded, threatened and cajoled the Judge and the game wardens but finally paid a $50.00 fine. The roll of bills he produced would far exceed the combined annual salaries of the wardens and the judge.

Stomping heavily from the court, he warned, "Ya were lucky Oinie. I've been tried for murder twice in Chi town and beat the rap. The two of em didn't give me as much trouble as this stinkin fish business. Better enjoy while ya cin, cause ya ain't doin it agin. I'll be fishin the dam after you're dead an gone."

"Go shoot someone," Swift replied tiredly, "but break a game law and we'll be there."

"Don't think your half bright," muttered Saltis. "The next time ya try ta take me ya better come shootin."

Reporting the episode to Chief Warden MacKenzie brought a trip to Madison for Swift and a meeting with Governor Kohler Sr. Kohler was extremely concerned about what was transpiring in the northern part of the state.

His concern was sharpened when told of the attitude of the local people and judicial system toward these unsavory characters. "You say Joe Saltis threatened to kill you Ernie?"

"Well yes, me and any other warden standing in his way."

"What do you propose we do about Saltis?"

In his straight forward way, Swift replied, "I think we should call his threat and I'll kill him if necessary."

Turning to MacKenzie, Koehler asked, "What do you think Mac?"

"Gosh Chief, I think Ernie's right. We have some really good men around the state, men who will not buckle under pressure. I'd like to pick a crew to assist Ernie and go after Saltis. He's the most troublesome of the bunch. If we put him in his place the rest will be less hard to handle. As to killing Saltis, it may be the only way and I'll certainly back Ernie if it should happen. But Ernie explain to the Governor the climate of the courts toward these people."

"I'm afraid the local courts would side with the wild element should it come to a shoot out. That has been the history up there since the gangs have taken over. I believe we are the only agency taking any action against them."

"Ernie, you can depend on the state to back you as long as I'm governor. Go ahead boys, we're going to rout that element out of Wisconsin. If necessary, I'll declare martial law and send the National Guard up there to restore order. Mac if you need additional funding to pull this off, I'll personally see you get it."

Soon the governor's words were echoed in the news media through-out Wisconsin and the Midwest. He had drawn the line. The hoodlums knew they were at war in Wisconsin.

Mac and Ernie went about picking the crew to take Saltis down. The

92   *The Saga of Ernie Swift*

men picked were experienced wardens, good woodsmen who had proved their mettle through the years.

There was A.J. Robinson of Rhinelander and Barney Devine of Webster, both would later become Chief Wardens; Kelly Jones of Ashland and Stuart Hayner of Eagle River. Buck Johnson stationed at Portage , a crack shot who often drew Indian Chief heads with a 22 rifle volunteered to kill Saltis. MacKinzie decided against this because Johnson's known skill with firearms should it come to shooting may make it look like an execution.

Governor Kohler's warning carried through the larger newspapers brought about a temporary truce slowing the number of complaints received on Saltis and other mobsters in the area.

Inexorably the Chippewa River Refuge drew Saltis back as Swift knew it would. In the middle of August, when he was fairly certain Saltis had been fishing, the selected men were called together at Hayward. A plan of attack was laid out taking advantage of their superior woodsmanship and the element of surprise. With no thought of backing down from a shoot out they added lever action rifles which all were proficient with to their arsenals. Leaving their cars about 12 miles above the dam, the men launched boats and traveled via water to about 1 mile above the dam. Dusk saw them setting up pup tents before a brooding rumbling approaching thunder storm. Beating the storm, they hurried inside listening to the rain and hail pounding against taut canvas. Despite the night long downpour they arose when the pale sullen light penetrated the openings in the tent flies.

Dressing hurriedly, leaving the tents, they cooked over a sizzling smoky fire, the smell of bacon frying mingling with the arid smoke.

As the rain slackened, they kicked dirt over the smoldering ashes. The woods were dripping and the walking difficult. The long awaited rain had finally bought relief to one of the worst disastrous droughts of the century. They splashed through the sopping wet sooty stumps and rampikes the hell bent for leather logging and uncontrolled fires of the era had wrought.

Making their way toward the dam the scrub brush continued to drip as though the rain had not stopped. Regardless of working their way carefully through the sodden mess, they soon were soaked and blackened with sooty grime from the recent fires. Pushing through the last of the dripping bush they entered a gravel pit topping a bank above the dam to observe the area below.

Bingo - Their spirits soared-wet cold bodies suddenly warm with anticipation. Saltis's crew were fishing the refuge area.

Binoculars swinging they scanned the bulky figure of Saltis and two other men dressed in dark raincoats busily casting into the turbulent Chippewa.

Further approaching the dam, the sudden flush of a Sharp Tailed grouse so plentiful in the burned over north startled the men. Rising practically under their feet, it rose, pumped heavily a few times, set its wings and sailed in a soaring arc against the pallid overcast skies past the intruders to the refuge, landing in the scrub growing tight against the apron wall.

Waiting with baited breath frozen in place, the wardens watched the grouse fearing their discovery before they were in position.

Not wise to the way of the woods, the three men after a brief glance at the grouse continued to fish.

Relieved the wardens moved to their rendezvous point on a bluff up the road from the dam to wait where the gangsters habitually parked their cars.

A steel casting rod nestling under his arm, Saltis led his boys up the trail. Gunny sacks, they carried and dragged, bulged and writhed from the large fish inside.

Approaching the parked cars, Saltis' happy countenance suddenly changed, his cheek twitching at the sound of rolling gravel from above. Spinning swiftly he faced the specter of a grimy, elfin, grinning, red-head sliding to a stop a few feet from him. His steely gaze directed a 30-30 rifle at his mid section.

"What the? Oinie! Wh, why the artillery?"

"You told me the next time I come for you to come shooting. Well, we're here."

Glancing desperately up and down the road for support from his underlings brought Saltis further consternation. The gravel still cascading down the bluffside revealed three other men sliding down. More rifles were directed steadily at him and his two partners who now held their hands in plain sight slightly up and forward indicating surrender.

The wardens turned their attention to the roadside as a figure suddenly appeared, working slowly through the sopping brush, the stiff rain coat scrapping harshly against the resisting brush, giving away his position. "That you Joe?"

"Christ man, a hell of a guard you are. They've already got me." Disgustedly he spat. "Might as well come out."

A slight man pushed through the thick brush, his pronounced limp helped to entangle him in the clinging brush. The submachine gun he carried became so entangled in the bush he stood perplexed gazing down the muzzles of several rifles.

Devine's sharp command rang through the area. "Drop it. Go on, drop it. No need to get it loose. Just let go of it, damn you."

The machine gun loosely teetered in the clutching branches, slowly turned and dropped clanging as it bounced several times on a rock pile sliding to a stop in the ditch line. Picking it up, Devine waved with the rifle. "Ok, over by Joe. Move!"

Saltis, staring at Swift, cursed softly under his breath, dark eyes darting up and down the road muttered, "how'd you guys get in here enny way?"

"By water. Now Joe just slowly slip that Colt out of your pocket with two fingers on the stock, and damn it be careful because we've come to take you and we don't care how we do it."

Down the road, Barney Devine's determined steady voice echoed Ernie's order. "Okay you guys, let's have your guns. Pull them slow and mighty easy like your life depends on it because it does."

With Jones and Devine keeping the two covered, Hayner sidled cautiously up to them collecting the handguns. "Ernie did you catch what Saltis said? There must be more guards along the road."

"Ya, why don't you stay here with me. Al, you and Barney go down the road and disarm them."

Hayner herded the two over near Saltis. "Move you guys. Over there near your boss and damn it don't give us an excuse to shoot."

"Ok, Ok, don't get so damn hostile," muttered one as he started toward Saltis. "Christ you'd think we'd killed some one or somethin.'"

Turning to the complaining man, Ernie studied him closely. "I know you. Aren't you Koffman, Potatoes Koffman"

"Ya. What's it to ya?"

"Well just thought I should know you." Ernie knew Koffman as a king pin of the beer wars, as famous as Saltis and MacErlane, a celebrated gangster and killer from Chicago.

With the three bunched up guarded by Swift and Hayner, the others moved silently and steadily down the road drifting silently into the roadside brush for concealment. Rifles at port arms, they slowly slipped through the dripping brush. Moving ever so slowly around the first bend they approached an unsuspecting tall lean man impatiently pacing up and down the road, a Thompson submachine gun cradled comfortably in his arms. He slowly caressed it as though making love to the inanimate lethal object.

At Robinson's deliberate order, "You're covered. Drop the gun" The man stiffened. Hesitantly he slowly turned to face the tall lanky deliberate man facing him. Disbelief showing on his face, his indecision vanished when Devine's voice droned from across the road. "There's another rifle over here. Do as your told." The stubby weapon dropped almost silently into the mass of soft grass between the wheel ruts.

Robinson approached rifle steady. Deftly sliding a handgun from the man's pocket he asked, "How many more are there?"

"Three"

"Where"

"Scattered tween here and the dam."

"Put your hands behind you. I'm going to cuff you. Now we expect you to just stay here and keep your mouth shut. We already have Saltis so just play it cool."

Continuing down the road the episode was repeated until all were disarmed and marched up the road.

Using the mobster's vehicles they were transported to the Sawyer County jail at Hayward.

Municipal Justice H.O. Moreland fined Saltis $50.00 and Ed Morrison and Joe Sedovich $25.00 each. The District Attorney refused to prosecute on gun charges in spite of the fact the possession of machine guns had been prohibited in Wisconsin since May of 1929, to deal with people of this kind.

The August 15, 1930 issue of the Milwaukee Journal carried the story of Saltis arrest with a giant front page headline. **"Joe Saltis Trapped by Armed Wardens."** In contrast as in the past the northern Wisconsin newspapers including the Hayward paper, made no mention of the arrests or the unsavory element in their midsts. Their papers only spoke of the much needed rain. They speculated that the long drought was perhaps over.

During the years between 1930 and 1933 Saltis remained belligerent but toned his game violating down somewhat.

Arrests were made occasionally with Swift visiting the Saltis camp, ordering people in when they killed deer, grouse or took illegal fish.

Saltis's scruples had not improved however. According to a Chicago newspaper story in 1931, he had the unmitigated gall to show fraudulent papers identifying himself as a Wisconsin Conservation Warden. The claim was made during a vagrancy trial in Chicago. It was obviously feast or famine for the pushy gang leader.

Chief Warden MacKinzie made a scathing news release stating, "Joe Saltis never has been and is not now, a deputy conservation warden in Wisconsin."

Late in July of 1930 on a balmy summer day, Warden H.B. (Happy) Haugan of Loretta hiked warily down the road to the Winter Dam. Unthinkingly he laid is hand on the handle of his ever present Billy Club protruding prominently from his rear pocket. The familiar wood reassured and comforted him. He far preferred it to carrying a handgun. Fully aware, he was approaching a hazardous situation he forced himself to continue past the black Lincoln parked below the bluff. The car, a sure indication that Saltis or some of his cohorts were again fishing the refuge encompassing the stilling basin below the dam.

Haugan had Chief Warden MacKenzie's orders running through his mind to watch the dam, as he approached the three men, unassumingly casting into the frothing waters of the Chippewa.

Haugen's "Good morning boys, catching any fish?" was answered by a sturdily built man in his early forties who arrogantly grunted, "What's it to ya?"

"Well, it's like this fellows, I'm a game warden and you're all under arrest for fish-ugh." Haugan's breath whooshed out, his sentence unfinished as the man's hand dipped in a blur into his leather lined jacket pocket where a German Luger pistol appeared like magic and was jammed unmercifully into Haugan's ribs.

"Wha the? Hey put that thing away."

"Shut up. Who ya think you talkin ta enny way. Know who iam?"

"Not really. You probably work for Joe Saltis."

"Ya damn right we do. If ya think ya can hassle us you're wrong. I"m Lefty Koncel and no damn hick game warden's gonna put the make on me."

Startled as name recognition hit him, Haugan swallowed hard. Koncel's reputation as one of Saltis star Lieutenants and known murderer had followed him to the north woods, where he now managed Saltis camps on Barker Lake.

Regaining his composure Haugan stalled for time to think and give Koncel time to drop his guard.

His compromising statement caused Koncel to relax slightly. "Mr. Koncel, I didn't really know who I was contacting here. Perhaps I should just leave." Pointing up the trail he took a turning step as to leave. His turn however did not stop, his hand darting to his hip pocket drawing his trusty

96 *The Saga of Ernie Swift*

billy. The blurring preposterous move took Koncel off guard. Haugan's speed and skill with the billy now paid dividends as he swung for Koncel's head aiming for the home run.

Koncel ducked just enough to save his life as the club struck a glancing blow to his forehead stunning and dumping him heavily on his back. The blood flying from Koncel's head bathed Haugan's face and torso as his 180 pounds of unleashed fury landed full on Koncel's chest, knees first. In his stunned state, without breath, Koncel did not realize his gun had dropped, and Haugan had scooped it up. Mind reeling, gasping for breath, he gazed at the angry man with the star shaking and poking the club at him. "M mi gun, my gat where's it."

"Right here," shouted the berserk madman patting the gun stuck under his belt. Jabbing Koncel in the ribs savagely with the club, he demanded, "Get up, get up damn it. You're going to jail. Get up before I crack your head like an egg."

Dazedly, Koncel staggered to his feet.

Turning, Haugan menaced the others waving his club to accentuate his commands. "All right, everybody turn your guns in here." Walking warily among them, he collected the guns.

Guiding the three up the trail with his now respected club, Haugen took Koncel in his car and had the others follow him to Hayward where each paid $50.00 fines.

Shortly after this encounter, Lefty Koncel was shot to death by a rival gang in Chicago.

All wardens from around the area were aware of the problem at the Winter Dam and were making contacts whenever possible.

So it was on the first of August 1930 newly appointed Warden Louis (Pat) Oshesky approached the dam. (Pat would later be involved in the misguided shootout directed by FBI agent Melvin Purvis in 1934 against the John Dillenger gang at Little Bohemia near Manitowish Waters.)

Watching three fishermen casting into the refuge area, Oshesky recognized Joe Saltis as one of them and approached him first.

Pat's gruff voice announced, "Im a game warden and would like to see your licenses. You know you're fishing in a refuge."

Saltis, a huge grin on his face retorted, "Well now sonny, aint ya a bright penny. We're not fishin."

"I should advise you I've been watching you for some time. All of you were casting from time to time."

"Ha! Bright one, we got no bait on the hooks."

"No bait? What are you doing here then. Pull your lines."

Upon checking their lines, Pat realized he had walked into what was set up to be an ambush. The lines rigged with sinkers, had no bait, lures or hooks.

Bewildered Pat blurted, "Ok, I see you have no hooks on your lines. What the hell are you doing here?"

Again the devilish grin appeared, Saltis jowls quivering with mirth, "Waitin-just waitin-fer an old friend."

"Old friend? What old friend?"

"Ya know, ma old friend Oinie."

"Your waiting for Swift?"

"Ya," Saltis added meaningfully, "I understand he wants to take a swim."

Leaving in confusion, Pat immediately reported what had transpired to Ernie. Swift immediately reported the incident to MacKinzie.

About two weeks later a hot muggy August day brought Happy Haugan back to the Winter Dam. He found four heavily armed members of the Saltis gang fishing the refuge.

Narrowly eying the now famous billy club jutting from Haugan's hip pocket they submitted to arrest without a fight.

Approaching their car they attempted to talk him into riding into Hayward with them. Wisely distrusting them, he ordered them to follow him to Hayward to pay their fines.

However, upon reaching the city, they gunned their black sedan past Haugan's Model A Ford. Chasing them into the country, he soon lost them on the dusty roads.

Checking later, Haugan found out the four had been staying at the Saltis camp. Upon checking there he found they had left the state.

As time went by the groups remained but became less noticeable. They continued to violate the game laws only slightly inhibited. Their status in the area remained high. Wardens were daily criticized by the local population for bothering the communities mentors. Then in September of 1933, John Helsing, a young forest patrolman of Radisson, working for Forest Ranger Sam Ruegger of Winter drove out of Winter on routine fire patrol. His patrol carried him to the Winter Dam road.

Rounding a turn he came upon a shiny large black Lincoln auto with two men in it. In a cloud of dust, it slewed to a stop in front of him. He watched a huge bear of a man slip silently out of the car, shotgun in hand. He observed the giant take several careful steps toward the ditch, raise the gun and fire into the low brushline. Immediately a grouse began fluttering its death knell in the dense brush. Lunging frantically forward the man snatched the still fanning head shot bird. Turning he strode swiftly back and unceremoniously threw the bird through the open window into the back seat. Turning the man fastened his gaze on and stared blankly at the vehicle parked behind him.

Quickly Johnny left his vehicle and trotted to the defiant appearing man who bellowed, "Who the hell are you?"

Not knowing who he had contacted, Johnny replied, "I'm a forest patrolman and you just shot a partridge during the closed season."

"Ya, whatcha gonna do about it?"

Well, I'm going to turn you over to Sam Ruegger, my boss. I'll have to take your partridge."

"Like hell ya will. What authority da ya have," the man roared.

Gulping at the broadside, Johnny dug frantically through his pockets finally coming up with the small forest protection badge he had been issued. "This is my authority."

Stamping about the road, the man was obviously perplexed. He did not know the badge carried no arrest authority.

Sensing the brute's indecision, Johnny capitulated. Bending to look into the car, he pointed at the driver, a medium-sized young man, "give me that bird." Silently the sullen pale faced man handed two grouse out the window.

"Now I'd like some identification."

Without comment the man handed Johnny a card. Quickly he wrote on his notepad, Edward Szumoski, of Barker Lake, Hayward, Wis. Turning to the hulking man, he said, "and you sir."

"Hell ya know who I am."

"No sir, I don't."

"Well christ, I'm Joe Saltis and by christ, ya soon will know of me."

"Joe Saltis," said Johnny almost to himself as he jotted the name down, walked behind the black Lincoln to copy the license number. "You two will have to follow me into Hayward."

The upward rush of blood blackened Saltis' face as he roared, "Like hell I will."

Unsure of himself because of lacking authority, Johnny hesitated and turned to Szumoski. "You can come to Hayward with me then."

Szumoski looked to Saltis for orders, "What ya tink."

Perplexed, Saltis muttered, "Oh go with em. They can't pin anthin on us enny way. I'm not goin. I suppose that damn Ruegger will sic Swift on me. Well let em come. We'll see if he can take me. I'm sick of these dumb yokels and their so called game laws."

Johnny took Szumoski to Sam Ruegger who personally knew him and delivered him to Hayward and Ernie Swift.

The following day found Johnny Helsing and Sam Ruegger on their way to Barker Lake with Swift. Armed with a warrant for Saltis and Edward Szumoski, Swift explained that Edward was the son of Joe (Radio Joe) Szumoski, who had been brought in from Chicago to replace Lefty Koncel in managing Saltis' resort after marrying Saltis' sister.

At Barker Lake their car rattled to a stop in a cloud of dust, scattering a bunch of chickens busily feeding in the yard. Sitting on the porch were four mean-eyed, pasty faced city type men who were obviously underlings of Saltis.

Leaving the car the three stopped below the steps. Addressing the group, Swift said, "I want to see Joe." Menacingly one of them silently nodded toward the door.

Swift and Ruegger entered and as prearranged Helsing stayed on the porch. Passing the four men on the porch, Swift and Ruegger were followed by them. Automatically fanning strategically out behind, they drew their guns to protect their leader.

Upon a call from one of the men, Saltis entered from a back room. His bloated face cryptically revealed he was on a drinking binge. Swaying slightly he grasped a kitchen chair to steady himself. The quart bottle of moonshine whiskey he carried was dwarfed by the huge fist clutching it, "Oinie, wassa the matta Oinie?" Groaning slightly, he lowered his huge bulk into a complaining swaying, squeaking kitchen chair.

Nodding to one of his boys he rumbled, "Give Oinie a chair."

Swift ignored the proffered chair feeling more comfortable standing under the stress of feeling trapped. His voice projected surprisingly steady as he battled his inner turmoil. "Joe you were shooting partridge yesterday during the closed season. Eddie and you are going to have to come to Hayward and take care of this matter."

"Aw Oinie, schit down. Less hava drink. Ya always get so hard about these things. Hell whatsa coupla partidge tween friens. Ya aint gonna push this are ya?" Splashing two water glasses full from his bottle he shoved one toward Swift as he lifted the other in a salute. "Bottoms up" and downed the drink in one great swallow.

Swift shook his head in the negative. "I mean it Joe. You're going to appear in court."

"Come on-n Oinie. We cin work together on these" Reaching out he gulped the second glass. Slopping booze into the glass again some splashing on the table due to his unsteadiness, he glared at Swift. "Now let's get down to bushiness. Looks like I misjudged ya. Maybe your not a boy schout but a bushiness man." Reaching for his hip pocket he produced a bulging wallet and withdrew a large stack of bills. Fingering out a hundred dollar bill he slapped it onto the table. "Thake it Ohinie."

Standing as tall as his five foot eight inch height would allow Ernie simply nodded in the negative. Sam Ruegger standing near the door blinked in awe. The depression had been tough. It was the first one hundred dollar bill he had ever seen.

Gazing blurry eyed at Swift, Saltis shrugged his shoulders and laid another bill beside the first, glanced at Swift and laid down still another and another until there were ten bills laying side by side. "It's yourn Schwift." Gesturing expansively with his ham like hands, "Take it, take a grand. Whadda I care? Jess lay off me en mi boys."

"I'm not for sale," muttered Swift.

"Everybody's got a price, God damn it."

Without passion, Ernie nodded and answered, "no."

"Ah can't believe yar that stupid."

"The state pays me," Swift replied feeling strangely heroic thinking of his annual salary of $1600.00. Stretching himself even taller, he continued, "Eddie and you have to come back to Hayward with me."

"Oinie, Oinie, juss slide these bills ina yar pocket. I'm not buying ya off. No one will ever know. We cin just firget thesch."

"There's no use arguing Saltis, the answer is no."

Face further darkening, Saltis lunged to his full six foot three catapulting the chair into a corner where it collapsed, wooden pieces ricocheting around the room.

Everyone stood transfixed in silence as Saltis stared at Swift hate mirrored in his dark eyes. "Ya stupid bashtard, da ya know how easily I could kill ya?" With a mighty heave he sent the table flying to the side where it caromed off the wall knocking a hole through the plaster. Stumbling through the door and down the porch, he gestured wildly with both huge arms, "Come here Oinie. I wanna show ya sompin."

Scattering a bunch of chickens, busily scratching in the dusty yard, he swiftly and deftly drew his 45 Army Colt and blasted away. Boom, boom, boom. In spite of his ineberiation three running chickens were sent tumbling headlessly to the ground where they thrashed raising large clouds of dust. Turning he stared at Swift. "Get tha idee?"

"Yeah, I know Joe, but I came here to get you and Eddie. I won't take you with me right now. You sober up and appear this afternoon at 5 p.m. Bring Eddie along." Turning he motioned Rueggar and Helsing to the car. They left the porch and strode swiftly away, their backs exposed to the guns that could cut them down. They walked swiftly past the three chickens still furiously fluttering their wings.

Turning as he entered the car, Swift repeated his earlier command, "5 o'clock Joe. Be in court."

The three left shirts glistening with sweat in spite of the coolness of the day, Saltis's words ringing in their ears. "Dammit, I'm not schooing up. Christ, I wash tried three times in Chi fer merder. Ya think ya can pin thish dumb rap on me?"

When five o'clock rolled around the three enforcers and Municipal Justice H.O. Moreland were surprised to see four large black sedans roll to a stop at the courthouse. About a dozen men dressed in black suits without guns showing flocked into the courtroom. Saltis now seemingly stone sober advanced to the judge's desk. The nine caret diamond on his huge finger caught the light of the strong September sun glaring through the unshaded window.

In a subdued manner, he explained he would like to plead not guilty to the charge and have a jury trial right away.

Moreland explained that he was only there for arraignment and he was establishing a hearing date of September 20th. He shocked Saltis when he set bail at $1500.00 and told him he would be required to post it immediately. Unable to post bail, Saltis and his men milled around while one of them went to get someone to post the bond.

While waiting, Saltis true nature showed through. Always a braggart, he continued to flash his huge ring, even though he didn't have enough money to post bond. Finally holding his hand up for all to see he said, "Just a little gift from mi boys." Finally a man arrived who owned a resort next to Saltis who by presenting the deed to his resort to cover the bond showed his admiration and trust of the gang lord.

Shortly a meeting convened at Hayward of District Attorney J.C. Davis, Mac MacKenzie and Swift. It was their consensus that it was time to take Saltis on and rid the north country of this menace. A warrant was issued charging Saltis with being a repeat violator.

A Milwaukee Journal story of the day related the state's intent. According to officials the state intends to file on information at the Sept. 20th hearing alleging previous violations by Saltis and listing them. Under Wis. law convictions in the courts of any state of the U.S. may be made on the basis for the habitual violator charge. It is for this reason that Saltis' Illinois court record is being carefully investigated.

Served Time Twice

Saltis has served time twice in Illinois - 60 days for carrying a gun and 30 days for conspiracy to violate the prohibition laws. These terms are important to the Wisconsin habitual violator case, as the law specifies that for a man to be so charged he must previously have served time.

Chief Warden H.W. MacKenzie is squarely behind the state's attempt to imprison Saltis. He revealed that the conservation commission records are replete with official reports of wardens going against the guns of visiting Chicago gangsters to arrest them for game violations. The most spectacular of these involved one of Saltis' arrests at the Winter Dam in August 1930.

"Polak Joe" has defied the Conservation Department to prevent him from fishing where he chooses. In court after a fishing law violation he had belligerently warned Warden Swift that "Next time you better come shooting."

Thus the stage was set for a hard fought court trial. Saltis hired Attorney Glen Douglas of Spooner who was born and reared in Winter and had an established reputation for defending and clearing people charged with game law violations.

While opinions of the people varied wildly, Saltis definitely held the advantage. Therefore an impartial jury was hard to pick.

Finally the 12 man jury got together and as fate would have it, chose as jury foreman Gustave Ankaberg. Ankaberg was a man who had worked for Sam Ruegger as a towerman. Several years before Sam had fired him for being unavailable at his tower when they had a large fire. He had left to attend a moonshine still he ran near the tower.

Enraged at Sam and Conservation Department employees in general he was placed in a position where he could get even, and as it was finally discovered, gain financially.

The evidence was unimpeachable so Saltis' only chance of acquital was his influence on the jury. Although the first vote was 11-1 for conviction, Ankaberg hung tough and slowly turned the jury around. Saltis and Szumoski were found not guilty.

It was later revealed that Ankaberg was contacted during the trial by the mob at the Giblin Hotel where they were sequestered for the four days of the trial. Ankaberg was paid $500.00 to sway the jury. Other jurors were threatened. Even though these facts later became widely known, no further action was taken.

Again the mobsters had triumphed but the call was close enough so that Saltis withdrew somewhat. Becoming more elusive, he continued to violate the game law. Although somewhat muted, he could not contain his belligerency. The threat to Wisconsin wardens and rangers remained.

Johnny Helsing was appointed a full -time conservation warden by Chief Warden MacKenzie in 1936. (He received the Haskel Noyes Warden of the Year award in 1948 while stationed at Winter.)

The fire season being a constant threat in late September after the

Saltis trial obligated Swift to assist Lief Stiero, the forest ranger with a fire lane bridge. Stiero and Swift began a bright September day hauling planking toward the bridge between the east and west forks of the Chippewa River.

Any auto traffic on these lanes were viewed with suspicion by wardens or rangers because they generally took you only into wilderness areas. Any autos were scrutinized closely for hunting and fishing activities and because arson was a constant threat during this era of disrespect for the fire laws. This threat existed through one of the greatest droughts in U.S. history.

Upon sighting two vehicles approaching them far in the distance in one of those rare areas where one could see over a mile ahead in the burned over forest area, Stiero brought the vehicle to a stop. The two sat silently observing as one of the vehicles pulled over and parked. The second large vehicle turned off into a logging road.

New to the area, Stiero asked, "what happened to the second car? Is there a road there?"

"Yeah, there's a tote road that ends a little ways in the woods. Let's go on up. Don't have time to spend here. Another hour and we'll have fires to respond to. They're probably hunting grouse. If they're just starting out and have no birds, we'll just send them packing."

Passing the large black sedan they saw a dark complexed man setting in it turn and stare at them. Parking they walked back to the car where a well-dressed man now stood staring quizzically at the two.

Swift asked, "what's that car doing in that tote road?"

"There's no car back there."

In the meantime Stiero had circled the car. "No guns here. Ernie."

"Ok, let's walk back to the road and see what's going on. There's a little opening a few hundred feet up that road. There's a small creek there. The bridge is out. That's probably where they parked their car."

Hiking briskly along the trail they spotted the dark two-door sedan parked in the clearing. Unaware they were being watched three men scurried hurriedly around the car grappling to remove something heavy from the rear seat.

Curiosity aroused Swift and Stiero continued toward the car undiscovered by the intent workers. Finally two men behind the car grunted and carried something into the tangled brush and new growth poplar sprouts.

The man still at the car suddenly looked, up surprise showing on his face, as he dug furiously at his waist band.

Seeing a flash of steel, Ernie thought, damn it he's trying to hide a gun. Wrong. As the blued Colt pistol swung free of the man's coat it was pointed at Ernie's belly button as he stuttered, "wha tha, wha the hell youse guys want?"

Panic running through him, Swift stumbled back stepping on Lief's feet entangling the two. So entangled were the two men they stood at the mercy of the distraught man with the gun.

Concentrating on controlling his emotions, Swift blurted, "Ah, ah, we're just out here to make sure no fires are set."

"Fires? Your lookin fer fires? Hey Jim these guys er lookin fer fires!"

Finally regaining some little composure, Swift recognized what the men were struggling with. The door of a safe remained in the car. They had disrupted some mobsters disposing of evidence.

Seeing Swift's intent stare the gunman slowly moving the gun back and forth to cover both of them suddenly lunged forward jerking the two men's hats down over their faces so hard it almost broke their noses. "None of yar damn business what's goin on here. Tray ta look and I'll drill ya. Who're ya guys anyway?"

Realizing lying would do no good, Swift replied, "We work for the conservation department. We've had a bad fire season. We're out here to fix a fire lane bridge so firefighters can get through."

Now all three of the men encircled them, guns drawn, jabbering among themselves, trying to decide what to do about the intruders.

"Ok move it," one of them shouted, pushing and guiding the beleaguered two out of the clearing into an open floored patch of mature aspen and spruce. "On your knees, get down."

Fear filling their hearts, the two complied. "Now on your faces! Get down."

Face down, leaf mold strong in their nostrils, they were searched. Stiero's truck keys were pocketed by one of them. Finding their credentials the men went over them carefully. One of them, a burly, giant went back to the car and returned with a brown paper bag and a stubby pencil. "Let's see now," he said as he copied their names. Obviously not skilled at writing they methodically worked their way through as a team, one writing the other spelling. The s, w, the i, he continued until their names and addresses were copied.

Dropping their wallets and credentials on the ground they left one man to hold them in the prone position where they listened and prayed for their lives.

A shovel could be heard digging into the rocky soil. A terrific struggle ensued back at the car. A thud was heard and felt in their breasts accompanied by a squeaking of the overloaded auto springs as the heavy door was unloaded. With grunts echoing through the woods, the safe door was rolled back into the woods.

Finally the digging and scrapping stopped.

Gathering back at the prostrate men the gangsters began arguing what to do with the interlopers.

One said he thought they saw him well enough to recognize him. "Wha are we gonna do with these son a bitches? Think we should kill em." Distraught wringing his hands, he walked around repeating "what are we gonna do with em."

One of the others joined in, "Ya think yar right. Can't just leave em. Let's kill em and bury em with the safe. No one'll ever find em. Think they can finger us?"

The third man, the youngest voiced his disagreement. It was obvious he was afraid of killing. "Does Wisconsin kill ya if they ketch ya fer killin? Hell, I don't wann die. I'm too young. Don't wanna be hounded fer murder. Don't think they got a good look at me anyway."

The Saga of Ernie Swift

Sensing their indecision, Swift bargained for their lives. Being careful to keep his eyes averted he lied. "I couldn't recognize any of you. You jerked my hat down too quick. Besides we want to live. If you let us go we'll never mention this to anyone."

A savage argument ensued, their future looking bleaker as they raged on. Both expected the slugs to begin pounding into them. With the argument finally cooling and quieting to a whisper the one arguing for their lives knelt beside them. "Keep your eyes down or I'll drill ya. Promise not ta tell anyone about what happened here?"

Relief flooded through Ernie. At least he was being given one last chance to plead for their lives. "Yeah. Ya I told you that. We'll keep quiet about this won't we Lief."

"Ya, sure will. We'll do anything we have to, to live."

"Well, geeze guys let's let em live. Don't wanna murder rap hanging over me." He turned to look at the others standing silently to one side. Finally one nodded his head toward the road. The kneeling man pushed the gun hard against Swift's temple, "Now God damn it, we mean it. We'll let ya live. Remember we got your names. Ya squeal, we'll be back and blow yar brains from here to kingdom come and back. Ya hear me?"

Fear sapping their strength, both nodded their heads and gasped, "Yeah, we'll keep quiet. Let us live."

"All right. ya lay here for five minutes till we're gone. We can still shoot ya from near the road. So damn it lay still and don't be a lookin round."

Two of them moved to the car. The motor roared, the car spun its wheels throwing leaves and rotting debris as it shot to the road, turned on the fire lane and stopped near the other car.

Laying side by side Stiero and Swift engulfed in anxiety waited what seemed like an eternity. Finally Steiro could stand it no longer. He whispered, "Let's get up and run for it."

"No you damn fool," whispered Swift, "there's a man in back of us yet. Don't move a muscle."

Several more uneasy minutes passed before the last man could be heard walking through the leaves. Ernie again whispered, "wait till you hear the cars gun out." Finally their ears told them that one of the cars had started, then the other. Among roaring motors, flying gravel and shifted gears the cars wheeled down the road and out of the region.

Swift, assured they were gone, whispered, "think they are all gone. Now get up and run like hell." Both sprang to their feet and ran haphazardly through the broken patches of popular and spruce. Finally assured the hoodlums had left they circled back to the truck. The vehicle had been searched, the contents of the glove compartment emptied and strewed about. Jackets left in the vehicle had their pockets turned inside out.

Swift grinned, "what are we going to do now, Lief."

He replied, "I don't know about you but I'm going to Hayward and mail my life insurance check. Been carrying it around in my wallet."

Stiero recovered a spare truck key he carried fastened under the hood. All thoughts of bridge repair forgotten they returned to Hayward.

While Lief mailed his insurance payment Swift stopped at the candy store and bought a St Paul Dispatch newspaper. Bold headlines proclaimed, **"$85,000 Express Robbery South St. Paul."**

Showing the newspaper to Stiero, Swift exclaimed, "There's our boys. Let's drop over to the DA's office."

District Attorney J.C. Davis was incredulous at their tale. "My God, you two are lucky to be alive. I'll call the St. Paul police."

As the sun set the following evening, Hayward was invaded by eight St. Paul detectives, who while interrogating Swift and Stiero, told them of the happenings in Minnesota. Eight heavily armed men had hijacked two railroad express safes and fled. Investigation later revealed the gang had opened one safe, looted and dumped it in St. Paul. Not able to open the other and wanting to put distance between themselves and St. Paul they split. One car heading south the other hauling the 400 pound uncracked safe to Round Lake near Hayward. At their familiar secure Round Lake haven where they had lived through the summer, they blew the door off the safe with TNT.

The next day the 400 pound safe and door were dug up and brought to Hayward.

Swift's call to Chief Warden MacKenzie so disturbed him he went directly to Acting Conservation Director Ralph Immel to obtain relief for his beleaguered wardens in the north.

Agreeing drastic action was needed Ralph called FBI Agent Purvis in Milwaukee. Purvis was an experienced law enforcement officer who had shot and killed the notorious gangster and killer Dillenger. Well versed in the history of these many gangsters in the north and the threat they presented Purvis directed Immel to get the affected Conservation Department personnel and their families out of the Hayward area.

MacKenzie's order soon followed. Against his will Swift took his family to the Mendota State Soldier's Hospital in Madison where he lived in a doctor's quarters for three months. Lief Stiero and Johnny Helsing and families spent their three months at Camp Douglas.

Luckily the threat's on Swift's life were taken seriously. Several weeks after he left, a black Packard purred to a stop in downtown Hayward. A well-dressed, well-spoken driver entered the Karibalis Pool Hall where he asked, "does anyone know where I can find Ernie Swift?"

Charlie Taylor, an elderly Indian who often hunted wolves with Swift, answered, "Sure I take you to his house. He's a friend of mine."

Politely the young man said, "That's awfully nice of you."

Nearing the car, Taylor hesitated spotting two sinister looking characters in the back seat. Looking through the window his glance took in an assortment of machine guns, sawed off shotguns, pistols, rifles and boxes of ammunition. Mouth dropping, he stopped, bolted to the ground, realization stealing into his consciousness as to why these people were looking for Swift. "Wait, I-I don't know if?"

His lament was sharply cut off as the rear door slammed open. Staring at the open door he was unaware of the young man behind him until he was unceremoniously shoved into the car. "Get in there you half breed son of a bitch." Threatened by the two armed burly men in the back seat, fear drove him to direct the way to Swift's house.

The Saga of Ernie Swift

At the house, held at gun point, he was told to knock on the door. "When Swift opens the door," the man snapped, "get the hell out of there or you'll get killed too."

After much knocking with no one appearing they forced Taylor back into their car and drove around town asking for Swift. Satisfied he was out of town they left the area. About 60 miles south they dropped Taylor off in the tiny village of Bruce with a final warning. "Tell anyone about this and well make a good Indian out of you."

The following January as a result of a bungled gem robbery, the men involved in the St. Paul robbery were apprehended in Omaha, Nebraska.

In Omaha, Ernie positively identified the four culprits who had threatened he and Steiro. They were sentenced to two years in prison. Two of them stood further trial in Wisconsin. They were convicted of the murder of John Beale, the Chief of Police at Marshfield. Earlier that year, Beale had interrupted them robbing the Marshfield Brewery. In Wisconsin, one received life in prison, the other 25 years.

Meanwhile the FBI and Attorney General's office were busy working the northern part of the state to rid Wisconsin of their unwanted guests. Some left but Joe Saltis hung tight. He liked Wisconsin. In 1933, with his finances drying up due to the end of prohibition, he sold his resort to satisfy his creditors. Drifting back to Chicago, divorced and penniless, he died on skid row.

Ernest Fremont Swift's battles did not end with the demise of the mobster rule in northern Wisconsin. In 1935 he moved to the Poynette Game Farm where he hardly started propagating foxes and raccoon when he was called to Madison. Promoted to Deputy Director of the Conservation Department, he toiled under the tutelage of hard driving Harley MacKenzie who now was the director. He remained at this position until promoted to Conservation Director in 1947.

Controversy after controversy plagued him as an administrator partly because of his uncompromising manner in protecting the resources. Far ahead of his time in conservation he fought all who stood in his way including many of his old friends, established conservationists and his past warden associates.

An effective writer, he put his talent to good use writing "Problems of Wisconsin Deer," in 1939 and "A History of Wisconsin Deer," in 1949.

Serving five years as Deputy Director and seven years as Director, he dealt with many controversial issues. When all else failed, he went to the legislature. To protect the hunting and fishing license revenues financing his department, he convinced a legislator to introduce a bill to finance state parks from real estate taxes. So startled was the legislature they hurriedly retreated and made a deal agreeing to drop the license issue in exchange for tabling the real estate tax increase.

Being popular with the legislature more than made up for his often being at odds with the Conservation Congress and other department employees. In three legislative sessions, a record 79 of 100 bills, he proposed were enacted through the able guidance of Assistant Director George Sprecher. Many of these laws still serve the cause of conservation. They also added

$5,000,000 to his budget.

He battled public opinion and steadfastly marched forward in closing inefficient fish hatcheries.

Lamprey eel had invaded the Great Lakes seriously reducing the Lake Trout population while the commercial fisherman having considerable political clout clamored and lobbied for a law allowing the use of fine mesh gill nets. They wanted to make legal anything caught in them. Raising their ire, Swift successfully battled them to a standstill.

During the long winter of 1930, Swift had observed large numbers of deer dying of starvation and exposure in the deep snow and overbrowsed northern deer yards. Solving this problem became a millstone around his neck with many former friends violently disagreeing with him. On the positive side he came to know and become friends with the famed conservationist Aldo Leopold. Agreeing that to maintain a healthy deer herd they fought the battle of killing does and fawns to reduce the herd to the winter carrying capacity of the range. Many wardens that Swift had worked with split with him on this issue. Predictably he forged ahead with no thought of backing down. Soon there were antlerless deer seasons along with antlered seasons. Though it took years with many setbacks, Swift's deer policy eventually set the stage for further management refinements that would see a tremendous increase in the Wisconsin herd.

Despite what it personally cost him, Swift proceeded with other unpopular causes such as reorganization of the conservation department.

The Conservation Commission backed him at first. Later they too became concerned and divided on many issues of the times wondering if they could contain him. One commissioner was heard to say, "perhaps we have more of a director then we need."

He joined and became a personal friend of Sigurd Olson as together they battled to protect the Boundary Waters Canoe area and other valuable wilderness areas.

Though Swift's policies were generally right and eventually prevailed, his administrative years were fraught with stress and so trying that when offered the job of assistant director to the U.S. Fish and Wildlife Service by President Eisenhower in 1957 he accepted.

His new job, created for him was to act as liaison between the federal government and the states to conserve timber and wildlife in the United States.

While this seemed an ideal position to accomplish a great deal he immediately came to odds with his organization. Not wishing to play politics but to contribute to conservation he doggedly dug, in fighting oil drilling on federal refuge lands.

Ernie's penchant for plain speaking, snipping of red tape and stepping on politicians toes brought him to odds with his boss, Director John J. Farley. Openly he criticized the duck clubs in Ohio, Maryland and California that would allow the baiting of waterfowl at a time when the duck population was so low that shooting over bait could endanger them.

Farley made a speech to a large group of conservationists assuring them the federal waterfowl baiting laws would be upheld. The next day he instructed Swift to write letter that would make enforcement impossible. Swift refused and of course the letter was written by someone else. Upon seeing it Swift retorted, "If you sign that letter John you better buy a one way ticket to China. They will come shooting." The letter was never sent.

After a year of not being able to bend to the political pressure daily faced he fairly jumped at the offer of a job as Executive Director of the National Wildlife Federation.

The Federation took advantage of Swift's dedication and never yielding fervor in protecting the resource. The largest conservation organization (3,00,000 members) in the United States and Swift flourished under his tutorship. Now he got to practice his religion. An effective writer he was now in his heyday writing articles, essays, booklets and a newsletter. He traveled extensively touting conservation and preservation of the environment in his uncompromising way.

He finally persuaded the Pentagon to rescind their policy allowing the military to indiscriminately take fish and game on their reservations much as Joe Saltis had at Hayward in the late 20s and early 30s.

After retiring and returning to Wisconsin in 1960 he continued to write from his Rice Lake home. He gave inspirational speeches, still blunt and to the point. He spared not the political system nor high business consortiums.

More impressed by progress then awards, he never the less won many; the first Haskell Noyes Warden of the Year award in 1930; a man made lake in Tracy, Minnesota (his birthplace) was dedicated as Swift Lake, he received the Nash Conservation award, The Aldo Leopold Award and Medallion, American Forest Products Award, John Muir Gavel, a citation from the Gordon MacQuarrie Foundation, a youth conservation camp was dedicated to him near Minong, he was inducted into the Wisconsin Conservation Hall of Fame in 1979, he was elected to the National Wildlife Federation Conservation Hall of Fame in Washington, D.C. joining other notable conservationists such as Theodore Roosevelt, Aldo Leopold, Ding Darling, Rachel Carson and John J. Audubon.

He published his best writing in 1967 "A Conservation Saga." The book tells of the conservation struggle, past, present and future of outdoor America. The book on a par with Aldo Leopold's "Sand County Almanac" is required reading for all trainee wardens and other people going into protection and conservation of the Natural Resources and Environment so they may know the people and problems that preceded them. It will prepare them to as Swift would say "float their own stick" in conservation. Although the challenges are great today conservation, was a rugged two-fisted battle in the past. It was men like Swift, Leopold and MacKenzie that broke the trail and left big tracks for future consevationists to follow.

Ernie Swift carried the conservation torch until his death in 1968. He was laid to rest at Hayward where this epic saga began many years earlier.

Chapter 10

Exhaust Whistle

In the early summer of 1937, as they returned from checking fishermen on some Marinette County lakes, Ernest Meress and Carl Mirsch talked about the law that allowed people using cane poles to fish without a license. Seeing many cane poles tied to cars and boats, Ernie was disturbed that most were never checked.

Wisconsin Statutes at that time proclaimed that to stop a car a law enforcement officer must sound a siren. Red lights were not required. State monies being extremely short, very little equipment was purchased for wardens. Wardens therefore became improvisors, making, borrowing or begging equipment.

Through a friend who was a Detroit, Michigan fireman, Marinette Warden Art Bye had picked up several Detroit exhaust whistles. Used for fire trucks, they were large and unwieldy devices about two and a half feet in length. The whistles, mounted alongside the car motor, were attached to the manifold and operated on exhaust from the manifold. The sound made by the whistles was awesome, comparing favorably to the locomotive steam whistles of the time. Art gave Ernie Meress one of these to use as a siren.

Making their way east along Highway 32 in Marinette County, Ernie and Carl conversed about wages and checking people using cane poles. Ernie, a short squat man with an unpredictble temper was concerned about a recent development concerning their wages. Driving the '36 Ford at a leisurely pace, he expounded on a waiver of wages signed by all wardens, who agreed not to collect $25.00 of their monthly wages.

"You know Carl, I don't think the state can legally force us to sign anything like that waiver."

"I don't know. Everybody signed of their own free will."

"Free will? You either signed or were layed off."

"Yeah, but without enough money the state really didn't have much choice. The waiver stated right on it that we were signing of our own free will."

"Yeah, I know, but you know how things like that go. Hell, Carl, no one would dare not sign. It was made pretty clear either sign or go home without a job."

"Well, for the good of the department I can see why we had to take the cut. God, I sure could use the money. But I guess what's done is done."

"Guess you're right, but $100 a month just doesn't reach."

Thinking deeply, Carl mused, "You're right. We were having trouble making it on $125 a month. Guess we'll just have to tighten our belts for a

110

year. Maybe next year, we'll get a raise."

"Well, they promised this would only go on for a year; but you know now that they've got the waivers signed we may be stuck with this for a long time."

As they approached a slow moving car towing a trailer carrying a wooden rowboat with cane poles tied to it, Ernie slowed, looking them over carefully as he slowly pulled past.

"You know Carl we should stop cars like that. They never get checked while fishing because they don't need a license."

"Sure they could have over the bag limit or undersize fish. With the size limit on panfish, I'd bet most of them are in violation. They may even have bass or muskies. I know we're missing a lot of business."

Passing another car with poles tied to it, Ernie again eyed them. "Did you see them look at us? Hell, Carl, they're loaded. Maybe we should stop them."

"Go ahead if you want to. We're in Marinette County. You know what your courts will accept here."

"I've never done it before. Would you do it in Langlade County?"

"Oh, no. I know my judge would frown on us just stopping cars. He wants us to have good reason to believe a violation exists."

"Well, I've got reason. Look how guilty they look."

"It's your county Ernie; I know we're missing a lot of illegal fish. If you want to stop some of them go ahead. You're the one that must prosecute them and explain to the court."

Thinking deeply, Ernie drove a little faster as a new thought excited him. Gaining on a large dark sedan pulling a trailer and a rowboat, he looked them over very carefully. Two young boys held four cane poles to the side of the car through the open rear window. The driver, a large, hefty middle-aged man turned to look apprehensively at the approaching car. Turning, he talked animatedly to the slim, middle-aged woman seated beside him.

Pulling closer, Ernie said. "See that. They sure look suspicious. I know they're loaded. What do your think Carl?"

"Well-l-l as I said before, it's your county; stop them if you want to."

Glancing ahead to see if the traffic was clear, Ernie pulled slowly into the passing lane. "Might as well stop them. We'll never know if they have anything illegal otherwise. Get ready Carl. When I get alongside, I'm going to give them the siren."

Finally beside the car, Ernie pushed the clutch down to disengage the motor, raced the engine to get a full head of exhaust and pulled the lever allowing the exhaust to enter the whistle. An awesome deafening roar erupted into the stillness of the wild rugged spruce swamp. The dark sedan swerved sharply to the right, and disappeared as it careened over the road shoulder, down the steep bank, and came to a sudden stop in a perilous position. Teetering on two wheels the car was about to tip over into the swamp.

Seeing the car disappear, Ernie shouted excitedly, "What-t-t happened Carl?"

"My Gaw-w-d, they went off the road. Stop 'er Ernie."

Screeching to a stop, Ernie shouted, "Get out Carl! Quick get over there!"

Throwing the car door open, Carl jumped onto the road running as fast as his legs would carry him around the trailer to the underside of the dangerously teetering car. At the side of the car, he braced himself to steady it. The frightened occupants scrambled out the upper side. Carl, a well-built young man six feet tall, had all he could do to keep the car from tipping into the swamp.

Ernie, his normally swarthy face now ashen, came running to the scene. Jabbering excitedly, "What happened? Why'd you run off the road?"

Carl interrupted, "Ernie this car is going to tip over. We need help."

Turning, Ernie luckily spotted a car coming. "Hold on Carl, I'll get help."

Wildly waving his arms, he threw himself in front of the oncoming car to make sure they would stop. Five husky young men got out of the car. Spotting the teetering car valiantly being held up by Carl, they scampered down the incline to help.

With all holding the car up, a decision was made to unhook the trailer. Ernie and Carl steadied the car as the five young men pushed the trailer back up onto the road.

Straining, sweat glistening on his forehead, Ernie braced and pushed with all his might. His mind raced for a way out of this predicament. *God, I hope it don't tip over. How will I ever explain this.* Turning he spotted the five men gathered around the trailer. "Think we can push the car out fellows?"

Gathering at the front they questioned whether the car would tip over when they began to push.

"I don't think it will tip over," offered Carl. "I held it up alone for quite a while. Go ahead and give 'er a try. Ernie and I can hold it. Take it slow at first."

With a lot of grunting and groaning by the men the car began to move. Inch by inch the car moved up the steep bank, while Ernie and Carl pushed until weak, covered with perspiration the exertion causing spots before their eyes as they grew weak.Finally, with the car firmly on the roadbed all stood gasping for breath.

Relieved, they gathered around the car. The young men left with many thanks still ringing in their ears.

Suddenly the tall woman came charging toward the backpedaling Ernie. Towering over his five foot 10 inch frame, she bore down on him. "What were you trying to do, kill us?"

"W - Well, I didn't think anything like this would happen. Glad to see everyone is okay."

"We're okay, no thanks to you. I think you should be arrested. What kind of thing made that God awful sound. Almost deafened me. You could have killed or injured the children." Turning, she glanced at the two boys who turned away attempting to hide their broad grins.

"Aw, Ma, we're okay. It was kind of fun."

"Fun, I'll give you fun. It scared the daylights out of me." She turned

Exhaust Whistle

to her husband for support. The beefy man screwed his face up not quite able to stifle the half smile, "Now Mama, no harm has been done to us. The car is not damaged. Everything is back on the road; we're okay."

Taking advantage of the unexpected turn of events, Ernie held out his hand to the man. "My name is Ernie Meress. I'm the warden from Marinette County. Sorry this happened, but we were stopping you to check your fish. This is Carl Miersch, the warden from Antigo." Relieved to see the man offer his hand in return, Ernie shook it vigorously holding on so long, Carl felt his face flame in embarassment for his friend.

Finally looking down, Ernie realizing he still had the man's hand, dropped it like a hot coal. Recovering fast, he asked, "Where are you from?"

"Suring. My name is Mick Perterson. I own a bar there, ""The Frontier."

"Oh, I know where that is. We'll stop over some time, hey Carl?"

"Sure. We'll give you a little business."

The hefty man's easy going personality was made to order for Ernie who not so subtly capitalized on it.

The woman, pacing back and forth, finally realizing she had been out manuevered, retreated to the rear and stood glowering at the wardens.

Ernie continued to butter the man up to lessen the impact of the incident. "We normally don't stop cars like this but we know many people using only cane poles take a lot of illegal fish."

"I have to tell you I'm 100% for you wardens. I have always supported your work. I know you have a difficult job."

Color slowly beginning to return to his face, the fear slowly ebbing, Ernie continued, "We work around Suring all the time. Now that we know where your place is we'll stop in. Sure appreciate your feelings after what happened."

The conversation became almost jovial because of the good natured way the man had accepted the incident.

Apprehension completely gone, Ernie inquired, "What made you run off the road like that anyway?"

Laughing the man replied, "You know I've been around a little. Spent some time in Chicago and some other large cities. I've traveled extensively around the United States, even sailed across the pond during the big war. I've heard all kinds of sirens, steamships whistles, whistles on factories and fire whistles, but when I hear a train coming down the road, I'm getting off."

Later in the retelling around the state, Ernie always related how scared Carl had been.

Chapter 11

Hyper Hypodermics

Summoned from his supper table by the incessant ringing of the telephone, Jim Chizek impatiently lifted the receiver.

The mellow voice of John Kasner of the Portage Police Department greeted him. "Jim we've got a complaint that a fellow is hitting cars with a coon. He's standing alongside Highway 51, swinging away. He's knocked the windshield wipers off several cars. Can you come down?"

Knowing John's sneaky sense of humor, Jim questioned, "Should I bring the raccoon strait jacket?"

"No kidding. This guy is actually hitting cars with a coon."

The sincerity in John's voice further increased Jim's suspicions. Sincerity usually immediately proceeded the falling of the hammer. "All right John, I'll bite. Go ahead what's the punch line."

"This is no joke this time. This guy is really doing it. Can you come down?"

Realizing the hook should have been buried deep by now, Jim asked, "Can you grab the guy?"

"Sure, will do."

"Bring him to the station. I'll be right down."

Arriving at the police station, Jim spotted the old rusty beat up Plymouth of Gene Robins parked in the dimly lit parking lot. Gene was known as a habitual fish and game poacher. Jim had arrested him a number of times for such things as shining deer, shooting deer and blasting fish. Usually belligerent when contacted by law enforcement officers, he was doubly so when drinking. Previous encounters gave Jim an advantage. Thus prepared, he entered the station.

Approaching the dispatch desk he said, "Hi John." Glancing at the holding area, he observed Robins sitting in a forward bent position. Robins, a moderately tall well-muscled man in his mid-twenties, wore slightly soiled overall jeans. Dark matted hair dangled like ropes before his eyes. "Don't tell me Gene is the coon man?"

"Yeah. His car is outside. You want to talk to him?"

"Sure do." Approaching Gene, Jim asked the incredulous question, "Were you hitting cars with a coon?"

Glancing up, Gene's breath struck Jim directly in the face. The yeasty stench of booze was overpowering. "Yeaah, scho what? Didn't do anythinnn wrong."

"Where did you get the coon?"

"Drivin dawn to Portache on 51. Thiss dumb coon crashed the road. Sctopped on the schide. Goot out and piccked 'em up."

"You just walked up to him and picked him up without getting bit?"

"Yeaah. Put 'em in the trunk."

"I don't believe you could catch a wild coon. Furthermore, if you could, he'd chew you up good. Unless the coon is sick or hurt, he'd chew your arm right off. Pound for pound they're one of the meanest animals going." Shaking his head in disbelief, he continued, "Where's the coon now?"

"In my car trunk outschide."

"Were you hitting cars with him?"

"Yeah. Guess scho. Didn't do any damage thouggh – well, guessh the windshielld wiper flew off one car."

"What about the coon? Don't you think you hurt him?"

"Hah! Can't hurt a dumhb coon. I huant them all the time. Tough as leather."

"Well, come on, let's get the coon, and Gene, I'm charging you with taking a raccoon during the closed season. That's the charge until I discuss this with David Bennett."

"Whoosh's Bennett?"

"You should know who he is. You've been in enough trouble. He's the district attorney and I don't think he'll think much of your behavior."

Entering the partially lighted parking lot, the two hesitated. Glancing momentarily at the car trunk, Jim thoughtfully said, "You open the trunk and I'll get a blanket from my car to wrap the coon in. Don't want to get bit."

Standing tall on the balls of his feet, swaying forward and back, Gene confidently spat. "A'll get the mangggy critter for ya."

With a quick step toward his car about 30 feet away, Jim commanded, "No leave him alone, I'll get the blanket."

The loud squeak of the old rusty trunk stopped Jim in midstride. Quickly hustling back to the open trunk, scanning the dark interior he saw a very large adult raccoon hudding defensively in the darkest corner. "My God, you were handling that animal with bare hands. It's funny you have any arms left. Don't touch him, I'll get the blanket."

Hurrying toward the car, Jim was suddenly anchored by a fierce deep ripping growl. Turning, he saw Gene had the raccoon by the neck holding him at arms length in front of him. Defensively, the raccoon growled a deep thundering growl so savage it made Jim's skin quiver. Biting and scratching fiercely, the raccoon worked up and down Gene's arms embeding deep bites. Each bite was followed by savage jerks, his rapier sharp teeth sinking to the gums. Temporarily frozen by the unexpected sight, Jim was undecided, should he return to Gene or get the blanket. "Let him go. Let him go."

Gene's face, distorted in a grimace of pain and disbelief, tightened his stranglehold. "No damn coon is going to get the bescht of me. I'll choke the blashed critter to death." Cursing loudly, he applied more pressure which resulted in a more furious response from the beleagured animal. Struggling to escape, the enraged raccoon attacked more furiously. Spurting blood soaked Gene's chambray shirtsleeves and splattered darkly on the parking lot.

Jim yelled at the top of his voice, "Let him go for God's sake." Making his decision toward the safe side he jerked the car door open and grabbed the army blanket. Turning, he repeated, "Turn him loose." He sprinted back to the bloody apparition struggling with the raccoon in the pale light. At close quarters the raging battle was even more gruesome as Gene desperately attempted to choke the animal. The raccoon snarled terrifyingly, ripping and tearing Gene's arms even as he held the raccoon further out to keep the struggling animal from reaching his face.

Hurriedly Jim whipped the blanket around the raccoon, quickly wrapping the animal and jerking it from Gene's grasp. "My God man, don't you know better than that?"

Holding the struggling raccoon, he briefly looked over Gene's injuries. Arms deeply bitten and scratched from the wrists to the shoulder, shirt sleeves tattered and blood soaked, Gene stood in a trance examining himself. Lowering his arms brought forth a steady dripping of blood onto the parking lot.

Turning his head, he gazed stupidly at the carnage, "Aw. It's not so baad."

Shaking his head, Jim snapped, "Not so bad? That's booze talk. You're chewed up good and you're going to the hospital." Quickly depositing the raccoon in his car, Jim proceeded to herd a protesting Gene into the station.

"Not going to any doctoor, don't believe in theeem, don't like 'em."

John came hurriedly around the counter, "God, Jim, what happened."

"Oh. Gene wouldn't listen and grabbed the coon. He got chewed good." Turning to Gene, he began to patiently explain to him what the result of such animal bites could be. "Gene you've got to go to the doctor." Voice more comforting now, he continued, "That coon is not normal. He must be sick or you couldn't handle him the way you did to say nothing of catching him in the first place."

"To hell with you. I'm not going."

John joined in. "That coon could be rabid."

Gazing belligerently at the two, Gene snorted, "Sho what is rabid?"

Jim replied, "Rabies is a fatal disease. Unless treated, people with it die. We've had a lot of rabid animals recently."

The circumstances began to sober Gene up — his slurred speech clearing. "Don't give a damn. That coon ain't got it. I'm not going to no doctor."

Jim's voice raising slightly in anger commanded, "You're going Gene. You're under arrest and my responsibility. You're going to the doctor. John call Chief Riley. He should know what's going on here."

As John dispatched the message to Francis Riley, Jim attempted to wrap some of the worst bleeders on Gene's arms with bandages from the station's first aid kit.

Jerking viciously away, Gene spouted, "Get away from me. Don't want any help." As if a sudden thought had crossed his mind, his face reflected concern, "What do they do for rabies anyway?"

Replacing the first aid kit in the cupboard, Jim answered, "They give the person a series of shots through the stomach wall."

A loud thump startled him. Jim turned to see Gene sprawled prostrate on the floor.

"My God! John, he's passed out. Come help me." Struggling the two men half carried half dragged the limp man outside. The fresh cold night air immediately brought consciousness back as Chief Francis Riley arrived.

"What's going on fellows? What's wrong with this guy? John, you better not leave the dispatch unattended. Better get back."

"Okay."

Quickly, Jim briefed Riley on the unusual happenings. "I think we should get Gene to the hospital right away."

Nodding agreement,he replied, "You're right. Let's get him into my squad."

Still hazy, Gene was assisted into the squad. With red lights flashing and siren wailing, he was whisked the nine blocks to the hospital.

Gene had become sullenly quiet as he allowed himself to be assisted into the building and elevator. Finally able to stand unassisted, he went into a dead faint and collapsed at the first movement of the elevator. The two were still struggling to get him on his feet when they reached the emergency room floor. Swiftly, one on each side, they assisted him into the emergency room, where Dr. J.J. Saxe (called Bluie by his friends) waited as a result of John's call.

Inspecting the severely mutilated arms, Bluie commented in his down to earth, sometimes sarcastic way, "I can't believe you'd be this damned stupid. Anyone who'd tangle with a coon should have his head examined. However, we won't do that today. We'll concentrate on your arms. You know coons are one of the dirtiest animals around. We'll have to watch for infection. That coon could be rabid too. Jim, you better pen him up and watch him for at least ten days. If he shows any sign of sickness, contact Doctor Corsco. That's your doctor, isn't it Gene?"

Completely subdued, Gene's answer was muted. "Yeah. Do you think the coon could be rabid Doc?"

Hustling around inspecting, cleaning, bandaging and ministering to the unfortunate man, Saxe replied, "Could very well be. We've had a lot of rabies in animals this year." Nodding to the nurse, he continued, "Some of these bites are very deep, we'll need sutures." Turning back, he saw Gene collapse in the chair. The three rushed to hold him in the chair.

Bluie scoffed, "What's wrong with you? Come let's get him on the cot. Do you have some aversion to needles?"

"Yeah, sure do. Can't stand em. Even the thought of them bothers me. I've always been that way. Please no needles."

Nevertheless the patching continued and the many stitches required kept Gene in a semi-concious state.

Bluie, exhibiting no compassion, commented, "You've brought this on yourself by what you did to that poor coon. Now, you're suffering the consequences. Now hold still."

Treatment finally complete with bandages extending from wrists to shoulders, Gene, sighing a sigh of relief, sat up. At the approach of the nurse, he turned and spotted the gleaming hyperdermic on the tray.

Conditioned, all turned to look as Gene experienced the inevitable, collapsing limply on the mattress.

"Lockjaw shot," Bluie winked.

Gene did not feel the prick that delivered the medication.

Describing the circumstances of the incident to District Attorney David Bennett, Jim explained Gene's fear of needles and what he had already experienced. "What do you think Dave? Should we charge him with cruelty to animals?"

Dave chuckled, "Cruelty to animals? Seems the animal was more cruel to him. That Bluie, I can just imagine him treating the poor guy. Why don't we just charge him with possessing the raccoon during the closed season? Jim, I'm concerned about you in this case. Be sure and watch that raccoon close. He was under arrest when this happened. Make sure you touch all bases on this one."

Appearing in court the following day, Gene charged with the illegal possession of a Raccoon and as a repeat violator was fined $200 or 30 days in jail, plus revocation of all licenses for one year. Having no money, Jim delivered him to the Columbia County jail.

After delivering the raccoon to the Poynette Game farm with instructions to Manager Bill Ozburn to watch the animal closely, Jim began worrying about Gene. On impulse he called Doctor Corsco to tell him of the incident. Doctor Corsco, being on the conservative side, decided not to wait. He would commence the series of rabies shots immediately. Jim told him of Gene's fear of needles.

Corsco replied, "I don't care. I'm not taking a chance with rabies. I'll administer the shots at the jail. Please keep me advised of the raccoon's health."

Several days later, Jim received a call from Bill Ozburn who said the raccoon was definitely sick. Thinking of his own protection and assuring all his steps were documented, he called Sheriff Peter Boylan. The two drove to Poynette, shot the raccoon in the back to perserve the head and rushed it to the State Hygiene Laboratory in Madison. They left instructions to quickly test the animal for rabies and any other disease that could be carried by a raccoon.

Doctor Corsco, now informed the raccoon was being tested, continued to administer the daily shots. The inevitable fainting episodes continued. The day before Gene was to complete the series of shots Jim received the lab report. "Rabies negative. Hepatitis positive."

Chapter 12

The Thirties in Northern Wisconsin

They gathered at eight o'clock that cold October day in 1930. All stopped at Jim's house on State Highway 70. The deer hunt would be planned and started here. The Tiller brothers, Curt and Lester, arrived walking the several miles up the highway, hiding their guns when encountering cars. Riding the old work mule was Lad Check, Jim's brother. Finally, Gordon Darling, Jim and Lad's brother-in-law, rattled in with his old Model T Ford truck. They laughed and joked as Anna, Jim's wife of a year, banged the pots and pans, making a lunch for them.

"You'll have to settle for canned venison. We're out of fresh meat. It's about time you guys got some."

Pacing nervously, Lad guffawed, "Guess I could have brought some along. Got some left from last month. Paid dearly for it too."

Laughing, Jim chidded him, "You could call it that - thirty days in the county jail. They ever get the bars back in the cell?"

"Ha! Ha! They gave up after I jerked them out the third time.

Bet the sheriff's wondering what happened to the distributor off his car." Gordon chuckled. "He should have known better than let me out early that last day. Gave me time to take it off."

Jim turned, astonishment showing on his face, "You stole the distributor off the sheriff's car?"

"Sure - How else did you think I could get that old junk to run? Hasn't run in a couple years."

Lester's hearty laugh burst forth. "Last time I saw you run it you ran out of gas - remember? You dropped pebbles down the gas filler to raise the level enough to get home." All whooped at this.

"Just the same," Jim said, "Be awfully tough if we couldn't get a little piece of jump meat now and then."

Curt, his boyish face showing admiration for the older men, chimed in, "Yeah. Government sheep."

The Depression had hit them hard. None had worked for the last year or more. Some food was raised in their gardens and on their small rocky pine stump studded farms. All were young without any finances. Money was desperately needed to get started on the poor farms that they dared hope would eventually support their young families.

Anna's cheery voice announced, "Come on you guys – time to eat." She scurried around placing the food and plates on the old table, the rickety chairs creaking barely holding the weight of the men.

"Don't have much to offer. Guess it will tide you over till lunch though. Can't hunt on an empty stomach."

She was always amazed at how much meat and coffee the young men could consume. She was not to be disappointed this day. Three quarts of venison and a mountainous pile of potatoes covered generously with milk gravy literally disappeared before her eyes. The two quart pot of boiled coffee was also consumed.

"My God! You guys sure eat. We never ate that much meat in a month at my home."

As they lingered over the last of the strong coffee, she made sandwiches. Home made bread and the fourth jar of venison were quickily slapped together. She smiled at the way they had buried and hid the glass jars in the moss of the nearby swamp.

The fast moving conversation changed from hunting to the national scene. "Heard on the radio last night Lucky Luciano and another guy shot each other up. Down in Indiana. Guess Lucky was bringing in a load of bootleg Scotch from Canada. Hear he's trying to join Capone in Chicago. Boy, they play for keeps! Honor among thieves-Ha-shoot the hell out of each other. Lad and Gordie served more time for shooting a couple of deer than any those guys ever will."

Gordon retorted, "Could have got more too – if Lad had swung at that game warden. That dang hogs leg, he poked at us looked like a cannon!"

Grinning widely, Lad mused, "Guess you're right. I didn't know we had backed over his foot. He was really mad. Should have known better than to stand behind us. Especially when that other guy jumped out in front of us. Doggone gun might have gone off. Scared me!"

Jim joined in, "Too bad about Hougan's foot though or was it Boomer's? Not anxious to see game wardens. But without them we wouldn't have any deer."

"Wouldn't have backed up if I'd a known he had his damm fool foot stuck in that frozen rut. Didn't want to break his foot. Guess he got over it all right. It was nice of them though to let each of us have a quarter of venison. At least we had a little meat. Let's get going. Where we gonna hunt?"

Putting the cup down sharply, Jim, the natural leader, laid out the plan. "Davis Lake - Don't want any shooting till we get back there. They may be watching us after the show you guys gave them. It's about four miles back in the woods. Not much chance of anyone hearing shots back there. Don't want anyone else to get pinched. Let's have a home brew before we leave. I've got just a few bottles left. Enough for each to have one." Striding swiftly outside he soon reappeared, arms loaded with bottles, a milk bucket swinging widely on his arm. "Had em cooling in the snow." Setting them on the table, he inserted one into the bucket. A pop and fizzle followed.

"This stuff is a little wild." He chuckled. Draining the foamy liquid into a glass he unceremoniously passed the bucket. "Had a few blow up in the basement last summer. Almost gave Anna a heart attack! Ahh! Good though."

Hesitantly Curt asked, "Can I have one too?"

"How old are you now?"

"Fifteen."

Looking over his glasses and smiling, Gordon drawled, "Aw. Give the kid one. If he's old enough to hunt, he's old enough for a beer." Lad passed the bucket to Curt. "Okay kid - have a beer."

After the beer was drained from the bottles, Jim moved the men with a wide wave of his arm. "Let's get going. It's getting late. We'll walk straight south to the lake. Then start hunting."

Picking up their rifles leaning against the house, they left the yard, the clickety clack of shells being pushed into the guns and levers working seemed unusually loud. Jim led them south at a brisk pace through the open field of whiteness into the deep wilderness, sunshine reflecting brightly from the new powder snow. "Little early for snow. Usually don't stay on the ground like this till the middle of November—about the start of the deer season."

"Two weeks early," mused Lad. "Makes good hunting. At least we can see tracks."

They fell silent, intent on their thoughts in the enormous subduing silence of the deep woods. After about an hour and a half of hard walking, Jim motioned them to a stop. "Okay. This is where we hunt."

Catching up with the group, breathing hard, Lester panted, "Let's make that meat drive right off the bat. Put Jim on the good stand. He's a good shot."

Agreeing, they immediately started off as though in their own backyard. The wilderness was not unfamiliar to them. They had hunted here often. Reaching the stand, Jim fell silent and still, listening to the small sounds of the forest. A red squirrel cried out in anger at the intrusions of his hemlock timber home. The challenge continued and grew in intensity as he came closer and closer. His back to the wind, Jim silently cursed at the din. He wished the squirrel would stop so he could better concentrate on the small revealing sounds of the forest. The shout that started the drive quieted the squirrel. Immediately, the brush in front of Jim began to crack as something passed through breaking twigs. *Coming*, he thought snapping to attention, raising the rifle, to the ready. Staring intently in the direction of the sound, there was movement and a fleeting glimpse of a huge whitetail with antlers of a tremendous size. Thoughts flashed through his mind, *My God, he's a big one; can't get a shot. He's not taking the usual runway. Whoops. There he goes. Almost too late — Now!*

In desperation, he threw the rifle to his shoulder and fired at the glimpse of the deer swiftly disappearing over a small rise. The deer was instantly swallowed up by the jungle of balsam and cedar. *Hang it — Missed him— Not much of a chance.*

The drivers shortly gathered excitedly around him.

"Get one?"

"What did you shoot at?"

"No doggone it. I missed —biggest buck I've ever seen too."

"You sure you missed?" asked Lad.

"Yeah - Never touched a hair. We'll take a look though. Wait - I think I see him"

"Come on - He's gone - He wouldn't be standing around here. Probably in the next county by now."

Staring intently at the deep swamp. Jim threw his right mitten into the snow. "No. There's something out there - See." He pointed out the spot. Everyone looked, breathes bated.

"Right there."

"Aww - that's an old rampike - that's all."

Jim kept his eyes riveted to the spot. "Damn it. That's a deer. He's standing there looking at us. I'm going to take a shot at it." Raising the old 44-40 rifle brought everyone to silent, rapt attention. The dull boom was still reverberating through the silent wilderness when a violent thrashing sound emittted from the swamp.

Lester ran toward the downed buck. The others followed helter skelter. "Be damned he was there all the time." Stumbling through the last of the rotting logs, he came upon the huge white tail. "You got a beauty."

"My God," exclaimed Jim. "I knew he was big but not this big." Jerking his antlers from under an uprooted stump, he counted. "Eighteen points - what a buck! We'll never drag this devil out of here."

Bewildered at what had transpired, Curt blurted, "What are we going to do with him?"

Lad, unperturbed, replied, "We'll hang him. Don't want to waste time dragging anyway. Looks like a good day to hunt."

Shaking his head in agreement, Jim knelt and opened his jackknife to begin gutting. "Hold his leg up. Roll him on his back. That's good. " The knife made long sure strokes as he opened the belly allowing the guts and blood to spill forth and stain the whiteness of the snow. Gasping, he complained, "Jackknife is usually all I need. Could use a bigger knife on this beast." Washing his hands in the snow and standing up, he motioned, "Help me drag him to that cradle knoll. We'll drain him. "

Meanwhile Curt was making his second rope throw at a high limb in a thick cedar. "No need to. He'll drain when we hang him. Ah, got it. Drag him over here." Two of them grasped the antlers and yanked the buck the short distance to the tree. Curt tied the rope securely to his antlers.

"Okay. Come help me. Up - harder, he's heavy - ugh. That's right, get him up high. Don't want the coyotes or wolves to get at him. No one will see him in this thick tree. Heck, no one gets back here anyway." Silent now, he was engrossed in making the rope fast.

"I'm hungry. Let's make a fire and eat."

"Just like my kid brother," retorted Lester. "Always hungry and wants to camp. Oh well, I'm hungry too."

Turning he kicked the nearby hollow tamarack rampike. Large pieces flew through the air landing in the snow. They quickly gathered them together and kindled some of the small slivers at the base of the tree. The dry wood sprang swiftly into a roaring sucking chimney fire.

Curt stared dreamily into the colorful flames. "Always like a tamarack fire. Prettiest thing agoing. Look at the tiny colored torches flying out all over."

Lad, pacing restlessly, spoke, "You go ahead and eat. I'm gonna take a walk up to that next little swamp. Check for sign." Shouldering his old octagon barreled 30-30, he strode swiftly off.

The hunters sat around the beautiful warming fire toasting frozen sandwiches on sticks, a rite as important to these men as the hunt itself.

Suddenly Lad burst gaspingly out of the thick brush. "Game wardens!"

The camp came to life as though a hand grenade had been dropped. "Did you see them?"

"Sure they're wardens?"

"Yeah! - Close enough - Even saw the badge! Yelled at me to stop. I ran like the devil! Chased me over a mile. They're on my trail right now."

"Where's your rifle?"

"Threw it soon as I could." Calming down somewhat, he continued, "Listen - you've got to get out of here. I'm the best runner. The rest of you skedaddle. Head for home. I'll go back. Lead them off. Get going - now!" Leaving that thought, he bolted back into the brush he had just exited.

Galvanized into action, the scared hunters hustled into a single line and trailed briskly north. They took time to lay a track northwestward. The track bypassed Jim's house to intersect Highway 70 a half mile from the house, to throw off any pursuit. Not a single car was encountered while following the highway home.

Sitting around anxiously wondering and worrying about Lad was nerve wracking. Had they caught him? Was he okay? Was he on his way to jail? Quickly they checked to see if any venison remained in the house. Anna washed the jars emptied just that morning. ""They may search us.''

After the meeting at the camp, Lad hurried down his back trail knowing he would meet the wardens soon. Tall and slim with long legs he was confident of his running prowess. Rounding a spruce thicket, he stopped staringly dead in his tracks. About 20 yards away intently trotting on his trail was the tall, thin warden. He also stopped. Momentarily the two faced each other — reading the challenge in each others eyes. Lad dove for the thickest part of a nearby spruce and cedar thicket. Falling he scrambled wildly on all fours under the low hanging branches clearing the thicket at full tilt. The maneuver saved him. The warden tried to follow bouncing off the thicket, falling twice in an attempt to get through.

A shout echoed through the still forest. "Stop or I'll shoot."

The hair prickled on the back of Lad's neck. Fear temporarily clouding his mind, *got to get out of here! He might do it!* this thought implanted in his mind, he ran as though Satan was breathing down his collar. Slowly, he put more distance between them. He began to think again. *Got to lead them south or east. Away from the rest of the fellows. Head for the river.* In another ten minutes, the Flambeau River was in sight. Momentarily stopping, he listened intently. He was relieved. No pursuit. *Wait! There he is again.*

About 200 yards behind came the determined warden doggedly trotting on his trail. Glancing up, spotting his quarry he, sensed victory and sprinted. Lad sucked in his breath, thinking *boy that guy can sure run.* Wheeling, he lunged for the river. Shell ice rattled and sent a shower of crystals cascading around him. *Whoops— can't cross. Not completely frozen over. Got to get out of here.* Retreating from the river brought Lad dangerously close to the warden who made a grab missing by inches. Ducking instinctively to the side, Lad again crashed into the heavy brush where he seemed to have the advantage. Fear fogged his mind again, *Doggone near got me.* Heading south, he picked up the pace. There were open hardwoods now. The warden was always in sight. The fast pace carried them several miles further to the edge of Priest Lake.

He thought clearer now. *Get to into the thick stuff again. I do better there. Besides he may take a shot at me out in the open.* Picking the nearest thickest cover, he drove forward. *Will that guy never give up? Must have run three or four miles already.* Swinging west, he thought, *Head for Perch Lake. I can make it. Surely he can't go that far.* The race continued through swamps, open hardwoods and popple. Whenever Lad broke into the sparse stands of timber the determined warden appeared in pursuit. Cutting east of Perch Lake Lad thought, *My last chance. The guy may catch me yet. Head north. Surely he can't go another four miles to Highway 70.*

Digging in hard, his stag boots slipping often in the new snow, his mind lamented, *damn boots wore so thin — don't have any grip. Good thing I made some bars on them with Solo the other day. Gives me a little traction anyway.*

The dogged race continued north. Lad was not now trying to lead the warden anyplace in particular. Slowly gaining, he ran the last four miles to the highway. *Think I've lost him.* He reached the highway about a mile west of Jim's home. *Don't want to leave a track to the house.* Stopping he listened intently. *No noise. Home free.* Bursting enthusiastically into the house, Lad cried out, ""I did it. Got away from them." They thumped him on the back to show their happiness. A happy clamour arose. "Was it close? Was it Chuck?"

Chuck Lawrence was stationed at Park Falls. Chuck later was to head up the Federal Fish and Wildlife Service.

"Don't think so. Don't think Chuck could run like that. Almost had me a couple times! Haven't got time to talk now. Gonna go back and get my rifle."

"What? Don't do it. They'll still be back there."

"Yeah — could be. Only one chased me. Don't care. I'm not leaving my old 30 - 30 back there. Just hope they haven't found it." a proud possession, the long barreled octagon 30-30 was one of his few possessions allowing him to feed his family. Without another word he banged determinedly out of the house. His face as cut from marble, he cut across the field for the second time that day thinking, *got to hurry — Getting late — Need light to find the rifle.* Holding a steadfast pace, he arrived breathlessly where he had thrown the rifle. Darkness was settling in the deep silent wilderness as he began his search. Luckily his memory was good. Frantic scurrying around in the gathering darkness brought success. The rifle lay snug under a tight thicket of cedar where the snow had not penetrated. Hurriedly shouldering the faithful old friend he struck briskly north. He had gone less than 100 yards when breaking out of a strip of hemlock a sixth sense stopped him. Cocking his head, he listened breathlessly, *Something wrong! Heard something! Someone is around.* Staring intently to his right where his ear directed, he saw the movement. *Close!* In the twilight the warden was barely visible. With bated breath, they faced each across barely 30 yards of sparse spruce and balsam.

"Stop! — I'm a game warden — you're under arrest!"

For the second time that day Lad spun in his tracks and lunged for the underbrush his mind not as cluttered this time. *Different guy. He couldn't keep up the first time. Not so long legged. I'm not throwing the rifle this time.* Heart hammering he dug in and ran as if a pack of wolves was hounding him. *No circling this time. Getting dark. Head straight north.* After about two miles of steady pounding he stopped. Catching his breath and gathering his thoughts, he listened as best he could, his breath coming hard, his heart hammering in his ears, somehow he had complete control of his emotions. *No sound. Must have outdistanced him.* Waiting, waiting with bated breath, he let fifteen minutes slide by. *No noise. No pursuit. Be hard for him to trail me in the dark. I'm okay now.*

It was pitch dark when Lad tiredly pushed the door open the second time. All were jubilant.

"Get away okay?"

"Get the rifle?"

"See anything of the wardens?"

"Got the rifle okay. Damn it that other warden chased me. Sure glad this day is over." Sighing, he sank into the old car seats improvised as a davenport. "Got anything to drink?"

Smiling broadly, Jim replied, "Sure have. Paw walked across country with a bottle of moonshine this morning. Not aged yet. It'll be okay though."

With that Anna began to pass out glasses.

"Don't need glasses - Just pass the bottle. Say how do you suppose they knew we were hunting back there?"

Anna slammed a glass down sharply. "Only one way - Jonathan must of seen you cross the field from home. Saw him go to town with his new Model A Ford. Probably went to a phone to call the warden. Only one in the neighborhood who would squeal! Only one who has a car around her to get to a phone."

"Damn him," retorted Gordon. "He'll never get my vote for town chairman again. Bet he's still mad at me."

A flash of annoyance crossed Jim's face. "He should be! You had no right to shoot his turkeys."

Lad turned, a look of exasperation on his face. "What! He shot Jonathan's turkeys?"

"Sure, right off the barn roof, where they were roosting."

"Took them home too." Gordon chortled, lifting the bottle in salute. "Still think he's awfully touchy. We were hungry!"

Lester broke in. "Sure thought we were going to jail. Pass the bottle." The lamplight danced and cast eerie shadows on the wall as the bottle passed, hand to hand until empty.

Not drinking, Curt remained serious and subdued. " Are we going to get that big deer?"

Jim dropped the bottle unceremoniously into the empty oil drum near the wood cook stove. "Don't worry - I'll get him. Too big to drag by hand. I'll take the old mare back and drag it out. Wait till it cools off around here. Think the wardens found the deer?"

All agreed it was possible. If they followed out the track it would be no trick.

Anna opened the door slightly and peaked out. "The wind's picking up. Thought I noticed the window shades blowing. Getting cold in here. Better get some wood in Jim. That old stove barely keeps up anyway."

"Yeah. I'll do it now. Time for everyone to go home anyway."

Three weeks later, one week after of the close the deer season, Jim drove and lead the old mare north into the woods. The old horse easily walked through the eight inches of soft new snow. Watching closely all the way for man tracks, he painstakingly worked his way toward the deer. When near, he carefully tied the horse. Slowly and deliberately, he circled the half mile of heavy swamp around the deer, his mind working on an alabi. *If they catch me back here I'm just out for a walk. Got to be sure there's no one around before I touch the deer.* Reaching the trail coming in from White Rock to the east, he stopped. The search became minute here. *I think this is where the wardens came in — no sign.* Relieved he moved on completing the circle. Untying the horse he led it forward. His arm was suddenly jerked upward as the horse lunged, her legs flailing the air. Hanging on desperately, he jerked the rearing animal down. "Whoa — whoa. Okay girl. Know you don't like what you smell." Calming her down he tied her for the second time. Consoling her with his quiet voice, "Wait right here girl. - It'll be all right." Proceeding to the deer, he made a cursory inspection. It was in good condition. *Well now. What a beauty! Frozen stiff as a poker."*

Working swiftly now, he untied the rope. Using a nearby tree as a snubbing post he lowered it gently to the ground.

Jerking on the antlers, he puffed and gasped as he backed the short distance dragging the deer to the horse. The balky horse backed up nervously against the tied lines. Determinedly, Jim brought the deer around and finally tied the rope to the evener. Carefully untieing the reins he slowly worked his way along the horse, petting and quieting her with his firm voice. "It'll be okay old girl. Just stick with me and you'll be in clover." Once behind her in muted voice he commanded, "get yup," Letting her have her head trotting behind he continued to calm her. "Easy old lady. You're getting a little old to act like this." His deep chuckle was swallowed by the awsome silence of the forest. Calming down, the old horse finally came to a walk. The deer behind her became second place.

A broad smile on his face, Jim swung the horse into the yard. An excited Anna met him exclaiming, "My God! I've never seen such a deer. He's huge - what a rack of horns." Chuckling Jim brought the horse to a halt beside the scale. Unhooking it he rolled it on. He slapped the sliding weights back and forth with a clikety-clack. "238 pounds - after hanging three weeks - a prize if I've ever seen one. Should keep us in meat all winter." Later that year the antlers were sold to a sport (a city slicker with enough money to mount them) at the unheard of price of $5.00.

Chapter 13

Sturgeon Bonanza

Conservation Warden Jim Chizek was working on some drains he was constructing on his Lake George home near Portage, Wisconsin. He was planning on finishing that evening of September 13, 1964 when his gracious wife Shirley called from the house. "Telephone Jim."

Brushing the cement dust from his trousers, Jim sighed, "I'm just about finished here. Take their number and I'll call back."

"This guy says it's real important and won't give his name. You better answer it. He says he has some important information for you."

"I'll be right in." Dropping his shoes outside, Jim walked in stocking feet to the phone. "This is Jim. What can I do for you?"

"I would like to report some violations on Lake Wisconsin."

"Who am I speaking to?"

"That's not important - I -ah would just as soon not tell you. I don't want my name divulged. I'm afraid these people may get even with me somehow. I just don't believe in what they're doing."

"Okay. I'll take the information from you. Go ahead."

"Got a pencil? Write their names down so you're sure you get it right. They have a bunch of illegal lake sturgeon at the Bait Shack on Lake Wisconsin. They have seven of them hid in their ice house. Listen close now. As you walk in, go clear to the end of the ice stacks. Near the wall, close to the ceiling, there are three fish. They are shoved between the ice blocks. Take a flashlight with you. You'll see where the sawdust has been disturbed. Got that?"

"Yeah. Go ahead."

"Okay. At the end of the ice blocks, turn right and go three tiers down the opening and turn right. Stop right there and look between the blocks on your left, up high. You'll be able to spot where the rest of the fish have been shoved between the blocks. I don't really know who the fish belong too. I think the owner of the resort is in on it. Maybe some of his employees. I'm sure you can find out."

"I'll try right away."

"Wait. I'm not done yet."

"Didn't mean to interrupt. Go ahead."

"This is just the beginning. Thirty-three sturgeon went to Illinois with some fishermen from Oak Forest. Don't know their names. But I do know they took them to the locker plant there. Don't know the name of that either. It's the only locker in town. If you go there, you should find them."

"How many people were there who took fish to Oak Forest?"

"Four. These fish were all big, would be legal size fish if the season was open. The sturgeon have been biting like hell on the lake. They're getting most of them straight across the lake from the grade near those high banks."

"When were the fish caught?"

"Yesterday. The fishermen went back to Illinois last night."

"How do you know where they are taking them?"

"Never mind. You'll just have to take my word for it."

"Just a minute. Do I know you? Your voice sounds familiar. I would like to talk to you. Make sure I've got all the information correct."

"Look, I gave you all the information I have. I can't risk talking to you. If you check this out, you will catch them, I guarantee it. I'm going to hang up now. Good luck." The phone clicked and was dead.

Jim reviewed his notes briefly and called his special warden Milt Henke who lived near Poynette, and made arrangements to pick him up in fifteen minutes.

Enroute to Lake Wisconsin, the two wardens discussed the information and how to proceed. Jim drove at a swift pace. "You know MIlt, I believe whoever called had everything written down. It seemed he was reading it to me. I have a feeling the info is good."

"God, do you think the fishing is that good, that they can catch that many sturgeon on hook and line?"

"Does sound almost impossible. But, I've seen those sturgeon really go on a feeding binge a few times before. The guy's story had a ring of truth to it."

"How are we going to do this Jim?"

"Been thinking about that. I'd like to see who's around the resort. Let's just go in and have coffee like we have in the past. After we look it over we'll just put it to them. Can't get a search warrant on what we've got. We'll just have to get consent to search. We may be able to search without consent. It's a public place. The ice house is not connected. What do you think of that?"

"Is it a public place when their house is connected to the business? They live there you know."

"Yeah. But I still think we can search the ice house. They may let us. We'll see." Pulling into the resort the two wardens walked into the dining room and sat at the counter where they could observe inside and out.

The owner approached Jim from behind the counter with a nervous gleam in his eyes. "Hi guys. How are you doing today?"

"Pretty good Jake. We'll have coffee. How's the fishing?"

Serving the coffee, one black and one with both cream and sugar as he was accustomed to, his answer was nonchalant. "Oh, they're bringing in a few. Nothing to get excited about. Excuse me, got a minnow customer."

Leaving the diner to the two, the wardens eyed who was present. Two men worked cleaning the boats outside and a middle-aged women walked back and forth clattering pots and pans in the kitchen.

Milt was anxious. "What do we do now?"

"I'm trying to determine who's here. You know the owner, Jake Bliss. Well, those two cleaning the boats are Frannie Houle and John Binch. The lady in the kitchen is Jake's mother-in-law, Mrs. Joe Kuchinski. When

Jake comes back, I'm going to put it to him. Let me do most of the talking. You stay close to the ice house door. Stand so you can see through the door on the other end as well. If anyone tries to go in you go with them regardless of what they say. You know where the fish are. Beat them to them. When Jake comes back, I'll pay the bill while you pick up our flashlights. Okay? Here he comes."

"Yeah. Guess so."

As Jake entered Milt walked slowly to the car.

Jim laid the money on the counter. Jake picked it up and laid it on the cash register shelf. "What are you guys up to today. Going to check the lake?" Milt had reentered now with the lights. Jake's eyes glinted as he glanced furtively toward the lights.

"No, we have a complaint that you or some of your guests have some illegal sturgeon here."

Taken aback, Jake darted from behind the counter. "Now wait a minute. We don't have any illegal fish here. I don't know of any. If they're here, they're not mine." Milt had moved to the door which was near the ice house door.

Jim continued, "Well Jake if you don't have anything illegal here you wouldn't mind if we looked in your ice house?" Turning, he walked outside to the ice house door, where Milt already stood like a sentinel.

Jake raced past both to practically block the door. "Now wait a minute Jim. I'm not letting you into the ice house. That's private property. You can't go in there without a warrant."

At a fast pace, a slightly built man of about 30 appeared. "What's going on here Jake?" It was Kike Couter, a local hanger-on, and ex-con who was always ready to give legal advice. Jim sighed; he knew this meant trouble. Kike was sure to enter the situation.

Jake pointed, "These wardens think I've got some illegal sturgeon in my ice house."

Kike snapped to attention and turned insolently toward the wardens. "The hell with them. You don't have to let them in. In fact, they can't even be on your property. Tell them to get the hell off."

Jim's jaw clamped tight and his lips began to twist. "Kike, you know better than that and besides this is none of your business. Just get out of the way."

A crowd began to gather including the two boat cleaners and Mrs. Kutchinski . All began asking excited questions.

Jim turned to take command. "Now listen everyone. We're not arguing anymore. We're going to search the ice house."

Kike stepped in front of the wardens. "You can't do that without a warrant."

Jim's lips were twisting noticeably now. Shaking his finger menancingly under Kike's nose he spat, "Kike, ever since you arrived you've been telling me what to do. I don't need your jailhouse advice. Now, I'm not asking you, I'm telling you get out of the way, and go home unless you want to go to jail. I'm sure with your experience you know I can do that." Turning, Jim motioned to Milt. "Come on, we're searching."

Temporarily buffaloed, Kike stepped quickly aside. Proceeding down the narrow passageway between the piles of sawdust covered ice, followed by a protesting Jake, Frannie, John and Mrs. Kutchinski, they did not pretend to look but went directly to where the first fish were to be. Flashing the light and reaching up, Jim slid his hand between the ice blocks where the sawdust was obviously disturbed. Feeling around he withdrew a small rock sturgeon. There was silence now as he reached twice more and came out with two more fish. He turned to the others. "Milt, you continue the search; we're going outside. Okay, everybody out." All stepped outside into the sunlight, eyes squinting.

There stood Kike, hands on hips, "Now you've done it. If I were you Jake, I would sue these bastards."

Milt came blinking into the sunlight with four more sturgeons in his hands to hear Jim's now shouting voice, "Kike, I'm telling you now, damn it, that this is the end. You either go home right now or go to jail." With a swift stride he reached for Kike who backpedaled.

"Oh, okay I'm going home." He disappeared swiftly behind the resort. However, he had riled everyone to the point where they were willing to argue. All started to yell and talk at one time.

Again Jim menanced them, "I've had about all I can take of this. Whose fish are these Jake?"

"Kike says we don't have to talk to you."

"I'll tell you what Jake, you don't have to talk to us if you don't want to. I'm telling you further that you are all in possession of these sturgeon. If you don't tell me who they belong to or who took them, we'll be in a position where we will have to arrest all of you. I know all of you are connected with this resort in one way or another and with the fish. It's your choice. I've had it. It's either way right now."

It was obvious that Kike had made an impression. They were still beligerent and babbled on.

Jake pushed forward, "We've decided that if you want to look foolish in court go ahead, arrest us all."

Jim reached for his citation book. "Okay. You keep them back there Milt. Get your identification out Jake." There was finally silence as Jim methodically wrote one citation after another. After the seventh and final citation was written, Jim stuffed his book in his pocket. "Come on Milt, let's go."

Jake had settled down and was now pale and approached Jim. "Do you have to give us all citations for these few fish. Can't we talk about it some more?"

"I tried to talk to you earlier. See you in court on Monday."

Jim swiftly led the way to the car where the wardens slammed the car doors and drove away. Milt was silent and pensive. Finally he sighed, "Are we okay Jim? Can we arrest all of them like we did?"

"Looks like we'll find out. Hell, I'm not going to stand there and take that crap. Wish I would have pinched Kike too. I was close to it. If he had gone just a little further, we may have given him another trip to the big house. Let them talk to the court. We can always deal later if we have to. I'll explain what happened to the district attorney. He's a good man. We'll work something out. Let's go over to my house and write up an incident report while everything is fresh in our minds."

"What about the sturgeon that went to Illinois?"

"We'll give the warden down there a call and see if we can't get them back along with whoever took them."

Arriving home, Jim immediately called the Illinois warden. He explained what had occurred on Lake Wisconsin. The warden agreed there was only one locker plant in town and said he would investigate immediately. Within two hours, he was back on the line. He advised he could find nothing. He said the operator of the plant had let him look around. There were no sturgeon on the premises.

Disappointed, the wardens discussed the case as they wrote their report. Jim drew in air and let out a huge sigh. "You know Milt there's something wrong here. All the information that guy gave me was correct. I can't remember a time when I've gotten any more precise information. Doesn't it make you wonder?"

"Yeah sure does. Those fish were right where he said they would be. Do you think the Illinois warden could be covering for them?"

"God, I would hate to believe any warden would do a thing like that. I suppose its possible."

"Well, Jim, they say there's one rotten apple in each barrel. Could we go down there and see?"

"Guess we could. Wouldn't have any authority though. We would still need help from a warden down there. It's too far anyway. I think I'll call Marshall Stennet of the Federal Fish and Wildlife Service. See what he thinks." He immediately dialed Marshall who was stationed in Madison.

"Good to hear from you Jim. Shoot. How can I help?"

Jim explained what had happened and how the warden in Illinois had stated he could find no fish. He also voiced his doubts about the Illinois warden because the information had been so good. "What do you advise Marshall? Think you or one of your agents could check this out for us?"

"We sure can. I, like you, have a hard time believing one warden would do that to another. On the other hand, heard of things like this happening between states before. I don't think it would hurt for one of us to look around. Tell you what, it's too late tonight to do anything. First thing tomorrow I'll have our man down in Illinois take a look at that locker plant and call you."

"Gee Marshall, I'd appreciate that. We'll be in touch then. Okay?"

"Yeah. Goodby and good luck."

About nine-thirty the next morning, Jim was again summoned by the jingling of the phone. "Hello. This is Chizeks."

It was a federal warden returning Jim's call. "You called Marshall yesterday about some illegal sturgeon down here."

"Yeah. Did you get a chance to look?"

"Yep. Just came from there. I was waiting when they opened the place this morning. I've got some big boxes of sturgeon here for you."

"Good. I couldn't believe they weren't there. Did Marshall tell you of my experience with the Illinois warden?"

"Yeah. Guess I was surprised to find the sturgeon. But here they are. Don't know how many there are yet as they're all cut up. They weigh 540 pounds though. What do you want me to do with them?"

"First, did you find out who they were possessed by?"

"Sure, the boxes are all labeled. Got four names for you." Jim copied the names and addresses over the phone. "Maybe we could meet at the state line if it's not too much trouble for you. I'd like to pick up the sturgeon myself to maintain the chain of evidence."

"It's okay with me." Plans were made and they met at the state line that afternoon. The evidence was transferred and Jim returned to Portage just before dark.

The information was too good to keep. He called Milt. "This is Jim. Guess what?"

"You got the sturgeon."

"You're right. I've already picked them up. Can you believe this?"

"Sure. You always told me if you roll over enough stones you'll find something under one of them."

"Did I say that?"

"Hell, that's your favorite saying. What's next?"

"Come on up for breakfast tomorrow and we'll take the whole thing to the district attorney. Say about eight o'clock."

"Okay. See you then."

The next morning Jim led the way into the district attorney's office. "Good morning Dave." David Bennett was an experienced district attorney who worked well with game wardens.

"Good morning. I've been waiting. Knew you would be in. What did you do on Lake Wisconsin the day before yesterday?"

"You've heard about it?"

"Everybody in town is talking about it. What did you do arrest everyone in sight?"

"Guess it looks that way. We sure have a bunch of sturgeon."

"Come on in. We'll talk it over." The wardens spent about two hours reviewing the cases with Dave.

"Looks like you guys did a stroke of business. Why don't we charge them all? We'll ask them in court who took and hid the fish and go from there. As for the people down in Illinois, we'll charge them too. I'll write them each a letter and inform them they can post a bond by mail. Is that ok?"

"That's great."

Monday, at the Columbia County courthouse the seven defendants from the resort arrived in a subdued state. Judge Jim Daley read the charges of possessing illegal sturgeon to them.

Shaking his head, he stared at Dave Bennett and asked, "Did all of these charges come out of the same incident? How many sturgeon are involved here?"

"Your honor, I would like to explain the whole incident. It may be some of the charges could be dismissed. We would like to get at the truth of the incident." Dave went on to explain how the people had been uncooperative and had obstructed the wardens in their investigation.

At this point Jake Bliss stood up, "Your honor could I say a few words?"

"Go ahead Mr. Bliss."

Very subdued, Jake continued, "We admit we over reacted at the resort the other day. I like to think I'm a respectable citizen. We'd like very much to dispose of this matter swiftly and as cheaply as we can. It's true we all knew what was going on with the sturgeon. I'm sorry now as the resort owner I didn't put a stop to it. However, there were several who were more involved than others. We have talked it over. I, as owner, am willing to pay a fine. The several others involved are prepared to come forward and also pay fines. We feel the others were not involved to the point of being responsible. That's all I have to say your honor."

Daley, clearing his throat nervously, stared at the other six defendants. "This is an unusual procedure, but I guess what we are attempting is to get at the truth. Is Jake speaking for all of you?" All nodded in the affirmative. "Do you understand you can be represented by an attorney?" Again all nodded in the affirmative.

Directing his attention back to Dave, he continued, "We will take a 15 minute break for you, the wardens and the defendants to discuss this and come back prepared to resolve this issue."

In the discussion that followed in the hall, both Frannie Houle and John Binch admitted they had taken some of the fish and helped hide all of them including the sturgeon that went to Illinois. They identified the four fishermen from Illinois who had taken the 33 large fish.

The case was disposed of swiftly with large fines meted out to Jake, Frannie and John on the recommendation of Dave. The charges on the others were dismissed.

As Jim and Milt were leaving the courtroom, Judge Daley stuck his head out of his quarters and yelled, "Come on in here for a few minutes." As they were old friends, the talk was very informal.

Daley motioned them to chairs, "What the hell is going on here? Now the court has to do your work for you?"

Smiling, Jim replied, "It's about time you do some work. God, we had the damnest rumble going. Should have pinched that damn Kike Couter for obstructing. He would have brightened your court."

"You mean Kike, the guy I put away here a few years ago."

"Yeah."

"Should have brought him in. He still answers to the probation officer. I know him well. He can sure get under your skin."

Milt chuckled, "Never seen Jim so damned mad."

Daley turned to Jim, "How many sturgeon were involved?"

"Well, let's see, we recovered 540 pounds of dressed fish, about 33 fish plus 7 small ones, about 40 fish in all. Looks like they are better fishermen than you."

"Yeah. I've fished three or four years now and haven't caught a legal sized one yet."

Milt broke in, "What are we going to do with all those fish Jim?"

"I'll sell them. How would you like to buy some Judge? We could have a sturgeon feed at our annual law enforcement association get together. Bill Lovelace should be able to cook sturgeon. He does a good job on beaver."

"Yeah, that's a good idea. I'll take about 50 pounds of dressed fish. Now get out of here. I've got a trial."

On a snowy February day, Jim received a visitor at his home. Opening the door, he was greeted by a burley man of about 35.

"Hello, are you Jim Chizek?"

"Yes, come on in."

As the man entered he began. "I'm John Tobeson from Illinois. You called me about those sturgeon last summer. I sure don't think much of you sending a Fed into my area."

"What! You resent me. Well let me tell you something. What you did stinks. I've worked with officers from many states. Never have I encountered an incident like this." Jim's temper snapped. "Please leave my home. I don't even want to talk to you."

"Just a minute. Let me explain. The owner of that locker plant is a good friend. I asked about the fish and he said there were none. What more did you expect?"

"I expected you to follow through, look the place over. It didn't take but a minute for the federal officer to come up with the fish. I've already talked to some other Illinois wardens and I think you were covering up for some of your buddies. Now get out."

"Just let me say."

"I've heard enough, get out!" Moving toward John threateningly, he continued, "Get out or I'll throw you out. I can't stand to be around a crooked law enforcement officer." Shouting now, he repeated, "Get out."

Moving toward the door, John muttered, "B-But wait."

Jim pushed the door closed, partially pushing John out the door, "Wait nothing. Good-by." Jim fumed. "He resents me. Wait till Milt hears this."

Chapter 14

Bear Motel

Assigned to work the deer gun season of November 1976, special investigating wardens Joe Rubesch, Jim Chizek and Harry Borner checked into the Bear Motel, one of the suspected outlets for the illegal sale of deer. The Bear Motel near Augusta was also central to other near areas that were to be worked.

After working several taverns in the area, the wardens returned to the motel that evening to rest for an early start in the morning. As the owner of the motel was a suspect, the investigators were exceptionally careful. Ficticious names were used when signing in, voices were muted because of the paper thin walls, credentials were never left in the room when the investigators were out.

Tall slim Joe immediately began to get out of his heavy hunting clothing while Harry stretched his husky form on a bed. Jim turned on the shower in the bathroom to confuse any sound overheard, seated his six foot two form on the commode and started his tape recorder to dictate reports on the contacts of the day.

Suddenly three high powered rifle shots rang out immediately outside the room. Almost dethroned, Jim babbled, "What the H____ is that?" This comment was later to turn up on the tape.

Harry, a solidly built veteran warden at age 50, grabbed his boots yelling, "I'm heading for the woods."

Joe began hurriedly dressing. "I'll be out as soon as I can."

Grabbing his cane, Jim hurried, hobbling out of the room toward the motel office where he saw a man carrying a scope mounted rifle. The man entered the motel office with Jim following.

"What's all the shooting about?"

Tom Justin, the owner of the motel, bragged, "My boy just shot a deer."

Jim turned to the man with the rifle. "What did you get?"

"I don't know for sure. Shot three times and knocked one down. I think it was a doe. There were six of em. Didn't see horns on any of em. Did you Dad?"

"No. He shot the deer right out of the motel office. Can you imagine that? By the way, we're out of party permit tags. All we've got left are buck tags. Filled ours already. That means the deer is illegal. Do you have one? You fellows could take the deer."

Chuckling to himself, Jim thought of the ficticious tags he had in his pocket. *My God, I've got a half dozen — one for every area around here,* struggling back to reality he answered. "Sure be glad to take the deer. We've had tough hunting and don't have a deer yet." Nonchalantly, Jim walked over to the counter where the man had laid the rifle. "Is this the rifle you killed the deer with?"

The shooter, a slim man in his middle thirties, turned to Jim his face beaming. "Yep. It's my dad's rifle. I'm not used to the scope sight. Did pretty good though. One hit out of three isn't bad with a strange rifle."

Looking the rifle over, Jim commented, "Beautiful rifle." Making a mental note of the make and serial number for later identification, he laid it down. The group then moved outside to look for the deer.

Harry meanwhile made a beeline for a group of hunters who were busily chatting about the deer on the hill behind the motel. Seeing them, he charged into the Norway pine forest. He was sweating profusely, as he successfully beat the group into the woods. Like a good bird dog he cast back and forth until he cut a blood trail. Walking parallel off to one side so as not to leave sign in the new snow he followed the trail. After about a hundred yards of trailing he found a large doe deer. She was stone dead, laying outstretched in the whitness of the new snow now starkly spattered with blood. Quickly hunkering down in some brush nearby, he waited. Soon three hunters came hurriedly along the blood trail talking in hushed tones. "Here it is. It's dead. A nice doe. Quick, let's pull the guts out of it and get it out of here." They worked feverishly to gut the animal. "What are we going to do with it?"

"I don't know. We don't have a party tag." Tying a rope around the neck, they started to drag it out of the woods.

Harry in his bright hunting clothes, stood up and walked unconcernedly into the group. "Nice deer you have there."

"Where did you come from?" One of the startled hunters demanded.

"I'm staying at the motel. Don't you remember me?"

A tall hunter with a pockmarked face stopped looking him over carefully. "Oh yeah. I saw you at he motel. He's okay."

"I'll give you a hand dragging the deer." Harry volunteered. Laughing and joking the men dragged the deer toward the motel office. Harry's loud booming voice and his loud Santa Claus, HO, Ho, Ho, told the other investigators he was with them.

The shooter approached them hurriedly as they met in the parking lot. "I've found a fellow who says he will take the deer. These fellows are staying at the motel. They're all right." He turned to Jim. "Get your tag out and put it on the deer."

Jim untwisted the metal seal from his hat band, wrestled his belt knife loose, cut the gambrel and attached the tag. "Gee it's a nice deer. It'll make good eating. But what are we going to do with it? We were going to hunt in this area a few more days."

"Hang it in that pine tree," said Tom. "No one will see it here behind the motel. We will keep an eye on it for you. Come on we'll help you hang it up."

As they were hanging the deer, Joe appeared with his camera, half dressed red suspenders dangling at his sides, shoe laces dragging. "Looks like

136

an occasion for some pictures. Everyone stand by the deer. I'd like a picture of the whole crew." With much good humor everyone lined up around the deer for a group picture. Joe took several pictures and got addresses, so photos could be sent. While he was writing down addresses he also wrote down their backtag numbers for positive identification. "What did you say your name was? Ralph Justin? Oh, your father owns this motel then?"

"Yeah, I was raised here. That's why I generally watch that crossing where I shot the deer. They always cross there."

"Pays to know your hunting area," commented Joe.

"You're right there, but I have to end this happy gathering and get back to Chippewa Falls. My wife is expecting me." All gathered at Ralph's car. While good-byes were said, Joe recorded Ralph's auto license number for further identification. The investigators returned to their room where much kidding around and pummeling of each others backs took place due to the break.

"Got one without even trying, ho, ho, ho," laughed Harry.

"Jimmy get back in the can and start taping," retorted Joe. "Now you really have something to tape."

Several months later Warden Ken Larkin served a warrant on Ralph Justin at his home in Chippewa Falls.

Justin gulped when the warden told him of his mission. His mouth falling open, he said, "You mean at the motel that day last deer season? Those hunters at the motel were such nice guys. Can't believe they'd do this to me. Guess there isn't anything I can do though except pay up."

Chapter 15

Chicken-Chicken

In the early 1940s Ernie Meress was stationed at Leona in Forest County. The sale of deer and venison was prevalent because of the scarcity of jobs. Unemployed people often sold deer at prices ranging from $20 to $50.

Ernie, a fast paced conscientious warden in his late 20s, constantly worked himself into a frenzy even to the detriment of his health. A leader in his own way he often entered situations where only the blind would tread. His nervous speech and terrific temper when vexed were widely known. From that and his Italian ancestry arose many jokes to which Ernie responded with anger and torrents of words. Short and stocky, he often challenged men much larger when taunted.

Ernie had no trouble awakening this cold November morning. The pain in his ulcerated stomach made it impossible to lay in bed any longer. Stumbling from his messy bed, he slid his stocking feet unceremoniously into his tiny kitchen. His eyes fastened on the gallon milk bottle silhouetted against the blackness of the partially frosted window where he had left it to keep it cool. His hand shook as he poured the first glass of the day into the glass he always left on the table so he could easily locate it during the night. Gulping down the large glass, he sighed a long sigh of relief as the milk slowly put out the burning. Rubbing the frost off the window, he gazed out to a fresh snowfall of about four inches.

Pacing restlessly, he filled the tea kettle from the water pail. Placing it on the cookstove, he swiftly slid finely split maple firewood in through the uplifted stove lid and tossed in a half cup of kerosene. Striking a match on the side of the box, he quickly held the match to the kerosene and watched the fire flicker into life. As the fire grew in strength and the kettle began to rock and sing, Ernie paced, slapping his hands against his shoulders as much to ease his impatience as to stimulate warmth in his hands.

His mind was already busily contemplating the long day ahead. Thoughts tumbled through his mind as to how he would approach the twenty-two complaints he had scattered in notes on the table. All were of people possessing illegal deer being held for sale in the Forest County area. Pouring the hot water into a wash dish, Ernie continued to consider the handling of this many complaints as he washed up and thoughtfully scraped the stiff stubble off his face. Stalking to the table, he began to review the notes. The burning returned. Dropping the notes, he slopped the glass full of milk and again felt the soothing relief.

Pacing back and forth Ernie read notes, toasted bread on top of the cookstove and sipped milk. Pacing as he buttered and munched the toast, the chiming of the large clock drew Ernie's gaze. "God it's 5 o'clock, got to get over to the cabin and meet Koppy and Les."

At the rented log cabin several blocks from Ernie's home waited two men, Albert Koppenhaver, a veteran game warden stationed at Madison, and Les Tiews, a game aide stationed at Portage. They had reported to Ernie before the nine day deer season. This was to be their last work day. They were to assist Ernie on cleanup on this the day after the close of the season.

Al, a well-built sturdy man about 5'10" in height, let his hearty laugh rumble through the cabin as Ernie entered. Gazing quietly, he half choked at Ernie's appearance. "You look terrible Ernie. Run out of milk."

"It's not funny," Ernie grumbled. "Didn't get much sleep. Damn ulcer kept me awake."

Grinning Al, continued his easy jibs, "We slept well, didn't we Les? Course our consciences are clear. Haw."

Pulling on his wool black and white plaid mackinaw jacket, Les snickered, " Sure and we had sausage and eggs for breakfast. What did you have Ernie?"

"You know well enough what I had. I get so sick of toast and milk. By the way, do you have any milk left? My gut is starting to burn again."

Les, a tall slim fast moving man in his mid-twenties dressed as the others in wool stag trousers and plaid wool shirt, strode swiftly to the pantry for milk. While there, he heard Al's loud guffaw ring through the cabin. Poor Ernie is sure getting it this morning. Emerging with the quart bottle Les jibed, "Here Ernie, better than beer."

Grabbing the bottle Ernie snorted, "Wish you guys had an ulcer, then you wouldn't talk so smart." Unceremoniously tipping the bottle against his lips, he let the milk flow soothingly down his throat. "Ahhh," he signed deeply, "really good." He slammed the bottle smartly on the table. "Let's get down to cases." Pulling the stack of notes from his red and black mackinaw pocket he spread them carelessly on the table. "Can't believe the number of complaints I got from the ranger station. About twenty-two here. All have illegal deer. They're for sale too. Guess we'll just have to start with the closest and end up with the furtherest." Quickly putting them in order, Ernie stood sharply up. "Let's get started."

Al mused, "Boy, these people really kill deer. The people in Dane County would never believe this. Course without a deer season, it's hard for them to realize what goes on up here."

Les interrupted, "Do you think all these people actually have illegal deer?"

Impatiently, Ernie snapped, "Hell yes. I know these people. They don't give a damn. They've got them all right. Come on let's get going. You drive Kop. I've used my allowance for this month."

With Ernie directing from the front seat of the Model A Ford sedan, Les listened from the rear seat to Ernie's constant prattle about the ridiculous way people respond to the deer season, and about the regulations this year being almost unenforceable as antered bucks were not legal.

Ernie had no search warrants so searches were done with consent.

They merely stopped at the suspects' homes and asked to search. Ernie, well-known and respected by the local people permitted them. The searches went well.

After picking up illegal deer at the first two sites, they stopped at a ramshackle log cabin. While Al went to the front door, Les waited at the rear door. When the women of the house opened the door, Al's badge, spotted by a tall rangy, rawboned man seated at the kitchen table, brought an immediate response. Clad only in longjohns, he grabbed the plate of venison he was eating and bolted through the back door. Les, momentarily startled by the man slamming savagely through the door, dashed madly after him. Les' long legs and the advantage of wearing boots soon defeated the barefooted runner. Grabbing him roughly around the neck, he partially pushed, partially herded him back through the back door. A final push brought the man to the empty chair he had left. "There, sit there."

Ernie took over by writing the man's name and address down. The man continued to gaze at, size up and measure Les. Drawling, he said, "Never saw a man move so fast. I'm pretty fast too. Let's try it again with boots. Bet I could beat you this time."

Al guffawed as he slapped him on the shoulder, his loud clear laugh ringing through the cabin. "Pretty fast are you?"

Ernie interrupted, "We'll see how fast you are in court next Monday."

During all of this, a small redheaded boy about six years of age remained sitting next to Ernie. Quietly intent on all the happenings, his eyes fixed solidly on his father in the longjohns. "Paw You've got your underwear on inside out."

"Quiet Joey."

"But Dad your underwear is inside out."

Disgruntled by the interruption, the man objected. "What makes you think that?"

"Well Paw the brown is on the outside."

Silence prevailed, as everyone struggled to maintain the proper prospective under the circumstances.

Ernie loudly cleared his throat to aid in maintaining his composure. "Now where did you say the rest of the venison is. We've got to move along. We've got a long day." Glancing one last time at the man, he snorted, "Be in court Monday at 10 o'clock"

Joking and laughing the three continued to work north and east from Leona toward Armstrong Creek.

Al's hooting laugh still echoed through the car as they entered the driveway of the small log cabin. "Haw the brown is on the outside." Back near the edge of the clearing in the cutover area, a man in bib overalls methodically pitched manure onto a wagon hitched to a team of grey horses.

Al drove swiftly through the flock of chickens in the yard, scattering them in all directions with a wild clucking and squawking. The noise brought the middle-aged woman, who was sitting on the porch in a cloud of steam picking a large white chicken, to her feet. Turning she spoke to a young man in blue bib overalls as he emerged from the house.

The thin gaunt man in his mid-twenties, a questioning expression on

140   *Chicken-Chicken*

his face, met Ernie as he stepped from the car. "Hi there young man, is this the Pulaske place?"

Furtively glancing at the three lawmen he breathed, "Yeah, this is Pulaskes." Gazing nervously at the badge Ernie displayed, he continued, "Dad is back by the barn. Want to see him?"

"We sure do," Ernie replied. "We're game wardens and we have a complaint that you have an illegal deer here."

Startled, the man gaped incredulously, fight or flight flitting across his features. Speechless he shuffled one way and then the other, kicking snow this way and that. Finally with an insolent glare, he shoved his hands almost casually into his pockets and strode defiantly toward the barn. Glancing fearfully over his shoulder, he detected Les beginning to follow at a swift pace. With a muttered oath he darted toward the barn.

Les, expecting such an act because of the man's actions, dashed after him. The race was short and for the second time that day, Les grabbed and grasped a running man - this time by the overall suspenders. Digging his heels in sharply, snow slewing, he swung the man in a circle. Les' sharp eyes riveted on the knife that appeared in the man's hand as it was jerked from an overall pocket. Swinging harder, Les grabbed desperately for the knife hand. Making contact was a gratifying feeling that was soon replaced by surprise at the strength of the now berserk whining man. With both hands finally on the knife hand, Les twisted mightily and felt the hand relax slightly. Relief flooded his features when the knife slithered and disappeared in the trampled whitness around them.

Raising a right fist, he stalked the man, "Now, we'll see how tough you are without the knife." He gasped when he felt his upraised arm held as in a vise like grip. Glancing back, he realized it was Al who prevented his swing.

"Take it easy Les. He's disarmed.He'll be okay now." Pointing, Al announced, "There is where he was headed."

Following Al's pointing finger, Les saw the large tenpoint buck strung up in a poplar tree partially hidden by spruce and balsam trees behind the barn near the edge of the woods. "Don't look legal to me." Turning to the young man, Al demanded, ""Is it yours?"

Shaking his head in the negative the man searched frantically in his pocket to produce an unsnapped metal deer tag. "I, I've got the tag ri - right here. C - can I still put it on the deer? Th - that's all I was trying to do. To put the tag on. the knife was for that, to cut the gambrel. Y - you know. Please let me put it on."

Calmly his comanding voice taking control of the situation, Al answered, ""Won't do any good that buck is illegal." He continued, "What's your name?"

"T Tony. Tony Pulaske."

"Well Tony it looks like someone is in trouble here. "

Meanwhile Ernie was confronted by the large women with the partially-picked chicken in her hand. She loomed above Ernie as he approached. Jabbering excitedly in Polish, her voice demandingly rose to a shriek. Ernie tried desperately to communicate with her.

"Now, Madam, take it easy. I don't know what you're saying but we have a right to be here."

Menancingly she approached holding the chicken as though she might use it as a weapon. Her voice became more insistent and demanding as she gestured toward the driveway indicating by her actions that she wanted them to leave.

Holding both hands out in front of him to ward off any attack, Ernie continued to attempt communication. Obviously, she could understand no English. Turning his head vigorously from side to side, he reinforced his answer of no. "No. No. We're not leaving, Kubish!?"

Threateningly the enraged woman advanced on Ernie, her body and the chicken held in a stance of attack.

Glancing behind him, taking in what was going on near the barn, he let the words come sharply. ""Madam. There is an illegal deer behind your barn and we're here to get it. Kubish?"

More excited Polish greeted his statement, her arm cocked holding the chicken by the legs.

Ernie backtracking now, jabbered, "You folks are asking for more trouble than you are already in. Just put the chicken down and we'll talk about this." Glancing briefly over his shoulder at he others' approach, he was rewarded with a solid staggering smash across the face with the chicken. Staggered dazed from the blow, Ernie stumbled backwards grabbing at his mouth where the chicken had broken his lip. His hand smearing the blood over his face. Wiping and spitting blood, Ernie screamed, "put that chicken down."

Wham, the chicken slammed him across the shoulder. The woman advanced now, both hands on the chicken, swinging wildly at the retreating warden. Shielding himself with outstretched arms, Ernie backed away yelling at the top of his vioce. Blows rained on him. The beak of the chicken tore a large flap of meat loose on his nose and cheek. "Damn you, you're going to jail for this." Warding off some of the blows with his arms and backing away towards the others put Les in a position to intervene. Ernie yelled, "I'm liable to forget you're a woman and knock your block off. Cut that out."

Les stepped between them. "Now, Madam, please stop. You can't do this. " Wham, she hit him across the arms. Les found himself in the same position Ernie was earlier, backing away and fending off blows as they fell on his arms. Tiring, she often missed, which gave Les the opportunity to grasp the chicken and wrench it away from her.

Without the chicken her vitality disappeared and she visibly shrunk. She sidled over to her son. Sagging against him, she sobbed out questioningly in her native dialect.

Ernie lunged forward. As he mopped the blood from his face with a handkerchief, he intoned, "I'll tell you what, you're going to jail." Pointing he stammered, "You, you can't do this, you can't do what you just did." The words tumbled from his lips like a trip hammer. "No damn woman can do, no one can do" Almost at a loss for words, he began pacing back and forth in front of the two. His firecracker temper brusting forth with more words. "I, I'm not going to let you get away, by God. I'm telling you, you will pay dearly for this, look what you did to my lips, look at the cut on my nose."

Seeing the situation was going nowhere, Al stepped between them and became the negotiator for the second time that day. "Look, Ernie, it's all over now. Take it easy."

Ernie's pride and terrible temper was urging him on. "But look at my lip and my nose. I've got to get even for this. Get even hell. I'm going to get ahead. " His control was slowly returning. In the back of his mind, however, he grimaced. *My God. They'll tell the other wardens I got beat up by a woman with a chicken, Christ I'll never live this down.* Aloud he said, "I tell you Kopp the woman has got to pay."

"Oh, Ernie, it wasn't so bad. Let's just get the deer and get out of here."

"But Kopp she hit me with a chicken."

"Yeah, I know but I think we should just leave and not make this any worse."

Turning Al noticed the middle-aged overalled man approach from the barn.

Hitching up his suspenders, he drawled, "What's going on? You tangle with Mama?"

Al and Les were biting their lips to keep from bursting out in laughter.

Ernie's face darkened again. "This is no joke and your wife is in a heap of trouble. Do you realize what can happen to her for assualting a warden? By the way, what's your name?"

"John. Look Mr. Meress, Mama gets carried away sometimes. Especially when she don't understand what's going on. She doesn't speak English. We don't want any trouble. That's my deer hanging down by the barn. Can't I just pay a fine or go to jail and let Mama be? If I cross her, she may hit me with the chicken too."

Al, afraid trouble would again erupt, stepped between Ernie and the three. "He's right Ernie, hell let's just take the deer and get out of here. John, will you appear in court on Monday and take care of this?"

"Yeah, just said I would and Mr. Meress we're very sorry this happened." He spoke quietly to his wife in Polish. Looking older and shaken, the woman replied and John translated. "Mama is sorry she hurt you Mr. Meress." Raising her apron, she advanced toward Ernie. He began to shield himself and retreat.

John interjected, "No . She won't hurt you. She wants to wipe the blood off your face." Pleading, she spoke softly while wiping the blood from Ernie's face. The scene was touching as she daintily dabbed Ernie's face to clean away most of the blood. The badly split lip and the loose flap on Ernie's nose continued to bleed.

Al stepped forward throwing his arm warmly around Ernie's shoulders. "Come on Ernie." He led him away from the crowd. "Get in the car. Les will get the deer. Okay Les?"

Turning, Ernie was holding his stomach. "John, there's one thing you can do for me. Do you have any milk? My ulcer is killing me."

"Why of course Mr. Meress," purred the man, "it's the least we can do." Addressing his wife in Polish, he sent her hustling off to the house to return with a large glass of milk.

Driving out the driveway, Al slapped Ernie heartily on the shoulder, "Don't worry Ernie, we won't tell anyone that a woman beat the hell out of you with a chicken, Haw, Haw."

The rest of the searches produced illegal deer at all the other locations but without incident. Several days later, Ernie had ulcer time again. Checking his garage which contained 23 illegal deer, Ernie was exasperated to find someone had stolen all of them. He dashed to the house and called the sheriff. The sheriff responded, "Ernie hang up the phone and open the window. I can hear you."

Chapter 16

The Race

In the early 1960s things got out of control at Devil's Lake State Park in Sauk County. Parties by juveniles were loud and rowdy and fights ensued. Speeding was so bad one took his life in his hands walking the roads, especially during the night time. As usual when things got bad, the wardens were called in to restore order. These assignments were not welcomed by wardens because under normal conditions they were not well received in the parks. Also, much of this work was done at night when the problems were greatest. Usually, the wardens had already put in a full day in the field.

It was after 3 a.m. when things quieted down in the park on a dark, balmy August night, when the group of wardens working the park decided to call it a day and go home.

Jim Chizek, stowing gear in his auto, was startled by a park policeman chasing a tall slim young man running as though pursued by the Devil. Immediately behind the park policeman appeared warden Donald Beghin, the last man in the race. The chase continued swiftly past the park headquarters and over a large Indian animal mound that was mowed like a lawn. As Jim watched, Don passed the park policeman.

Hmm, he's doing pretty good. Looks like future chief warden material to me. Jim mused. Just before entering the woods the young man lost his hat, stopped, picked it up and still out ran both pursuers. *Oh hell. So much for Don's future.*

Built like a Popsicle, long and thin, the man hit the brush running so hard a person could imagine his feet throwing gravel and his skin being torn off by the solid mass of prickly ash he had slammed into.

Meanwhile, Jim was considering what his move in this spectacle should be. *No use to get in the race. He's too far ahead. Big dark woods he's entered. He'll be lost and scared. He may hear cars and work out to the north park entrance road that cuts through that big woods. He's hurt the way he hit that prickly ash. Wow! Wearing only blue jeans and a tank top, he'll be ripped and torn. He'll be all the more scared and it will give him more reason to get out of that scary woods and get his wounds dressed. I'll just take a little hike up the entrance road and see what happens.* He had only walked about a quarter mile north in the total blackness when he caught up with three young men. Although in full uniform with badge displayed, the young people did not recognize him in the darkness.

Carrying on a casual conversation, they walked slowly toward the park entrance. "What are you fellows doing at this time of night?"

"Oh, we're looking for a friend. He got separated from us earlier tonight. We've about given up on him. We're going to our car. It's parked near the park entrance."

Oh, oh! Lost friend huh, the runner. Got to stick with these guys.

The conversation continued the last mile to the park entrance where a light sign reflected a bright glint off Jim's badge. One of them half whispered, "Oh. Oh! The fuzz."

Irritated Jim snapped, "I'm a conservation warden. Is that your car?"

There was no answer as they walked to the car and began to unlock it.

Jim asked, "How about a ride down to the park office?" Thinking, *I've Got to stay near them somehow.*

The spokesman replied, "It's my car and I'm not going back into the park. It closes at eleven o'clock. We were chased out earlier. Besides its got loud pipes. The police told us earlier if we come back after hours or with these pipes, I'm pinched."

"But with me along no one will bother you. In fact you will be assisting a law enforcement officer. It's over a mile back to the park headquarters. A long walk in the dark. You won't be arrested, I promise that. Come on. How about a ride?"

"Well, okay. We'll drop you off and then head for our motel. Remember you promised no trouble."

Jim got in the back seat. The three young men squeezed into the front. Entering the park, the stillness of the night was shattered by the roar and backfires of the old car. Thoughts tumbled through Jim's mind, *My God. If that guy is anywhere around, he will recognize the rapping of these pipes. He may come out.*

After a quarter mile, there was a loud hysterical shout in the brush near the road. "Stop. Stop!" The driver braked sharply and the car bucked almost to a stop. Suddenly realizing what was going on, he accelerated again. he car jumped jerkily ahead.

Realizing what was happening, Jim yelled at the top of his lungs at the driver. "Stop this car. Stop this damned car right now," he raged at the driver. Intimidated, the driver slewed the vehicle to a halt. A tall, slim young man lunged wildly out of the thick brush at the edge of the road. He was completely disheveled, hair flying wildy, face a mirror of terror, blood oozing brightly from the corners of his mouth. His arms at the shoulders were torn and bleeding. The prickly ash had done its job well. Bolting wildly toward the car, his momentum carried him solidly into the side of the car with a thud that rocked the car.

Babbling and shouting like a wild man, he screeched, "Let me in, quick! The police are after me. Quick open the door."

Baffled the three men in the front seat were unable to respond in any way. They sat mute. Jim, alone in the rear of the two door car was frustrated, unable to do much. Shuffling forward on the seat, he yelled at the fat man at the passenger door. "Let him in. Open the door." As the door opened Jim attempted to push the seat and the man forward enough for the apparition to enter.

He urged, "Quick get in. Get in before they catch you."

146   *The Race*

The man pushing and scrambling to gain passage, shouted, "For God's sake, will you guys let me in and get the hell out of here? They'll catch me for sure."

Jim gestured him forward, "Come. Hurry up get in." Pushing the seat and the fat man as far forward as possible as he urged, insistently, "Quick. Come over the top. Hurry. Hurry up man!"

The encouragement and the man's panic drove further reason from his mind as he began to crawl over the top. Then, he hesitated and stopped. Incredulous eyes widening, staring at the badge. His committment had doomed him. Hands on the top of the seat, he could not retreat. Jim grabbed him by the wrists. Lunging desperately backwards, hurtling him over the fat man into the back seat. Twisting, Jim rolled him with a thud to the floor behind the driver.

Struggling desperately, spitting invectives, he screamed, "What the hell did you guys do to me? How did he get in your car? I'll kill all of you for this. I can't believe you would let me get in the car with a dumb cop."

Holding desperately on to his wrists, Jim spat back as he rolled heavily on top of him, "I'm not a dumb cop. I'm a game warden." Turning to the driver he shouted, "Now move this damn thing."

The three in the front seat went into a secretive huddle, hushed words were spoken of throwing the damn warden out and beating the hell out of him.

Jim thought. *Oh, oh. could be in trouble here. A little outnumbered. Don't let them dwell on the subject.* Reacting desperately now, Jim yelled directly over the back seat into the driver's ear, "Damn it! I said move this car. I mean it. Do it now or you will all end up in jail!"

Visibly shaken the driver heaved a huge sigh, "The hell with it. We're in enough trouble now."

Letting the car drift down the hill, he accelerated slowly. Jim holding the spitting, biting struggling, swearing man on the floor directed them to the headquarters. There they were met by the other wardens and chief park policeman Jack Allan.

Jim released a sigh of relief. "Jack take this guy out and for God's sake cuff him. We don't want to chase him again."

Jack, grabbing the man by the wrists as Jim slowly released him, quickly put the cuffs on. "What's your name?"

"None of your damn business." Without another word Jack shoved him against the wall and searched him. Wallet in hand, Jack slowly studied it, "Well Joe, guess you won't have to tell us your name." Glancing to the other policemen as he hustled Joe into the nearby squad, he asked, "Will you take him to jail?"

As the squad left, Jim shook his head in bewilderment. Clapping his hand on Jack's shoulder he asked, "What the hell is this all about? What's he wanted for?"

Jack laughed. "You mean you caught this guy and you didn't even know what he had done?"

"Yeah. I guess so. What did he do?"

"All I know is that he broke loose from one of the park policemen who was about to book him in the park office." Turning to Warden Harley Lictenwalner, Jack asked, "Do you know what happened?"

"Yeah. Evidently a park policeman responded to a call from the park office. The call was from a man in one of the cottages who said this guy was drinking and had molested his daughter. On the way out to the place, he spotted the man walking one of the roads and grabbed him. He also had beer in his possession. He brought him back to the park office to book him and when entering the door the man bolted and ran."

Turning to Don with a grin, Jim commented, "Looks like you're loosing a little steam. Thought sure you would catch him at first. Got to set a better example than that if you're ever going to be chief warden."

Don grinned, "Hell. I didn't do too bad in that race. I came in second."

In spite of his shortcomings, Don did become chief warden in 1974 where he served until his retirement in 1983.

Chapter 17

Bob

It was without a sense of destiny that Saturday evening of May 7, 1966 that District warden Bob Markle and Special warden Leo Stecker hid their state vehicle in an old tote road near the Bass Lake landing in northeastern Price County. Acting on a complaint of illegal Walleye spearing as they had many times before, the two settled down to a night of tedious waiting. There would be soft talk and coffee drinking to pass the lonely cold hours in this muted wilderness area. This night would be different as fate would step in to alter history and lives.

Bob, a 30-year veteran, in accepting a promotion had recently moved from Mellen south to Park Falls to command a three county area. Bob was a man among men. Known statewide as a good field warden who applied good judgement to a strict enforcement program, his contagious sense of humor and hearty body-shaking laugh carried him through many trying situations.

Leo, generally a deceivingly quiet reserved fishery technician, was quick to laugh - especially when relating his fishing exploits. Because Bob, was short handed and Leo had special warden credentials, he rode along to assist him this fateful night.

The muted conversation centered on Bob's upcoming retirement, which could be within a year. He voiced second thoughts about leaving a career and job that had become his love of life. He quietly spoke the thoughts of many wardens. Their family relationships suffered because of dedication to a job that controlled one's life. The job took time he could be spending with his devoted wife, Arlene and two children, Marilyn and John. He related he would like to have the time to visit his brother Stuart, a game warden stationed at Anaconda, Montana, and pursue his many hobbies. As only wardens can do, the conversation made the long cold hours short.

Suddenly the inky blackness was pierced by the blinding bright lights of a car moving down the desolate landing road. Squinting to allow his eyes to focus in the new brightness, Bob gently sat his coffee cup on the dashboard, picked up his binoculars and gently stepped out the car door. "Looks like we've got business Leo. Hmm it's just a little after midnight just as Joe said." Raising the binoculars, he scanned to pick up a vehicle license number. It was difficult as the plate light was out, and the plate was mud spattered. Concentrating on the plate he waited for the light carrying figures darting around the car to illuminate it. "Ah, got it. Leo I think I know one guy. It's John Johnson, I'm sure that's his station wagon." Several minutes later, a muted police radio confirmed Bob's identification. The stillness was violated by the scraping of a metal boat on gravel and the slight riffling of water as the boat entered.

Lowering his binoculars, Bob whispered, "They had the boat stashed in the brush near the landing."

Suddenly the darkness was broken by a strange eerie glow emanating from below the water surface. "Underwater light, " mused Bob, "they'll get a lot of fish. A lot of walleyes were on the gravel beds yesterday." As the light played out into the gravel spawning areas where the walleyes lay so vulnerable to the five tined spear, the spear handler stood upright and began plucking the flopping giants into the boat where they lay splashing and thumping.

Both wardens, accomplished fishermen, were repulsed by the irresponsible act being played out before them. "Don't take much of this to deplete a lake this size of walleyes," snorted Leo. ""God, I hate to see this. Look at the big females they're taking. Not many of those in a lake like this!"

Bob concentrated, his binoculars on the boat as it made a complete circuit of the small lake. "We'll get them Leo, they've got a ton of fish. Ah, they're coming in. Wait for my signal."

The harsh scraping noise intruding on the silence of the primitive setting seemed unbearably loud as the metal boat was pulled up onto the gravel landing.

The wardens waited as again the two silent men darted around the car carrying and placing things in it. Bob from his broad experience, giving full consideration as to how the court or a jury would view the case and how best the evidence and contraband might successfully be seized, held off. His experience in the past years commanded his thoughts. The courts were quick to throw out game cases. Lack of physical evidence or a small mistake in interrogation could doom a case. *Should we go now? No, they may throw a lot of evidence and worse vanish into the woods. Johnson is a slippery one. If he gets away it will set back resource protection years in this area. The court system's not too good right now. I'll wait till they're completely loaded before we jump them. We'll have them good.* ""Time to move up Leo, take it slow and easy. I'll take this side you take the other. Don't turn your light on till I do."

The stalk began. Suddenly the starter rotated the motor into life, the area was flooded by light as the car lights came on. Taken by surprise, the two jumped off the road edge. Bob whispered, "Let's get up there Leo, right now." A few swift strides brought him to the driver's side of the car. Disappointed, he realized both spearers were inside. Johnson furtively glanced toward Bob. Desperately reaching both front and back, he hastily locked the doors. Bob could see his mouth moving through the glass as he told the other man to lock his doors.

Turning on his large flashlight Bob shone it directly at Johnson's pale face. In a loud voice, he announced, "We're conservation wardens, open the door Johnson. You are under arrest for spearing walleyes." Seeing the indecision on Johnson's face, he commanded, "Get out of the car, now."

Johnson jerking his head from side to side in a desperate manner sized up his chances of escape. The tic in his pale cheek betrayed his fear and frustration. The decision was quickly made. Without speaking, he jerked the shift lever into drive and jammed the accelerator to the floor. Wheels spun throwing gravel in the lake as the car careened forward. Leo, directly in front of the car, taken completely by surprise jumped for his life. His wildly swinging left arm hit the radio antenna as the car barely missed him. The antenna dropped in the road.

Behind the car, a frustrated Bob unsnapped and drew his revolver. Held high, the gun roared twice in warning. Bob hoped the driver would stop, but the car continued to accelerate in a cloud of dust. A crack shot and a twice-wounded veteran of four World War II campaigns in Europe, Bob could have terminated the escape. Because of his temperament and law enforcement training he was not quick to endanger human life. He chose therefore other methods of apprehension more dangerous to the wardens. Sprinting toward his car, Bob shouted, "Come on Leo."

The starter was spinning the motor as Leo jumped into the car. There was no time to fasten the seat belts. Throwing twin geysers of debris, the car lurched forward in dusty pursuit. A veteran of many dusty chases, Bob knew the dangers present as he pressed hard through the blinding dust. Rubber burning and gravel flying they pursued attempting to gain on the car. A mile and a half from the lake, Bob navigated the left turn onto Bass Lake road. The taillights of the staion wagon were faintly visible ahead through the boiling dust.

Setting his jaw, Bob with exteme faith in the high powered pursuit vehicle he was driving pushed the accelerator hard. The danger was there and Bob was aware of it. Yet the many years of law enforcement would not allow him to break off the chase. The unwritten creed of law enforcement to continue was fulfilled. Bob knew if one violator gets away many more will run. With motor screaming the car hit an unexpected large frost boil common to the spring breakup. The car careened violently out of control to the left and into the muddy bank. Bob felt the sickening spin, but didn't realize he had been thrown from the car. It was over for Bob. He never knew he was pinned under the car.

Leo felt the dizzying spin as the car flipped twice endwise. The windsield exploded. Shattered glass and gravel sprayed inside raining off him like shotgun pellets. Movement finally stopped. Dazed, conscious, but severely injured, Leo found himself half way out of the upside down rear window which had popped out. Scared, dazed and bleeding, Leo groped and crawled slowly out on the hard cold gravel. Staggering dazedly to his feet, he attempted to gather his thoughts. *What happened? Where am I?* Slowly realization returned. *My God, I'm hurt — and bad. Where's Bob?* Weaving, feeling his way along the car in the total darkness, he squinted to focus his eyes on a figure slightly protruding from beneath the windshield and roof of the upside down squad. "God, that's Bob." Dropping weakly to his knees, he struggled desperately to extract his inert friend. Slowly realization seeped into his mind. *I think he's dead. Can't get him loose.* Feeling blindly in the darkness that suddenly seemed much colder and darker, he located Bob's arm. Feeling for a pulse confirmed his wildest fear. *He's dead!*

Stumbling around in a fog and knowing Bob was dead brought further confusion. *What do I do? The radio. Got to get help.* Again feeling his way along the car, he crawled under the space between the hood and the windshield. Groping inside with his hand, he located the radio mike. After several attempts, he realized the radio was smashed and beyond use.

He tried gathering his thoughts as he stood. *Got to get help. Bob dead.* It was hard to accept in spite of the evidence at hand. Glancing desperately around in the inky blackness that suddenly seemed even darker, Leo's glance riveted on the illusion of a house down the road. His heart jumped. *Could it be. Is help at hand?* Weaving forward toward this illusion in his confused state, and not sure if he was dreaming he was rewarded as he squinted to focus on the farm house. Spirit lifting, pace quickening, the thought of help nearby buoyed him the short distance to the house door.

The pounding on the door brought a welcome light and a sleepy-eyed young man in pajamas to the door. "What do you want? Do you realize it 's ten minutes to two?" Wiping the sleep from his eyes and centering his gaze on Leo' s distraught bloody face, he said, "My God man you're hurt. What happened to you?"

"G-Got to have help, Bob's dead. You got a phone?"

"Just take it easy. Did you have an accident?"

"Why— yes - we did. Bob-Bob Markle's dead." Pointing up the road. "Up the road a ways."

"You mean the game warden?"

"Yeah, a phone, you got a phone?"

"No, we don't, come on in. I'll take you to one. Just let me put on some clothes."

Within ten minutes, Leo was talking to the sheriff's office from a nearby farm.

Returning to the scene, he was soon transported by ambulance to the Park Falls hospital with severe lacerations of the head and five broken ribs.

Immediate responders from Phillips were Sheriff Paul Gehring, State Highway Patrolman LeRoy Larson and Warden Howard (Howie) DeBriyn. With Howie in charge, the area was soon filled with wardens from the northwest area and elsewhere assisting in the investigation.

Evidence was picked up through a step by step search along the escape route from Bass Lake. A number of walleyes, spears, an underwater light and a wet storage battery were found. Johnson's car was found at a house in Butternut. Meeting physical resistance from the occupant of the house, resident warden, Donald Nimmer impounded the car and had it towed to the sheriff's office in Phillips. There it was searched and sent to the crime laboratory at Madison for a further evidence search. Walleye slime and scales were found. Battery acid was identified as the substance that ate a large hole in the back seat.

After an extensive search, John Johnson was found in Park Falls and arrested. Charged with resisting a consevation warden, failure to stop for an emergency vehicle, possession of a spear, possession of walleyed pike during the closed season and transportation of walleyed pike during the closed season, Johnson pled not guilty and posted a bond of $250.

Eventually with the search of Johnson's auto ruled an illegal search by the court, these charges were dismissed. The other man involved in the

Bob

incident was never identified.

A fine man and his family paid the supreme price to protect Wisconsin's natural resources. Lost was the quick smile, the hearty laugh. Lost was a good man to walk the trail with, a man to have with you when the chips were down, a man among men. Remaining are his family and friends who will long remember Bob. An editorial in the Park Falls Herald on May 12, 1966 written by Publisher Bill Schwenler is appropriate as Bob's Eulogy:

"It is never an easy matter to lose a friend, it is much harder when that friend is a person who you must always look up to, look up because of the way he conducted his work and his friendship, and that is why you probably wait until that person is gone, wait until it is too late to let that person know just how you felt about him.

Such is the case with Bob Markle, barring none, one of the finest game wardens and warm human beings I have ever chanced to meet. Bob has made my job a much easier job in the short time he was with us. Bob always had the time and pleasant manner to straighten me out on any conservation matters when I needed help.

He was a man, the type of which all other men would have to be judged against, never angry, never mean. He was a man with a tremendous understanding of the other person, understanding which all of us could use more of.

But ahead of all this was the Warden Bob Markle. A professional man with a professional purpose about his work. A public relation director for the entire law enforcement branch of the Wisconsin Conservation Department, a fair man and a just law officer.

I have talked many hours with Bob, and never have I gone away from one of our discussions without feeling a little bit better about. . . well just about everything. His constant smile, his bit of wisdom, never failed to raise your depressed spirits. And yet many times he never knew how much good he had done for someone else.

The death of Bob Markle has taken from us a good warden, a great man. But from his family it has taken much more, and it's to them that I now express my own deep sorrow, and hope they understand that I too have lost an unreplaceable friend. One that will add meaning to my life and a pattern for my life for as long as it shall be lived.

It is appropriate for people and especially young wardens, visiting Ashland County to search out and find Markle Road (named in his honor) just west of Mellen. Stop here in the area Bob loved and meditate a minute on one of the giants in Natural Resource Protection who broke many trails for us.

Junk Yard Venison

Jim sat comfortably reading a Field and Stream magazine on a cold December evening of 1957, enjoying the comfort as only a game warden can who has put in long cold hours for days and months on end with little sleep or human comforts. Finally, the cherished rest of winter had arrived.

The ringing of the phone broke the lazy luxurious spell. Still in a daze from the total relaxation, Jim stocking footed to the phone.

Columbia County Sheriff's department dispatcher Jack Tessman's voice was apologetic, "Jim, there is a guy we picked up for vagrancy up here who wants to talk to you. He's kind of funny, retarded or something. Didn't know if I should have called you or not. Claims he knows of some game violations. It's up to you."

"God Jack. I hate to come out. I was ready to hit the sack. Oh well, I'll come up. It probably won't take long. See ya."

Arriving at the Columbia County Jail in Portage, Jim was immediately ushered into an interrogation cell by Jack.

"Jim, this is Elliot Richardson. Claims he's from Dellwood in Adams County. One of our officers picked him up hitchhiking on Highway 33 near Cambria. Stated he's walking from Fox Lake to Dellwood."

Thus Jim met Elliot Richardson setting into motion a string of strange events.

Elliot was short and slight, wearing disheveled mismatched clothing that was torn, dirty and generally worn out. His shoes were mismatched and he had no socks or shoe strings. His bare ankles revealed that he was wearing no underwear. His light overall type coat had one button. The red wind-whipped areas on his ankles, wrists and hands revealed that he had suffered from the cold. Still shivering either from the earlier cold or the nervousness he felt in these strange surroundings, voice weak and trembling he addressed Jim. "I - I'm sorry to bo - bother you but I really have something to tell you - if you'll listen?"

"Okay Elliot. I came down here to see what you have to say. I'll listen. But first is that all the clothing you have?"

"Ye - yeah. I It's off the junk pile. Y-you know the city dumps."

"Well tell me Elliot what brought you to this state of affairs? No money, no clothes and locked up in jail."

"I - I wa - was trying to get home. My mother lives in northern Adams County. She will help me if I can get there."

"Elliot why don't you start at the beginning and tell me just how you ended up like this."

"O - Okay. You know I've been in trouble all my life. I did hard time in Waupun about ten years ago. Got caught playing with a little girl. You know. Guess they called it rape. Got caught right here in Portage. Stole a car up in Adams County and drove through here. Ran out of gas on the south end of town. W - went to the Portage Police Department for help. They got me some gas. Right after I took off they realized I had a stolen car. They came after me. Never really had a full-time job. But anyway when I got out of jail I was on probation. Got in more trouble. Finally the probation department ordered me to work for Larry Marvin. He owns a junkyard at Fox Lake. Worked for him a year now. He's a big black man. I'm scared of him. He beats the hell out of me. He's always pounding on me. L - look at my face. Look here under my shirt." Pulling his shirt open he displayed large black and blue marks.

Jim was astonished at the sight. It was obvious the man had been repeatedly beaten. "Why does he beat you Elliot?"

"H - He beats on me for anything. If I don't work fast enough or long enough. He pounded me up a couple times for talking to the cops about things he does. I hope he doesn't find out I'm talking to you."

"Don't worry, I won't tell him. What kind of things does he do that I should know about?"

"I - I'm afraid to talk about them."

"Well, okay. What kind of work does Marvin do?"

"Oh, oh. He picks up junk all over the country with an old truck. I go along. He makes me do most of the loading. If I can't lift something heavy he kicks the B - Jesus out of me. If he thinks I didn't work hard enough he won't feed me for a few days."

"You mean you depend on him for food? Why don't you buy your own or leave?"

"Can't do that, the court ordered me to stay with him and do as he tells me. Th - that was the time they fixed me up. They did an operation on me. You know, so I won't bother girls. He never pays me anything. That's why I have to pick my clothes off the dump. Food too sometimes. Sometimes he just beats me because he likes too. Don't tell him I've talked to you."

"We'll make sure he doesn't find out. Now what was it you wanted to tell me?"

"Y - you are sure he - that is - you won't tell him? A - Ah, will you sort of protect me if I tell you?"

"Yeah, we'll protect you. Don't worry. Just go ahead and tell me what's bothering you."

Shakily, he proceeded. "W - well he's got venison. Larry has." He paused and gazed around as if to see if others were listening.

Jim reassured him in a firm even voice. "Go ahead Elliot. It's okay. We are alone here."

He began again, his voice firmer, "Well, I told you we sort of tour this whole area looking for junk in that old enclosed truck. When we see deer, he shoots them and makes me gut and load them and cover them with junk." His voice sounded more firm now. His demeanor calmer. "He has a bunch of venison over at Fox Lake right now. It's in a chicken coop at the junk yard. He sells it in Chicago to his renters. He has several tenement houses there. The meat he has on hand is spoiled. He took it to Chicago, but could not sell it because he had not taken care of it. It's in some barrels in the chicken coop. He's feeding it to the chickens. Do you believe me?"

"Yeah, guess I do. I'll go over first thing tomorrow morning and take a look."

His face lighted up. "Y - You are really going to check my story out?"

"Yes, first thing tomorrow morning."

"You know, Jim, I've told police officers things that Larry was doing. Never once did they believe me and check him out."

With a wave, Jim walked out of the interragation room. "I'll stop by and let you know how we make out tomorrow."

Reaching home, he thought of the way Elliot had acted and of the information received. *Don't know if I should believe him or not. Seemed awfully scared of Marvin. Haven't seen Bingo in a long time anyway.* With that thought he picked up the phone and called Mel (Bingo) Lange the warden at Waupan.

At 8 o'clock the following day the two wardens met at the small village of Fox Lake. After discussing the story told by Richardson the two decided to try for a search of the junkyard without a warrant because it would be hard to get a search warrant on the word of Richardson. The two drove over to the yard in Bingo's station wagon. Getting out of the car near an office type building, the wardens were looking around wondering how to proceed when a large black man about 6 foot 6 inches tall weighing about 275 pounds came out of the office building.

"Hi fellows. Is there something wrong?" Looking back and forth at the uniforms and badges, he appeared puzzled. He leveled his gaze on Jim. "You aren't police, who are you?"

"We're conservation wardens. We have a complaint that you have some illegal venison on your premises."

Taken aback, the snapping of the dark eyes reveled anger. "You guys are way off in coming here. There is no venison here."

Mel stepped forward. "Then you wouldn't mind if we looked things over?"

"No. You can't look. I don't believe you have the authority to do that. You need a search warrant."

Mel explained. "We can get a search warrant if you like. One of us will stay here till we get it issued to make sure you don't do away with any evidence."

"Well go ahead and look around then."

With the consent, the wardens looked in the office and around junk piles while working their way toward their real objective - the chicken coop.

Stepping up on the step of the coop, Jim was blocked by the huge shape of Marvin. "Stop right there. This is as far as you're going without a warrant." His eyes were ablaze now as they gazed down on Jim.

"Looks like this is the place where the evidence is Marvin. I guess you can stop us but you know as sure as God made little green apples we'll be back and with a warrant. I know there's venison in there we will get it one way or another."

"Well damn it, go ahead then." Upon entering the chickens flew in

156   *Junk Yard Venison*

fear and raised dust to the point where the one window was not furnishing enough light to continue the search. Standing still to let the dust settle, Jim was astonished at what he saw. Sitting in an old rickety rocking chair in the middle of the coop among the frightened chickens was an aged man peering back through the dust.

"What is this Marvin? Who's that man and what's he doing here?"

"None of your damn business. Make your search and get the hell out of here."

Jim appoached the dust covered old man looking as old as Methusalah. "Hello. Who are you?" It was as if he couldn't hear. Staring straight ahead, he said nothing.

Off to the side, Mel called in a loud voice. "Jim come here. Found some venison.

Jim moved to the open steel barrel that Mel was staring into.

"Look in here. The barrel is about half full of meat. Reaching into the barrel, he picked several hairs off the meat and holding them up toward the light of the open door he broke them in half. "Venison all right. We better look at the rest of these barrels." Metal covers were removed to reveal meat in all of the five barrels in the coop. Mel replaced the last cover. "Let's just roll all of them out of here so we can see better."

Marvin was gallant now, realizing there wasn't much he could do to avoid what was to follow. "Looks like you guys have the goods on me. Here let me help with the barrels."

With the barrels outside they could be examined more closely. All were dumped in an area where the wardens cleared most of the snow away and placed a large piece of plastic tarp. The result was a large pile of partly frozen cut up meat. It was impossible to determine how many deer had been killed to make the pile. The wardens picked out 27 pieces with legs on them.

Mel backed the car down to the piles.

"Looks like we've got a minimum of 7 deer here. You agree, Marvin?"

"Guess I can't argue with you. Now what?"

Mel reached into the car for his citation book. "We're going to charge you with the illegal possession of untagged venison." Writing in the book, he continued, "You'll have to come to Juneau with us where you will be taken before the Justice of the Peace."

Jim interrupted, "Before we go to Juneau we want to make sure we've got all the venison you have. I understand you have four houses here in town. Do you have any venison in any of them?"

"No. You've got it all. You can look if you like."

"I believe we should look Bingo."

Throwing the venison into the back of Mel's station wagon on the plastic, the three proceeded to Marvin's home. A complete search was made. There were 3 old people living in the basement of his home. A slop jar covered with a piece of plywood served as a toilet. The odor was putrid. When questioned, the old people would not reply to any questions.

Thinking this strange, Jim as they mounted the cellar steps questioned Marvin. "Larry what's going on with these old people down there. Do they live down there?"

"I told you guys before, you can search for venison but anything else on my property is my business."

Mel stumbled on the last step, almost falling into the living room. "Look Larry something else bothers me here. What are all those TV sets, stoves and furniture doing in your basement. Do you own them?"

"Will you guys just shut up and get on with the search?"

Jim's glance covered all accoutrements in the living room. "Boy Larry, you sure have a lot of nice guns in that big gun case. You must do a lot of hunting?"

"None of your business. Get on with the search and let's get the hell out of here."

Always a real gun enthusiast, Jim started toward the guncase.

Mel intoned from the front door. "Come on Jim, this place is clean."

Searching the other three houses, the wardens found renters on the first floor and three to four old people in the basement of each. Each basement was as cold, dank and dark as the first. All the old people were dressed in rags, using buckets as slop jars. Each basement had the same stench. None would speak to the wardens. It was if they were prisoners and afraid to speak with Marvin present. Every basement had large stockpiles of TV sets, stoves, refrigerators, freezers and other household furniture and appliances.

Marvin was extremely quiet while being transported to Juneau. When asked to plead to the charges brought against him, he pled guilty. Because he could not pay the fines for release, he was committed to the Dodge County jail in Juneau.

Jim and Mel talked over the strange case over coffee in a Fox Lake restaurant. They agreed that the piles of household furniture and appliances must be stolen, especially because of the way Marvin reacted when they were discussed. The old people living in the basements were a real mystery. Again, they agreed all was not right with what they had seen. Mel said he would talk to Dodge County Sheriff Schultz about it.

Upon his return to Portage that evening Jim again stopped to talk to Richardson. "Well Elliot you were right. We got Marvin with the meat. It was right where you said it was."

A look of disbelief rushed across his face. "Y - you mean you actually pinched him?"

"Yep, he's in the Dodge County Jail."

"B - But I've been telling the police about him for years and they'd never believe me."

"Did what you were telling the police have anything to do with all those household appliances he has in his houses?"

Elliot was pensive and quiet. Finally the words came weak and trembling from his lips. "I'm going to tell you all about Marvin. I trust you. Maybe it's time someone stopped what he's doing. You know all those cabin break ins that have been going on around here. Well he's the one. He's stealing all that stuff." Now the words were coming fast and sure, tumbling out of his mouth as though it was a great relief to unload. "Just last week he emptied a cabin along the Fox River."

Jim interrupted, "Was that on Highway F just north of the Marquette County line?"

"Yeah that's the place."

"How do you know he broke into the cabin?"

"Because I was along. Sometimes he makes me break in."

"Okay. Go on Elliot."

"About a month ago, he broke into a cabin on X on the Neenah Creek."

Again, Jim checked his story. "What was taken from the cabin?"

"Let's see now. There was a refrigerator, TV set, a brown davenport and chair, and 2 table sets. There was more but that's all I can remember."

It was obvious he was telling the truth because Jim knew of these break ins and his story fit. "Do you know of others Elliot. If so, tell me about them."

Break in after break in was related. Some Jim knew about, others he didn't. After about a half hour of this, Jim excused himself and left the room. Convinced that Elliot was telling the truth, he quickly called Sheriff Walter Geophert. Upon Walt's arrival and after a short discussion he took him into the interrogation room with Elliot. "Elliot, this is Sheriff Walter Geophert. He's a good man and will listen to you. Why don't you tell him of all those break ins."

Walt picked it up smoothly. "Yes, Elliot we will work on this with you. Jim says he believes what you've been telling him We work together a lot. Would you tell me about the break ins?"

"No - No. Jim, can I talk to you alone, please? D - Don't ask me to do this."

Seeing the response Walt arose. "Come out in the hall a moment Jim."

In the hall, a short discussion was held. It was decided they had better take advantage of the trust Elliot had for Jim.

"Okay Walt. You go on home. I'll just write down everything and give you the information tomorrow."

Jim walked nonchalantly back into the room with Elliot. "Evidently I made a mistake. You don't want to talk with Walt."

"N-No. I'm really scared of sheriffs and besides they never would believe me before. Why should I talk to them now?"

Jim consoled him. "Walt went home. I won't do that to you again. Will you tell me more of what Marvin has been up to?"

Nervous, trembling shakily, he began again relaying his story. As time went on, he again regained his composure and the words came swift and strong.

Thus began an interrogation that lasted until the first blush of dawn. Story after story of break ins, theft and the killing of deer were related. The scheme was always the same. Marvin with Elliot as his slave toured parts of the counties picking up junk. The acetylene torch they carried was effectively used to cut up articles to large to load. There were many instances where farmers usable machinery was cut up in out of the way places, hauled away, and sold as junk. Nearly 200 cabin break ins were related covering large parts of Columbia, Adams, Sauk, Green Lake, and Marquette counties. Both

Jim and Elliot were completely exhausted as the morning sun streamed through the east facing window.

Jim, picking up his reams of notes, ended the interrogation. "Is there anything else you should tell me Elliot?"

"W - Well y - yes. Larry also stole the game wardens' rifles."

Jim spun toward him excitement showing in his features. "What. When did this happen?" The previous deer season Jim's and his special warden's rifles had been stolen out of his car. Jim had been very angry about it as his was an antique rifle he'd received from his father. He had thought it stolen at the police station as it was the only time his auto was left unlocked. He had spent about 10 minutes at the station sending his daily deer season reports. The rifles were found to be missing the following morning.

"I - It was last deer season."

"Where? Damn it, that sounds like our rifle's."

"Y-you know where the levee runs west of Portage along County O. Right where the levee begins. Right there."

Jim recalled. They had indeed stopped to check some hunters who were shooting in the woods at that location near the end of hunting hours and left the car for about a half hour.

Elliot described the car even to the spotlight with a red lens.

"But, Elliot, the car was locked. How did he get our rifles in such a short time?"

"H - he just used his ring of keys he carries from junk cars until he got it open. Grabbed the rifles, relocked the car and left."

Jim was convinced now. "Good thing he didn't dig through all that gear in the back seat cause he missed my 10 gauge double magnum and my Model 50 Winchester auto shotgun. Where are the rifles now? Have they been sold?"

"The one was sold but the other one was very different from the other rifles so Larry kept it for his own. It's in his gun cabinet in his house."

Jim choked off an oath. "You mean when we searched yesterday my rifle was in that big guncase?"

"Yep."

"I damn near looked that case over. Hell I would have spotted my rifle anywhere."

Jim was enraged at the turn of events. He no longer felt like going home to sleep. He considered going right back to Fox Lake to look for his rifle. He had the dispatcher call Juneau. Marvin had paid his fine and been released.

Soon Sheriff Geophert arrived at the jail. Jim gave him the volumious notes he had taken. "Hell Walt, let's go over there and grab all that stuff we saw piled in his houses. "

Walt disagreed, "Look Jim, this looks like a big deal. It involves more than one county. We really should get a warrant to search those houses. We should involve all the sheriffs and DAs in this if it's to come off right."

"Guess you're right Walt. I'm pooped. Will you make contact with the counties and line this thing up. I'm going home to sleep."

Jim kept calling Walt the next several days. Getting the district attorneys and sheriffs together from five counties was difficult. Eventually a search warrant was issued by Dodge County to look for all the stolen goods in Marvin's homes.

Five sheriffs from Adams, Marquette, Columbia, Sauk and Green Lake counties descended on Fox Lake, along with Warden Bill Barton who had rode along with Sheriff Serles from Adams and Jim. The search was no surprise. Marvin gracefully ushered all from one house to another. All were clean. Not a single item was left in any of the houses. Jim's rifle was not to be found. It was determined that Marvin had made several trips to Chicago with his big truck. Dejectedly, all returned home.

Several days later Elliot was released from the Columbia County jail. He called Jim and asked if he would take him to Fox Lake to pick up his belongings. While he didn't have much, it was all he had in the world. Jim called Bill Barton as Elliot lived in his area. Bill agreed to go with Jim to recover Elliot's few worldly belongings.

Before they could get out of their car, pulling into the junkyard, Marvin came charging like a bull toward their car, "What the hell are you guys doing here? I've had enough of the whole bunch of you and, Elliot, if you get out of that car, I'll kick your brains out."

The wardens, prepared for such a reception, bailed out of the car and quickly faced Marvin. They thought the two of them would deter any violence. Wrong again. He charged straight at Jim grabbing him by the throat. Not to be undone Jim grabbed for Marvin's throat. Around and around they went on the icy ground, slipping and sliding and hanging on, each trying to choke the other off. Marvin hovered over Jim and it was just a matter of time before his size and strength would overcome him.

Bill drew his gun and grasping it by the barrel slid around the grappling pair trying to bust Marvin. "Hold him Jim! Hold him!"

Finally, both tired of the simulated Russian dance they had been performing, as though by signal stopped and backed off. Gasping, they faced each other trying to get their breath.

Marvin croaked, "What you guys want anyway?"

Bill gave Jim a chance to catch his breath. "All we want is Elliot's clothing and things."

"All right damn it. Pick his junk up and get out of here." Turning, he shook his finger at Elliot. "Damn you, you stay in that car, and don't let me ever see you again, or you know what will happen."

Standing off to the side like a wounded bear, he stared at the two wardens as they entered the little tarpaper shack where Elliot had lived. Quickly, while keeping a weather eye out the small window in case Marvin tried to approach Elliot, they cleaned out the few items of clothing scattered around stuffing them unceremoniously into a flour sack. They were about to leave when Jim spotted a small 6 inch shotgun chambered for .410 gauge. They hurried outside.

Jim had the gun in his hand. Pulling the shell out, he waved the gun at Marvin. "Is this your's?"

"You damn right that's mine. What are you doing with it?"

"This is an illegal firearm Marvin and I'm taking it to the Fox Lake police. They will hold it for the FBI."

"Damn you guys, you're just harassing me. You can't legally take that gun. I'll have you charged with stealing it."

He was raging and swearing when the three left the yard. Barely had they hit the street when Marvin's black Cadillac swung in behind them, riding their tailgate all the way to the police department. Both cars stopped as one - inches apart.

The three went into the police department with Marvin stalking stiff-legged behind them.

Jim explained to the officer on duty where he had obtained the illegal gun and asked that they hold it for the FBI.

The officer was unsure of himself, especially with Marvin glowering at him. "I think I better call the Chief down to make sure this is okay."

Jim shrugged his shoulders. "Guess we can wait awhile for him." Looking around Jim noticed Marvin had disappeared. To break the silence, the officer asked if they would like coffee. All agreed it would go good. Drinking their coffee, they were surprised to see a middle-aged man enter the station. He nervously went right past them into a back office without speaking. More time passed as they waited for the Chief.

Soon he arrived and greeted everyone. "What's the problem?"

Jim began to brief him when the back office opened.

The old gentleman came forward toward Jim. "Are you Jim Chizek?"

"Why yes, who are you?"

"I'm Bill Jackson. I'm the justice of the peace here. I have a complaint for you. It charges that you stole Mr. Marvin's gun.

Jim was rankled. "Let me tell you about that gun. It's illegal to possess and, damn it, Marvin's not getting it back. As far as that complaint goes you can wipe your hindend with it. I'm turning the gun over to your chief here. He will hold it for the FBI. Is that okay with you chief?"

"Why yes. That is an illegal firearm under federal law. I'll hold it here." Glancing mischieveously at the justice, he continued, "Looks like you'll have to get rid of that complaint."

Nervously, the justice agreed. "Guess the gun really wasn't stolen. I'll tear it up." Walking nervously to a waste basket, he hurriedly shredded and dropped in the pieces. He continued out the door with Marvin stalking haughtily behind him. As the tension eased, all laughed at the strange happenings over another cup of coffee.

Having returned to Portage, the two wardens were discussing Elliot and what to do with him. Bill agreed to deliver him to his mother's home in Adams County. Stopping at Jim's house, they picked up a few of Jim's old clothes and gave them to Elliot even if they were much too large.

Jim peeled off a few greenbacks and handed them to Elliot. "Here, this will keep you going for awhile."

Bill then dipped and produced a like amount. "Come on Elliot. I'll take you home."

The next day, Jim stopped at the jail to tell of his experiences. He was chomping at the bit because he had lost his rifle. The deputies were joshing him about how smart he was being in the same room with his rifle and not

162

getting it back.

Jim retorted angerly, "That wise so and so may wake up some night and find his junkyard on fire."

It was a remark that would long be remembered. About a week later, the junkyard and all the buildings in it burned to the ground. The old man in the chicken coop almost burned up because he could neither walk nor talk. The fire department carried him out in his rocking chair.

Shortly after this, authorities acting on Jim's and Mel's complaint moved all the old persons living in Marvin's basements. They later related they were old-age pensioners who routinely turned their pension checks over to Marvin. He treated them like prisoners and beat them when necessaary to keep them from telling of their predicament. They were deathly afraid of him and until then would not speak out against him.

As to Elliot for many years he lived with his mother who cared for him. Bill stopped in often to see that things were going well for him. Many times he brought food, clothing and good cheer.

Chapter 19

Ode to Odie

Conservation warden Jim Chizek was called away from his lovely wife on a sparkling bright August day in 1962 by the Columbia County Sheriff's office dispatcher.

"Jim, this is Jack Tessman. We think we have a drowning on Lake Wisconsin. Would you assist us?"

"Sure. Where do you want me to go?"

"It happened near Bill's Lodge, so guess you could go down there and. . . ah just a minute. Bob Hamele wants to speak to you."

"Jim?"

"Yeah."

"This is Bob. Could you bring your boat and pick me up. We'll go down to the lake together."

"Sure. Where?"

"At home. I have a few things to pick up. Want to change clothes."

Leaving Portage enroute to the lake, Bob briefed Jim on what he knew of the incident. "It seems during the night one of Bill's rental boats drifted into shore near Tiperary Point. Empty beer cans, a gallon wine jug almost empty, and a bunch of set lines are scattered in the boat. There are no life preservers or lights aboard. Evidently someone already towed it back to Bill's Lodge. What do you make of it?"

"God, sounds like Odie Jackson. He's always out on the lake monkeying with illegal set lines. I've been trying to catch him for years. He's a real river rat. Knows the river like the back of his hand. Never uses a light and always takes a jug of wine with him."

Pulling into Bill's launching site, they were greeted by a small crowd gathered around a small wooden boat. Bill, the owner of the lodge, was thoughtfully inspecting the boat when Jim approached. "Morning Bill. Is this the boat that drifted in?"

"Yeah, about a mile downstream near Tiperary Point."

"Who did you rent it too?"

Nervously turning, Bill looked sheepishly away gazing at the river as though looking for the occupant downriver. "We - Well I don't remember."

"Look Bill this is more than a game law violation. I think Odie Jackson had this boat. I've known for years he rented boats from you to put out his illegal lines. This time it looks like Odie may be in the river."

Sighing with relief, Bill turned resignedly back to Jim. "You're right. Odie had the boat last night."

Bob stepped forward to question Bill. "What time did he pick up the boat?"

"About eight o'clock, but he didn't leave right away."

"What did he do?"

"He sat around in the bar awhile drinking beer."

"What time did he leave?"

"Oh about ten or ten thirty."

Continuing, Bob pointed at the empty beer containers and the capped wine jug which contained a small amount in one corner as it lay canted on the bottom of the boat. "Did he get that stuff here?"

"Yeah, he bought a six pack of beer and the gallon of wine before he left."

"Was he drunk?"

"Well, hard to tell with Odie. He could hold a lot. Never showed it."

"Did you give him a life perserver with the boat?"

"He just took the boat on his own. I was busy tending bar. Told him the perservers were in their little cabinet on the pier." Walking to the cabinet, Bill swung the door wide and systematically checked his preservers. "They're all here. Guess he didn't take one."

"I notice there's no motor on the boat. Did he rent one?"

"Naw. Odie never used a motor. Just rowed. He hated motors." Bob gestured with upraised palms to Jim. "What do you think?"

"I feel he's in the lake. Let's dump my boat in and look around."

Launching the boat at Bill's landing, the two were soon patroling slowly along the shore. They stopped often to quiz people along the shoreline who may have seen or heard something unusual. No one had noticed anything of any importance. Several newly laid setlines were found attached to deadheads and stumps in the area. Several fish were released as the lines were picked up.

Jim recognized the lines immediately as Odie's. The workmanship on them might as well have been Odie's signature. As they searched, they noticed a large white boat touring slowly around the area. After some time, they hailed it and asked the operator, a young man of between fifteen or sixteen if he had been on the lake the night before and if he had seen or heard anything unusual. The blond crew cut young man was very courteous, but his nervousness showed through. He said he had been on the lake but had seen nothing unusual. He then proceeded across the lake to his rental cabin. Both officers wondered why the young man was nervous. They put it off to being nervous while in contact with law officers.

After nothing of consequence developed, the search ended. Odie had not showed up at home. Jim and Bob were now convinced that Odie was in the lake. Both were experienced in recovering bodies from the Wisconsin River. They knew the body would lay on the bottom like a blanket until the body gasses made it buoyant. Without knowing where the drowning took place dragging for the body could not be done. They would wait for it to float. The warmer the weather, the sooner one could expect it to float, especially if the victim had been drinking beer as the evidence indicated.

At daybreak the following morning, Jim again picked Bob up. The two launched the boat as the early sunrise streamed over the hills east of the lake. The water was still as a mirror with just a faint fog wisping along the surface, dissipating like ghosts as the sunlight became stronger. Cranking the motor into life, Jim backed slowly out of Bill's boat slip. "What do you think Bob? Will he float today?"

"No don't think so. Too soon."

Jim turned the boat gently downstream as though reluctant to break the sheen of the silent lake. He shifted his body into a comfortable position to start the long search. Over and over they moved and stopped and glassed the smooth surface. Nothing unusual was spotted. Toward noon the lake picked up a small chop and made glassing difficult.

They were about to pull into Bill's landing to discontinue the search when a large white boat approached at a tremendous rate of speed. Slowing abrutly it settled deeply into its own wash, rose slowly on a large wave and was directed skillfully alongside their boat. Grasping the gunwales, the officers were surprised to see the young man they had talked to yesterday. His face was drawn and looked tired.

Jim greeted him. "Good morning Ken. How are you this morning?"

"Terrible. I've got to talk to you. Didn't sleep all night. Got to get this off my mind."

Gently, Jim directed the conversation. "Go ahead. Is it something about Odie?"

"Y-Yes. Don't know how to start."

"Just take it easy and start at the beginning."

"I - I think I drowned the man you are looking for. Saw you out here this morning. Finally decided I had to tell you what happened. My folks don't even know yet."

Jim's face showed compassion. He had two young sons of his own. He hoped they could be as courageous as this young man. "It's okay. Maybe it's not as bad as you think Did you hit his boat?"

"No - Didn't hit it but almost." His voice became stronger and firmer now as though a load was lifting as he shared his terrible secret knowledge. The words tumbled out. Neither officer interrupted. "I was running around the lake that night in the dark with this-my dad's boat. I was all over the lake and up and down the river many times. Around midnight I came over here in front of Bill's and made a couple of large circles. Suddenly it happened." His hands shakingly grasped the steering wheel as if to brace himself to finish the story. "I was going wide open when suddenly out of nowhere this boat appeared right in front of me. Didn't think I could miss it. It was so close in the darkness. I jerked the wheel and just missed. It seems I was inches away. I looked back as I passed and this skinny old man jumped to his feet in the boat. He stared hard at me and shook his fist. I think he swore at me. The motor noise - you know- couldn't hear. I didn't go back. I was too scared. I went right home. Couldn't sleep all night. I didn't see anything happen but the wave from my boat might have made the man fall out." Seeming very tired he stopped, dropped his hands from the wheel and stared blankly ahead. "That's all. What's going to happen to me?"

Bob grasped the gunwale of the other boat and slid the two together so he directly faced the boy. "Did you have your lights on."

166

"Yes."

"Did he show a light?"

"No."

"Do you know for sure the man fell out of the boat?"

"No - But he could have."

"Let's go over and tell your folks the whole story."

"Do we have to?"

"How old are you Ken?"

"'Fifteen."

"Well, I really believe they are entitled to know and I'm sure they will understand."

The contact with the parents was a rewarding experience. The middle-aged couple were very understanding and supportive of their son. They were quite proud that he had come forward as he had. It was decided that if what the young man had described was true Odie would be as much or more to blame than he.

Jim and Bob agreed to renew the search at sunup.

Again arriving at the golden time of day when the bright sunlight makes its first appearance, both officers enjoyed a small part of the natural environment. The sun warmed them pleasantly. Both were want to dally. The enjoyment must be briefly felt however as they realized the grim task they were about. Sliding the boat gently into the silent motionless lake both men silently reflected briefly on what they were doing.

Finally, Bob broke the warm silence. "Think we'll find him today?"

Jim allowed the boat to drift silently. He was still caught up in his thoughts. Finally shaking them off, he replied, "Wouldn't surpise me if he's up. With these warm temperatures and a belly full of beer, they float fast." Picking up the binoculars, Jim continued, "Let me look around before we do anything. Might spot him." Swinging the binoculars around, he slowly covered the glassy smooth surface of the lake along the shoreline from near to far downstream. Suddenly the swing stopped, swung quickly back and held steady.

Bob noticed the movements. "Got something Jim?"

"Yep - Think so. There's an extra stump in that stump patch near Tiperary Point. At least I don't remember it. It's about a mile from here. Let's run down there. I think he's up."

Both men were apprehensive now. It's always good to find a body and have the unpleasant affair over with. The actual happening however is always taxing. Somehow both knew as the boat sped downstream that the search was over. As the boat neared the floating object, Jim eased the throttle back and swung gently toward the object. Although neither mind wanted to accept it there was definitely a man floating face down arms outstretched as though reaching for invisible help or as in supplication to someone of a higher order than us mortals.

Jim slid the boat quietly beside the body and killed the motor.

"Okay Bob grab him." Reaching gingerly out of the boat, Bob grabbed the man's belt. The motion of the boat pulling the body gently through the water tipping the body enough to expose part of his face to Jim, who was watching intently.

"It's Odie all right. Guess he's all through setting lines. Grab the portable radio and let the sheriff's department know we have him."

Bob used Jim's call number to relay the message to the Columbia County Sheriff.

"C225, Baraboo."

"Go ahead C, two and a quarter," boomed back the dispatcher.

"Please notify Columbia County we have Odie Jackson's body near Tiperary Point. Have them send the coroner and transportation for the body to the landing at Bill's Lodge.

"10-04, C225 will do." They then lifted Odie gently into the boat and layed him reverently between them on the deck. Cars along the nearby road were stopping and observing the recovery.

Gesturing toward the cars, Jim started the motor for the return trip. "Guess the word's out." Proceeding slowly, he lifted the binoculars to glass the landing. A crowd was beginning to gather. He shut the motor down and raised his eyes to Bob. "I'm not going in yet. It will be at least an hour before the coroner and sheriff arrive. I don't want to face that crowd of ambulance chasers and have them gawking at the body."

Silence prevailed as Jim let his mind drift over past events as the boat drifted silently and aimlessly downstream. He remembered how he had first met Odie one dark night here on the river. It didn't matter to either that Jim was trying to catch Odie setting his lines. Both knew what the other was doing there. Somehow it only mattered that they were both on the river that night. The river was spoken of in awe as an old dear friend. Both had remarked how damp it was at night - how damp it was every night on the river. They shivered together that night and shared something of the wonder of the river, it's peacefulness, its swift treacherous currents that one must never trust. These things too were spoken of and shared in quiet talk that night and many other nights by them - two people on opposite ends of a game which was being played all over the country on many rivers. It didn't matter to Jim that Odie was a violator and it didn't matter to Odie that Jim represented the long arm of the law. What did matter was that both shared the wonders of the river. So a kinship was born between them that was never discussed openly. Yet both understood the other's feelings and needs which were basically the same for each.

Yes, Odie I will miss you. I won't speak of you to your kin or mine. But I will always remember that we shared something that not many other people can share. How fitting it is that you should end your days here in the river.

His mind pictured Odie's satisfaction as he tied his lines to the old stumps and deadheads in the total blackness. Just two days ago his anticipation of what he would catch ran high and thrilled him. But even greater was the self-satisfaction of outdoing his friend the game warden. No, he had never told anyone of his true feelings toward his sworn opponent. To do so was to admit weakness. It didn't matter to anyone else how he felt anyway. Above even these things though was his deep abiding love toward the old river. Many nights of his lifetime had been spent on it. He knew the risk and took it willingly. The river had almost taken his life before.

One night many years ago his boat had moved suddenly when the anchor rope he had tied to a deadhead slipped. At the first sudden movement of the boat in the treacherous current, he had automatically reacted by trying to throw the set line in his hand. Too late, the long steel hook had caught in his jacket and jerked him out of the boat into the vicious current. The current spun him around like a silver spoon at the end of a fish line. The strong 30 pound line was not to break. He was drowning. Finally, struggling mightily, he managed to partially slip out of his jacket. The current mercifully turned him and completed peeling the jacket off. He drifted to a sandbar below and waded to shore. The river had given him a second chance that night.

Jim let his mind wander to that night just two days ago when Odie, enjoying the river again and moving from one setline location to another, heard the motoboat approach. At first there was just rage at this age when the river's peacefulness could be broken by one of man's many contraptions. Inventions had completely changed the face of his peaceful river and world. Odie could remember when there were no boat motors. He never had use for one and hated the noise and the confusion they created on his peaceful river.

Then there was fear. The roar of the motor was too close. Turning, he saw the large white hull riding high, bearing down on him. He knew he would be hit. Then somehow, miraculously he wasn't. Even in the darkness he could see the fear on the young man's face as they passed so desperately close. The fear turned to anger at this intrusion. Jumping to his feet, he shook his fist and uttered a curse at the hated machine. Then the wash hit, pitching his small boat, throwing Odie into the dark warm Wisconsin River water. Down down into the dark deepths. No sandbar would save him this time. Fear again hit like a sledge hammer. A poor swimmer and disoriented from the booze and from being thrown into the water, Odie struggled. Blackness above, blackness below. He lashed out desparetely to save himself. Fear and panic overcame him to the point that when he reached the surface several times in the blackness, he was unaware of it. Thrashing and fighting the terrible relentless giant sapped his strength. The river was not going to give him another chance tonight. He was suffocating as he attempted to breath the river water. The thrashing grew less now as he weakened. Suddenly there was no more fear. Everything was warm now as he moved peacefully toward the soft golden light. Everything was grand now as he was completely enveloped by the peaceful light. He no longer fought the river but embraced it and drifted within it in wonderous bliss. The river craddled and caressed Odie and claimed him in its warm loving arms. Odie was at peace.

Yes, Odie, it's right and proper that you should die in the river. I will never speak of this to others but I shall always carry your love for the river. For I to have the same need. Kind of glad I never caught...

"Jim, Jim a squad and the coroner just pulled into the landing."

"W-What - Okay Bob, we'll haul Odie in."

Chapter 20

The Hit

It was widely known around Exland in northern Wisconsin (pop. 189) that Robert Glasco had committed a multitude of game law violations over the course of many years. He was loner who lived off the land, by selling his ill-gotten game and fish to local people. Attempts had been made to apprehend him by many wardens, including special investigators. He had been arrested only once, for spearing fish, and then he walked out of the jail while being booked, much to the consternation of several wardens.

Harry Borner, a vetern conservation warden newly appointed in 1975 as chief of special investigations made Glasco a first priority and his personal assignment. After all this man had flaunted the law way too long.

Harry, a rotund hearty man, knew he would have to lay the ground-work very carefully if he was to trap this wily, exceptionally suspicious violator.

On November 12, 1975, Harry, full bearded, wearing wool trousers, plaid shirt and battered hunting boots, looked every bit the hard-bitten hunter.

Upon arriving in Exland, knowing Glasco worked for a surveyor in the area, Harry entered the Buckhorn bar, hoping to get some information about Glasco and lay a logical believable trail to him.

While eating a sandwich and drinking a soft drink, he asked, "Is there anyone in the area that does land surveying?"

One of the local hangers-on immediately picked it up. "There is a fellow who lives in a trailer house here that works for a surveyor in Birchwood."

"What's his name?"

"Robert Glasco," he replied and explained how to get to the Glasco place.

That evening, just after dark, Harry located the Glasco home. Parking his car on the highway, he trudged the 75 yards up a very muddy snow covered road to the trailer house. As Harry knocked on the door, he noticed a pert blonde woman silently staring at him through the door window. She opened the door slowly.

Harry asked, "Is this where Robert Glasco lives?"

From the rear a man spoke up. "Yeah, I'm Bob Glasco. Come on in."

Hat in hand, Harry stepped politely past the strangely silent woman into the kitchen. Sitting in a wooden rocking chair, Glasco fit the description Harry had of him, clean shaven, appearing taller than his five foot eight inches because of his wiry thinness; a man who gave the impression of fast nervous

170

movement, dressed neatly in wool trousers and a checked woolen shirt. "I was told at the Buckhorn to contact you for a land survey."

"Why, yes. I work for a surveyor. What's your need?"

"My bosses' bought some land nearby and asked me to find a surveyor in this area."

Robert seemed very interested. "What's your name?"

"Harry Hatfield. I'm from Bloomington, Minnesota."

"That's a long ways from here. What are you doing around this country?"

"Looking over my bosses' land and a place to hunt. Nice country you have here."

At the compliment, Glasco courteously ushered Harry into the living room gesturing to the sofa. "Sit down. I do survey work all over this country. Even go as far as Bayfield at times. Fact, is it's about all I know how to do. Besides, in this part of the country there ain't much else to do unless you farm or log. I don't really care for either. I like doing survey work even though it keeps me away from home a lot." Gesturing toward the blonde woman, he remarked, "Makes Mindy mad keeping my meals warm in the evening, specially when I don't show up until midnight." His wife smiled and went about making coffee.

Noticing several large deer antlers mounted on the wall, Harry tipped his head approvingly. "Beautiful antlers you have there. You must do a lot of hunting."

It was the opening Glasco needed to speak of things dear to his heart and he immediately began to tell Harry how he had taken the two deer.

"Killed 'em both in October. Just before the deer season. Can't seem to wait until November. Too much competition with the season open."

The fact he was talking to a stranger bothered Glasco not a wit. Evidently feeling secure in his home, he babbled on, relating numerous tales of his hunting and fishing prowess. He dug some dogeared photographs out of an old tin cupboard above the kitchen table - pictures of numerous game animals and fish he had taken. Obviously many were taken during closed seasons and by illegal means. Deer with antlers in the velvet and red coats indicating the animals were shot in the spring or early summer, sturgeon and trout that were obviously speared, shot or snagged. The tales were many and varied, but all were about violating on fish and game, including exceeding the bag limit on squirrels and wounding a bear with a bow and arrow, and how it got away.

Harry used the offered opening, "I have a bow and arrow along with me. Do you know of a place where I could hunt deer? I've hunted some already this year with no luck. Had a few shots but can't seem to hit them. Season is getting short."

Brow wrinkling in thought, Bob's response was slow and deliberate. "I'll show you how to get to the round barn. If you don't get a shot at a deer there tomorrow, there's is something wrong with you." Drawing a map on a piece of notebook paper with a stubby pencil, he said, "Maybe I should go along and show you where to hunt. I could do some trout fishing. They taste good at this time of year. Besides, the fishing pressure is down, so they are easy to catch."

Harry laughed, "Is this your home country?"

"I was born and raised around here. Worked in the oil fields out west a few years back, but I like the wilderness around here. So I came back. Besides, I like outsmarting the game wardens hereabouts. You know one time when I was between marriages, I was really down in the dumps. I had my dad drop me off by a little creek where I stayed overnight in a tent. Helped me get my mind straight. Had a great time. Went fishing. Caught a bunch of trout, fried them up and ate them. The next morning when I stuck my head out of the tent, there stood a beautiful ten point buck in the velvet. Dropped him with one shot from my twenty-two rifle. Dressed out and boned him on the spot. I had a whole packsack full of venison. The squirrels were moving so I went out for a while and shot ten. Dressed them and packed them in the packsack. To top things off I went out and caught 47 more trout. I had so much to carry I had to walk ten miles and get my car. Got to be careful you know. Game wardens are always watching me. I had a perfect couple of days. Quite an experience. Felt much better after that."

"Sounds like you really had a time. By the way you mentioned going hunting with me tomorrow. Maybe you could show me some of your territory."

"Yeah, not doing anything anyway. I could drop you off at the old railroad grade. You could hunt along it. There are about four good miles of hunting. It would be good deer bow hunting or you could shoot partridge or even squirrels."

Smiling, Harry agreed, "Sounds like fun. Let's plan on it. I don't know about the partridge and squirrels though."

Glasco shrugged, "Hell there hasn't been a warden around here in a month of Sundays." Glancing at Harry's belt knife, Gene asked, "Do you have a good knife to take along?"

Harry handed him his folding hunting knife. Glasco opened it and ran his fingers over the blade. Whipping his head back and forth disapprovingly. "Got to have a sharper knife than this. Wait a minute." At that he left the room to return with a honing stone. "Here sharpen it up."

Harry worked the knife over the stone repeatedly until finally Glasco nodded his head in satisfaction.

"You'll be out there all day, so bring along some sandwiches and beer."

Harry shrugged. "I don't drink beer as I have high blood pressure. I'll be here tomorrow morning. I think I better leave now. It's getting late."

With a flourish Glasco motioned toward the table. "Have some coffee before you leave. It's not that late."

"No thanks, can't drink coffee, I have an ulcer."

Glasco grimaced. "Is that right? I have one, too. I've had surgery a couple times but still have the ulcer. Mindy has one, too. Guess it's the fast life we lead. Ha Ha!"

Laughing heartily, Harry nodded agreement. "I really must be going, Bob. I have a motel in Radisson. I'll see you about nine tomorrow. Okay?"

"Okay. Can't wait to get a mess of trout. Better when they are illegal."

At nine the next morning, Harry arrived at the Glasco trailer where Bob was anxiously scurrying about. "Are you ready to go hunting or is it fishing?"

"Can't get my car started. We'll have to use Dad's. We'll take your truck over to his place." After a short drive west they pulled into a driveway leading to an old but neatly kept farmhouse.

Bob introduced him to his gracious folks who had immediately appeared outside the house at the sound of the vehicle. While they were talking, a tall, slight young man, a younger replica of Bob, joined them from the house.

"Harry, meet my brother Tom."

"You sure can't deny you are brothers." chuckled Harry. "Look like two peas in a pod."

Bob shut down the small talk with a grunt. "Come, let's get going. Haven't got time to waste."

Harry shrugged and started to get into the elder Glascos' car.

"Wait Harry, you follow me with your truck. That way neither of us will have to walk. Have more time in the woods."

Harry followed Bob to the abandoned railroad track where Bob stopped his car motioning for Harry to park his truck. As Harry stepped out, Bob shouted. "Come, jump in with me."

Glasco started the car with a jolt. "I'll drop you off up the road and you can hunt your way back to the car. And leave that dumb bow here. Can't kill anything with that."

Soon Harry was unloading his equipment, gun, shells, and lunch. Bob babbled all the while of the trout fishing in the area. "Trout are easy to catch at this time of year. They're on the spawning beds. Tom caught a twenty-two inch German Brown the other day. It was a meal for all of us. Delicious. Now Harry, you just follow the old railroad grade along until you come to your truck. It's only about four miles, so take your time. Just sneak slowly through the brush, and you will pick up partridge, squirrels. . . and you might see a bear or deer. Here, take these slugs and buckshot. They are good for deer or bear."

Harry visibly hesitated, "But are they legal to carry?"

Bob shrugged, "Oh well, if you see someone, just drop them on the ground. The warden can't prove you had them. If you kill a deer or bear we'll get it with the tractor. I'll hunt and fish my way home and meet you there."

"But that's six or eight miles back to your trailer."

"Oh, that's not far. I do this all the time. See you there. Bet I'll get more game than you."

Harry spent an enjoyable afternoon hiking and hunting the railroad grade. *Might as well play this like it's real,* he thought. *Glasco is too smart to fool. Besides, this is not too bad a way to make a living.*

After about five hours he reached his truck and drove to the motel at Radisson where he picked up his gear. While driving to Bob's trailer, Harry mulled over the case today. He knew Glasco was beginning to trust him. It was quite a feat considering other investigators had been trying to break him for years. Then a twinge of conscience began to nag at Harry. Associating with a man who was friendly but whom Harry knew would eventually have to be arrested bothered the warden. But, it was Harry's job, and he knew violators like Glasco were a serious drain on fish and game populations. A drain Harry intended to plug.

Upon arriving at the Glasco residence, Harry was greeted by both Bob and Tom.

"Well how did you do?" Bob asked.

"Not too bad," Harry answered waving three squirrel tails he dug out of his pocket.

Not impressed, Bob snorted, "They're worth fifteen cents each. Hardly worth shooting."

Laying the tails down Harry inquired. "Oh well, how did your afternoon go?"

Fidgeting laboriously, regluing some picture frames, Glasco evasively took off on a different tack. "Ya know, my wife and I refinish antique furniture. These three frames will bring a pretty penny. See that old clock with the pendulum? My wife restored it. It took a lot of sanding to get the wood clean. It was given to her. She has it sold for eighty dollars. Not bad, hey?"

Motioning toward a mounted squirrel, Harry inquired, "Nice squirrel you have there. Do you do taxidermy work too?"

"Naw, my brother-in-law, Tim Goodman, did that. He's has been mounting animals for years. Nice job, hey? I've several mounted animals, but it costs too much. Most taxidermists simply charge too much. Hell, Tim don't charge much. If you have anything you want mounted, bring it over."

Harry fished, "What I really want to mount is an eagle. Is it possible to pick one up in this country?"

At that, Mindy, joining them, replied, "eagles are protected, and you are really asking for trouble trying to get one. Ain't that right Bob?"

"Even I wouldn't monkey around with an eagle. You couldn't even show it after you have it mounted."

"Guess I bettter give up on the eagle then. Would it be possible to see some of Tim's work in case I have something to mount?"

"Why don't you stop and see him? It's on your way home anyway. Just tell him Bob sent you."

Harry nodded agreement. "Guess it wouldn't take long. I really must get started, it's a long way to Bloomington. I'll see you during deer gun season."

"Come the day before the season. We will have venison and mushrooms by then."

Harry smiled. "I probably will. Sure sounds good to me. See you then."

Harry left, shaking hands all around. After several miles of driving he pulled into the Tim Goodman residence. All was dark. As he was turning around to return to the highway a car pulled in and stopped near his truck.

A middle aged man shouted, "Looking for Tim?"

"Yeah. I would like to see his taxidermy work."

"I'm Brad Nedbrook, Tim's hunting partner. Who are you?"

174

"Harry Hatfield, a friend of Bob Glasco."

"Oh well, any friend of Bob's is a friend of mine. Say, do you have a pen? I'd like to leave a note for Tim." Opening the house door, Nedbrook walked in. Harry followed, handing him the pen.

Mounted animal specimens filled the room. A partially mounted, open winged beautifully colored wood duck sat on a table. Harry openly admired it. "When you see Tim please tell him I was here and will be back in the deer gun season? Here, give him my card. I better get going. I've got a lot of driving yet tonight."

Driving to Ladysmith he met the local game warden, Edward Manthei. He gave him a complete report on his activities with the Glasco clan.

Obviously tickled, Ed chortled. "Looks like we're finally in? The citizens in this area will sure be glad to see us finally bust Glasco. He's been a thorn in my side for years. Tim Goodman doesn't have a taxidermist license, so, he's a customer too. I will get a bird or animal to have him mount.'"

On November 26, after several days of the deer gun season had passed, Harry again stopped at the Tim Goodman residence, bringing investigator Paul Toltzien with him. As they approached the residence a middle-aged man opened the door. "Hi fellows, looking for me?"

"Are you Tim Goodman?"

"Yep. Who did you expect? I live here."

"I'm Harry Hatfield from Bloomington, Minnesota."

Tim motioned toward the truck. "I noticed the Minnesota plates. Don't see many of those around here. Ain't you the fellow that hunted with Bob Glasco last fall and talked to Ned?"

"Yeah, Bob is a good friend of mine. This is Paul Woodman another friend of mine. We're hunting deer up here. I brought a duck for you to mount."

Motioning to the open door, Tim replied, "Bring it in."

Returning from his truck he displayed the golden eye duck. "How much will you charge to mount this?"

"Oh about twenty-five dollars. It's a nice golden eye. In what position would you like it mounted?"

Harry pointed at a wood duck in flight on the wall. "That's a nice mount. Why don't you do it like that? How long have you been mounting animals?"

"About six years now."

"How did you learn the trade? Go to school?"

"Naw, I learned it through a sort of correspondence course put on by the North Eastern School of Taxidermy. I stay away from fish though, they're too hard to paint. I feel my work on animals is good. I like to work on fur animals. I get some specimens at Rice Lake from a fur buyer."

"What's the fur buyer's name? I'd like to pick up a badger for mounting."

"His name is Ben Weistman. Badgers are protected, but he may fix you up if you're careful."

"I didn't know they were protected, but I may stop and see him when passing through. How long will it take to mount the duck?"

"It'll be a while because I'm busy hunting at this time of year."

Jokingly Harry remarked, "It looks like you have it made here: a little business, a place to live, a cabin in the woods where you can live on venison the year around."

"Ha, Ha, you can say that again. Times are I get so sick of it I have to go to town and get a ring of red for a change of pace."

Harry walked briskly to the door. "We must get going. We're going over to see Bob. When can I expect to pick up my duck?"

"Oh, about the middle of February."

Shaking hands, Harry left. "See you then."

In the truck, Harry said, "What do you think of that, Paul?"

"Sounds like he lives off the land. I'm a little envious. Looks like we'll have a good case in February. Let's get over to Bob's place. I can't wait to meet him."

Harry's knock brought Mindy immediately to the door.

"Oh, it's Harry - Bob. Harry is here."

Bob, sprawling on the couch with only dirty shorts and a t-shirt on, yelled, "Come on in Harry. My God, some hunter you are showing up in the middle of the night. Suppose we could go out and knock one down with a light?"

Harry agreed. "Might be a good idea. Meet my brother-in-law, Paul Woodman. How's hunting?"

"Only fair." Glasco cautiously replied, looking Paul over throughly obviously bothered by the newcomer. "Nothing to get excited about. We did get four legal bucks among about fifteen of us. Tomorrow the people around here will be making big drives west of my dad's place."

"Yeah. Would you know of a place a person could kill a doe? Paul has a party permit tag he'd like to fill."

Picking up a notebook and a stubby pencil, Bob studiously began drawing a map. "With all the people hunting that area west of my dad's place, there will be a lot of deer rattling around. Look, I've marked some places to stand. You should get a deer without any trouble."

"If we don't fill Paul's tag tomorrow, do you think there may be an extra one lying around somewhere that Paul could pick up?"

"If it was closer to the end of the season, there would be lots of them. The hanky-panky really starts after Thanksgiving around here."

"I suppose Mindy has a big turkey ready for Thanksgiving?"

"Hell no. Around here we eat venison. We already have a shoulder prepared."

As there was no invitation to sit down, they said goodnight and left. Entering the truck, Harry asked, "Paul, what do you make of him?"

"Pretty cool, I don't think he likes me. Maybe we should let it rest for awhile."

Thoughtfully Harry commented, "Yeah, I think we will let it go until next summer. We really don't have a legitimate reason to be around this country. He may guess who we are if we keep pushing. I'll warm him up again next summer. I've got a lot of other leads to follow through on anyway."

The following July, 1976, Borner again knocked on Bob's door.

176

"Come on in," Bob greeted him. "Oh, it's Harry. What are you doing in this country?"

"Just passing through on a business trip. Thought I would stop and pick up the duck I left with Tim last fall. I tried to contact him several times by phone. Couldn't get an answer."

"Tim's been in the hospital. He was in a car accident. He's okay now though. You just missed him He just left here about five minutes ago. I know the duck is done. I seen it over there."

"Looks like you're going into big farming," Harry observed. "The backyard is full of animals. You didn't have all that stock last deer season."

"Yep, I'm making a little money on rabbits, chickens, and turkeys. We eat a lot of them ourselves. It's nice to have a change from venison once in a while."

"Have you shot any lately.?"

"Yeah, shot a spike buck a few days ago. They usually get good to eat around the first of July. Got to be careful, though, the warden starts to watch me about this time of the year."

"How has the fishing been?"

"Pretty good, got a nice sturgeon the other day. Shot him with fineshot. In fact I barbecued him with some of the venison on my new charcoal grill. How come you didn't come to fish with us last spring? You said you would."

"I still intend to . How about next month?"

"Fine. We could fish bass, walleyes or trout. I might even take you out for sturgeon,"

"Sturgeon - Ha, the warden will have both of us. Got to get going if I'm going to catch Tim. I'll let you know about going fishing. Okay?"

"Better stick around, I'm going after muskies tonight."

"Geez-wish I could. Got to get over to Tim's."

"Okay. See you next month."

Upon arriving at the Goodman residence, Tim cooly greeted him. "Hello."

"Don't you remember me?"

"Should I?"

"I left a duck here last fall to have mounted."

"Oh, yeah, you brought the golden eye. I sure had a hell of a time mounting that bird. Looks good though. Come on in and sit down." Reaching with a grunt he unhooked the duck from the wall. "See, here is where I had the problem. He was really shot up along the back. You must have really clobbered him."

"Looks good to me. You did a good job under the circumstances." Harry said, thinking to himself, *that dang Manthie really busted that poor duck.* "How much do I owe you?"

"I quoted $25 so that's what it is."

A check that could be used for evidence was quickly written and handed to Tim. "I appreciate what you've done. The price is right. How has the fishing been around here?"

"Haven't had much time to fish, but I heard it's not too good."

"Bob told me it's been good."

"Oh, Bob doesn't fish like other people. That's why he has better luck."

"Yes, he mentioned he was going out tonight to get some muskies."

"Yep, I'm sure he will spear them."

Harry feigned surprise. "I didn't think you could spear fish?"

"Ha, Ha, legally, you can't. It's easy to get them as long as the warden don't get you. Bob fishes the Chippawa River often. You just fasten a sealed beam car lightbulb to a long stick with the wires running to a car battery in the boat. Stick it under the water and row right up to the fish and spear them. The nice thing about it is the warden can't see the light very far. Better than shining flashlights all over hell. You sticking around?"

"I really have to move on. I'm on a business trip and have a long way to go yet today."

In August, Harry again stopped at the Glasco trailer. Mrs. Glasco opened the door.

"Hello Harry. Bob's not home."

"Oh, where is he?"

"He's working at the box factory in Bruce."

"I was hoping to go fishing with him."

"It would be nice to have some fish to eat," she reflected. "All we've had lately is bear meat."

"Where did you get the bear meat?"

"Oh, Bob shot one about a week ago. It dressed out about 400 pounds. So we will be eating it for a long time. Would you like to come in?"

"I'll stop back this evening when Bob is home."

Returning at 7 p.m., Harry noticed that Bob's car was not in the yard. Rather than enter, Harry waited in his parked truck. Lightly dozing, he was startled by the sound of footsteps. Two men came trudging through the mud in the driveway. Glancing at his watch, he noted it was 10:05 p.m.

"Hi Bob," he yelled.

"Oh, hi Harry, come on into the house. No need to sit out here. This is my nephew Steve Dodge." Stomping the clinging mud off their shoes, they crowded into the small trailer.

Harry commented, "Hear you have a new job? I suppose that means we won't be able to go fishing?"

"Yeah, even I have to work sometimes. It's okay though, Tom can take you fishing. He's not doing anything right now. He's over next door sawing lathes. You know we're moving? Mindy's folks don't want us on their land any more. My folks are letting us move our trailer to their place. So I'm a litle busy."

Nodding approval, Mindy began serving Bob coffee.

Harry commented, "Hear you had a little bear hunt here last week?"

"Yep, late in the afternoon last Wednesday. When I was taking care of the stock, I noticed the calves looking at something in the woods. A nice bear walked through the edge of the field. You know they hang out in the dump when they're in the area. The dump ain't far from here. So Mindy and I took a little drive. Sure enough there were three of them there. Picked out

The Hit

the biggest and let him have it with the 30-30. Went right down. Dummy me, I had only one shell so I was afraid to go near it. Mindy was thinking better than I. She had brought along another shell. I put that in the rifle and went down to where he lay. Shot him again. Looked dead. So we went home to get some tools to dress it. When we got back it was dark and all there was left was two splotches of blood and some blood in the muddy tire ruts. Tried to trail it with matches.. Finally I gave up, and we went home for help. The Curtiss brothers next door wouldn't go. Said they were afraid of a wounded bear in the dark. Went over to my other neighbor's place and talked his two sons into coming along. They were really excited. We took a flashlight along to trail the bear. That gol'dang bear went a long ways. Clean down to the lake. It was laying in the water. When we got close, it charged right at us with a roar. I waited until it was about 50 feet away, then shot it right in the chest. It dropped in about two feet of water. They drag easy in the water. Boy, when you hit land that's a different story. Like lead. Anyway, we got it dressed and loaded that night."

Mindy entered with the coffee pot and milk for Harry and said, "I'm sick and tired of eating bear. That's all we've had for a week."

Bob laughed heartily. "Don't worry dear, you'll have a change in diet soon. Come on Harry, we'll go over and see Tom. I'm sure he'll take you fishing tomorrow."

Leaving the house, the two walked to a small dark shed behind the neighbors' house. A knock brought a flood of light as the door opened. Upon entering, Harry noticed all the windows were blanketed so no one could see in, making the shed look dark. There were three people in the building. Tom Glasco, a medium-sized man called Steve, and a young man weighing about 300 pounds. All had bloody hands. Hanging from a rafter was the skinned carcass of a large deer. On the floor lay the hide and head of a buck deer. The hide was in the red coat, and the wrinkled antlers had eight points in the velvet. The big man with long hair hanging in his eyes looked apprehensive. "Who is this guy?" he snapped.

Steve laughingly joked, "I bet he's from the DNR. Wouldn't it be funny if he was an undercover warden?"

Bob retorted, "It wouldn't be funny at all. This is Harry, the guy I told you about. He's okay. He's a friend of mine."

"Yeah. Bob and I have been friends quite a while, and I sure wouldn't care to see a warden either. That's sure a nice buck you have there. Nice and fat. Be good eating." Picking up the head he pointed at the bullet hole beside the eye, "Boy someone is a good shot."

"Can't miss when the deer are showing like tonight. Even Bob can hit them, hey Bob?"

"Saw eleven deer between here and Birchwood."

Cursing, Tom struggled attempting to cut the deer with a swede saw. Harry volunteered. "Let me help you with that." Taking the saw, he success- fully severed the quarters with Tom indicating where to cut. Each hefted a quarter and carried them to the garage where they put it into a chest-type deep freeze.

Tom remarked, "By tomorrow it will be stiff enough to cut up."

At Tom's suggestion, they returned to the house where three small mongrel dogs very excited over the deer smell were busily sniffing everyone.

Bob laughed heartily and remarked, "Mindy, I told you we were going to have a change of diet. Even the dogs are excited. To celebrate we're going fishing tomorrow. Harry, come with me. I want to show you the boat you'll use tomorrow."

While walking through the dark cold night behind the shed, Harry dropped a little bait. "As long as your wife don't care for bear meat, maybe I could take some of it off your hands?"

"Sure you can have some, you may want some of the venison too. I have the boat hidden back here so no one will steal it. See the wheels I have rigged up? I can throw the front end in the back of my station wagon and with the wheels under the stern like that I can tow it down the road. Works real good. Traded a little venison for them."

Harry looked the rig over thoughtfully. "Think I can master it."

"Sure, nothing to it. You can fish all day and have supper here, then fish catfish after dark. Mindy saved some chicken guts for bait. Anyway, you're all set. " Raising his voice, Glasco yelled at the people in the house. "Come on down here and help move this boat. It's getting late, after midnight already. Harry's starting to yawn."

"That's right, I'm tired. I don't know how you fellows do it. Stay up all night and still get up early in the morning. I should go get some shuteye."

The three men wheeled out and loaded the boat into the back of Bob's stationwagon. All then went to the shed to clean up the mess. The deer hide was stuffed into a gunnysack along with the head after Tom cut the antlers off.

Suprised, Harry asked. "Why do you want the horns? You can't display them anyway in the velvet."

"Ha - the wardens won't see them. There's a good market for antlers in the velvet. I know where I can sell them."

Harry needed physical evidence soon. "Bob, what are you going to do with the bear hide?"

"Hides no good at this time of year. We threw it out. The head, Tim is gonna mount.''

"I really don't want the whole head. I would like just the skull if Tim isn't going to use it in mounting."

Bob thoughtfully replied, "I believe that can be arranged. Tim never uses the skull. Why'd ya want a skull anyway?"

"Oh, I would cook the flesh off it and use it in my den as a trophy."

"I've seen some people do that. I personally wouldn't be interested. I'll see what I can do." Meanwhile completing the clean up job, Tom carried a bag full of deer dressing out. He nonchantly threw it in Bob's car and slammed the door.

With a smile, he approached Harry, "Say, Harry, have you ever seen Bob's underwater light?" Reaching into Bob's car, he brought out a long pipe with a headlight attached to the end. Wires led from the light to alligator clamps on the other end . "Have ya seen one before?"

Harry feigned ignorance. "No, Bob explained it to me once though

180

and it's evident how it is used. You know guys, I'm really getting tired. If we're to fish tomorrow we better get us some sleep."

It was close to 3 a.m. when Harry finally put in a call to the new warden at Ladysmith, Omar (Curley) Stavlo to bring him up to date on the Glasco case. With a very tired sigh, Harry went to bed.

Few fish were caught the next day as they fished the Chippewa River downstream. The river being at a very low stage made the trip very difficult. In the evening Bob picked them up at the high banks.

Arriving at Bob's place for supper they found Mindy in a rare hospitable mood as she served a generous meal of bear meat and venison.

"Mindy, you're a wonderful cook, and I really like the way you prepared the bear with mushrooms and onions, said Harry. "Can't believe these are wild mushrooms. They're delicious."

At that point, Harry let his mind wander about the situation he was in. *Here I am eating a hearty meal with these friendly people. They are treating me like a king. Mindy really is a very nice person. Oh well, I'm paid to do a job. Guess I better just concentrate on that. After all they are stealing this area blind. If they keep it up, there will be no fish or game for anyone.* He was jarred back to the present by Tom's thoughts on eating bear meat.

"Some people won't eat it at all, but we all like it here. Except the diet is too steady."

Harry quickly took advantage of the conversation. "You know Tom, I'm really serious about getting that bear skull. It would make a nice display."

"Tim has the head. Can't see no reason why we can't get it for you. Let's get Bob's chores done so we can go fishin."

The men went out and hurriedly fed the stock and left for the river. Launching the boat Bob commented "You know Harry we might run into a spearing party tonight. My neighbor, Ed Hoeffner, will be out here some place."

Harry continued to steer Tom in their conversation to the deer Bob had killed. "When are you going to cut up that deer?"

"A neighbor, Ed Apple, is coming over to Bob's tomorrow to help Mindy cut up the deer. That way he will get some venison out of it. We work togther and share these things."

"If I wake up early enough I may stop and help Mindy cut up the deer."

"That would be real nice of you Harry."

"The fish were not biting so they pulled out at 11 o'clock."

Leaving the river, Harry hurriedly drove to Exland and made two phone calls from the public phone, one to Omar Stavlo and the other to supervising warden Larry Miller at Hayward. Filling them in briefly on the status of the case, he aslo told Omar of the spearing outfit presently on the river. Omar responded that he would go out and see if he could ambush them.

Mindy responded to Harry's knock the following morning at 9:30 a.m. "Come on in Harry. I'm just setting around drinking coffee and reading. Would you have some coffee with me? Here sit at the kitchen table."

"I'll have just a little. Ulcer you know. Thought I would stop and help you cut up that deer."

"Gee Harry, that's real nice of you. I was just sitting here trying to get up enough gumption to start. If I give you the keys to the Bean residence, would you go over and get the venison?"

"Oh, is that the neighbor's name? That big fellow with the long hair? I didn't catch his name the other day."

"No, that was Dan Becker, a friend. We always use Erwin Bean's deep freeze when ours is overloaded. Here are the keys to their garage."

"Okay, I'll be back shortly."

Next door, Harry immediately opened the deep freeze. The four quarters of the deer lay all alone as they had several days before. Digging the small camera from his pocket, he photographed the freezer and contents. The quarters were frozen together so hard it was necessary to pry them apart with a crow bar found near the deep freeze. Mindy was waiting with several knives and a cutting board when Harry returned with the frozen quarter. He laid it on the board where Mindy tried cutting it.

"It's too hard to cut. We'll have to wait for it to thaw."

"Okay, I'll go over and get the other quarters."

On the second trip, Harry photographed the house and the shed where the deer had been skinned and quartered. With the venison on the kitchen table, the conversation revolved around hunting.

Harry asked, "Could you tell me where the Exland dump is? I may try for a bear after tasting bear meat here."

Mindy explained explicity how to get there. Harry inquired of the people he had met around the Glasco home.

"You know Mindy, that Dan Becker, the fellow I didn't know the name of? Well, he was telling me the sheriff's department stopped him and searched his car for marijuana. He was laughing because they found none. Does he use drugs?"

"He uses marijuana all the time. I often see him high. My brother-in-law Chuck Dodge sells the stuff. He has 100 pounds of Columbian on hand right now. He's been trying to get Bob to sell it. I put my foot down and said absolutely not. I'd rather see him kill deer than sell dope. I really hate to see him kill deer all the time too. Deer are too beautiful to kill. I really don't have much to say around here. Last summer I had to cut up 17 deer myself. Bob and Tim killed them. I don't know how many more they killed; they never tell me. I know Tim took some and many others were given or traded to neighbors."

Drawing his hunting knife across the near quarter, Harry determined the meat was thawing very slowly. "Mindy, have you ever eaten bannock?"

"No, I believe I've heard of it. What is it?"

"A type of Indian bread. I always carry the makings in my vehicle. I'll go and get them and make you some while the meat thaws." Soon he returned with a paper bag of the makings. "Watch how I do this so you can make it yourself from now on. You'll really enjoy it."

Harry took over the kitchen and clattered around among the pots and pans. Soon the piping hot bannock was done. They sat down and ate it, washing it down with ice cold Seven-Up.

Mindy nibbled on the last piece. "Harry, that was delicious. I will remember how to make it. Bob will enjoy it. Guess that meat will never thaw." Testing it with a knife, she continued, "Still hard as a rock."

"Guess I'll leave then. I have a few errands to run."

Leaving he followed Mindy's instructions and drove to the Exland dump. He found and photographed the area and the gut pile where the bear had been killed. Notes were taken so he could later explain to the field wardens.

Later that day, Harry arrived at the Clarence Glasco house to find Steve Dodge and Tom Glasco talking. They convinced him he should drive to Bass Lake to fish.

As he was about to leave, Tom shouted, "Harry I want to show you something. " Leading Harry behind the garage, he pointed to a pile of white gallon size plastic jugs. "Remember I was telling you about jugging? Well those are the jugs I'm going to use. I will start the middle of next week."

"Isn't it pretty risky? Those jugs are awful easy to see."

"Aw, I put them out after dark and pick them up before daybreak. Wardens aren't out at that time of day. They really catch fish. Using forty lines covers a lot of ground."

Harry jolted his vehicle to a halt at Bass Lake. "You know boys, I"m so beat I really don't care if I fish or not. You go ahead. I'll camp out here on shore and take a nap."

Steve replied, "Go ahead, I know you've been doing a lot of driving."

At that Harry finally got a chance to lay down and rest. The case had worn on him mentally as well as phsyically. It's not easy to live a lie especially when there are so many people involved. At about 3:30 p.m. Harry awoke. The sleep had been good and he felt more refreshed than he had for some time. "Now I can go all night with these owlhoots. A few minutes later, their boat scraped to a halt on the nearby rocky shore. The fish were not biting. While loading the boat and equipment and traveling to Bob's place, Harry openly questioned their operations. Trust showing, they freely told of sins far into the past.

At Bob's home, he heartily greeted Harry. "Come on in, we're just about to eat supper. I know Steve and Tom gotta get home. But you can talk for awhile. Besides, you didn't finish your job. We've got to cut this meat up tonight."

Pulling up a chair, Harry sat down. "It was just froze to doggone hard this morning."

"Yeah, I know. We're having some of it for supper. I don't know how you two were going to cut that venison anyway? Our meat saw is all warped and needs pounding. I'm taking it over to the Herman Koz place right after supper. Why don't you go fishing catfish with Steve and Tom while I take care of the saw?" It was obvious Bob didn't care too much for conventional fishing.

After supper as they were leaving, a car with Illinois registration drove speedily into the driveway. It contained three men who were considerably inebriated. They were friends of the Glascos who were returning from a Canadian fishing trip. Bob inquired as to the fishing in Canada.

They replied that it was lousy. They were in a bad mood because they had been stopped and cited by the Canadian Mounted Police for possessing open intoxicating beverages in the car.

Bob consoled them, "Sounds like you had a bum trip. Sit down. We just ate but there is some venison left."

One replied, "thas'e why we schtopped. We knew we could depend on youse to have veniskon. That early stuffss the best. Ha. Ha!"

Steve and Tom burst into the kitchen. "Come on, Harry, it's getting late."

Harry made a quick pitch to Bob. "I'm leaving tonight Bob, and would really like some of that bear meat. It's important I get back to the Twin Cities. Business you know."

"Mindy, fix Harry a few packages of that bear and while you're at it give him some of the venison too. After all he helped us cut it up. Haw!"

At the catfish hole, several small fish were caught and thrown back. By 10:30 p.m., Harry was looking for a way to leave. "Boys, I'm tired and have a three hour drive ahead of me yet tonight."

"Let's call it a day then," Tom replied.

"Okay, we're going spearing later on anyway at Bass Lake. You tell that brother of mine if he's coming he better hurry up or he'll find me in bed."

Arriving at the Glasco residence Harry found the three men from Illinois more drunk than before. They talked freely of killing deer illegally and outwitting the warden. It was obvious they spent time here, and made themselves at home.

Harry delivered the message. "Tom said to hurry up Bob if you're going spearing yet tonight."

Bob laughed, "Just like Tom, always in a hurry. On the serious side though, suppose I'd better get going if we're to get any fish. Mindy has that meat ready for you. Finished cutting the deer up while you were fishing. Mindy, get those packages you fixed up for Harry."

Opening the refrigerator and picking up five large packages, Mindy explained, "I've marked the packages for you. The ones with a B are bear and these two with an S are venison."

Shortly after midnight, Harry taking his leave, met with Larry Miller, Omar Stavlo and Lynn Thompson south of Hayward. The evidence was marked and turned over to Larry. Harry told them all he could remember, including the Illinois license number of the car at Glasco's and advised confidential reports were to follow. It was decided to continue the investigation even though they had sufficient evidence to prosecute the Glascos. The investigation had broadened to include a number of other people.

As Harry finished summing up, he yawned sleepily, "Frankly fellows I'm beat and I'm heading for Lodi tonight as I have to be in the office tomorrow. This case will be the death of me yet."

Late on a September afternoon, Harry drove into the Clarence Glasco residence. The elder Glasco was working on a new building. "Hi Harry, what are you doing around here? On vacation?"

"No, just going through and thought I would return Tom's fish stringer. Took it home last month."

"Oh, Tom is over at Bob's up the side road."

"Oh, Bob did make the move then?"

"Yeah, you just follow that side road until you see the house on the hillside."

Driving down the side road, reaching Bob's new trailer site Harry parked. Bob and Tom were feeding the animals in the yard.

Spotting Harry, Bob walked out to the truck. "Oh, hi Harry, jump out of the truck. You can help us feed the stock."

"I see you are all moved. How's it going?"

"Okay so far, I don't have my electricity or well in yet. But we're getting by. Come I'll show you around the grounds."

"See, I made my own septic tank. Dug a hole 14 feet deep and put three oil drums in there. Put a vent in and ran the pipe from the trailer down here and hooked it up. Works real good. Come, I've got something else to show you." Walking over to his station wagon he returned with two bloody arrows which had deer hair on them.

"Well Bob, you must have scored."

"Yep, got a fawn last Saturday night. That's the first legal deer I've gotten for a long time. It was so small I didn't bother to tag or register it though. My tag is still not filled. Ha. Ha!"

"Sounds like you've been having fun."

"Yeah, Tom and I got a little jump meat since you were here. They were both forkhorn bucks. We try to save the does. The only reason I shot that doe fawn was cause I'll take anything with a bow. Come on in, it's time for lunch." After the meal winking slyly at Harry, he stood up, "We are going to Birchwood."

"Tom asked, "Is this going to be a legal trip or an illegal trip?"

Bob chuckled, "We'll make it a semi-legal trip; we'll take the artillery along as a backup." Upon leaving the house, Harry walked toward his truck at which time Bob yelled, "Well, you're going along with us, aren't you?"

"I didn't know what your plans were."

"Come on, you've nothing better to do anyway. Bring your bow." Harry got the bow and arrows and placed them in Bob's car. Bob took the driver's seat, Mindy the middle and Harry the outside. Tom got into the back seat alone. Harry glanced back and saw a .22 rifle in the seat along side Tom who was pulling a blanket over it. "Better cover this up."

Bob drove at a steady 23 miles per hour, explaining, "This is the speed to drive to see deer. I know as I've hunted like this for years." After about 10 miles of driving, two deer were spotted while passing a field near the road. Bob said "Get that bow and arrow, Tom and stick it out the window. Maybe you can still get a shot." As soon as Tom had them out the window, Bob slowly backed up.

Harry thought, *My God, what an operation. I wonder if they've ever killed deer this way?*

The deer bolted so Bob continued driving. Upon entering the village of Birchwood several more deer were spotted in a back field.

Bob said, "I can get to them. I know this area like the back of my hand. I helped survey this area. It's called the project." He freewheeled down many twisting dirt roads until they were at a circular turnaround. As predicted there stood the deer. Bob lurched the car to a stop as Tom slipped out the door and onto the top of the station wagon with the bow and arrow. Bob proceeded to put Tom in good shooting range. Zing - the arrow narrowly missed the doe. Quickly Bob grabbed for the .22 rifle and stuck it out the window ready to fire. "Hell, I can't see them anymore. "

After picking up the arrow, the driving continued. Bob bypassed a nice buck standing in the ditch. Braking to a halt, he whispered, "Quick Tom, get the .22 ready and I'll back up." Tom stuck the rifle out the window directing it into the woods to no avail. The buck jumped and was gone.

Tom pulled the gun back in. "Go ahead, we'll find another one. Wait! I see him. He's back down the road. " Bob applied a little too much weight on the brake pedal while backing up jolting Tom, the .22 went off with sharp crack, the buck bouncing into the woods.

"Damn, Bob, you're going to have to learn how to drive. You made the gun go off. It would have been a perfect shot too. I could have got him right in the neck."

"Yeah, we always shoot them in the neck Harry."

"Will a .22 rifle kill them by shooting them in the neck?"

"Drops them right in their tracks. Besides it saves a lot of meat. No sense in shooting them all up."

Circling the little block of timber the buck had entered. Bob mused, "May see him again," as he fumbled for a five cell flashlight he had under the seat. They made one complete circuit of the small block shining the flashlight along the edge of the woods, ever sweeping it back and forth. The buck was nowhere to be found. They drove some other roads sweeping the roadside with the flashlight. Nothing further was spotted.

Mindy complained, "I'm thirsty, let's go to Birchwood for a bottle of pop. Besides the exhaust fumes in here are getting to me. I'm getting a headache."

They proceeded into Birchwood stopping at a tavern. Everyone was hungry and thirsty and broke.

Harry said, "Here's ten dollars, buy us lunch and something to drink." Bob and Tom proceeded into the bar and came back with hamburgers and pop. They ate while laughing about their hunting experiences.

Bob said, "Let's head for home." He started out along Highway 48. "We'll still get a little jump meat on the way home." Fumbling under the front seat he hauled out a bolt action 30-30 rifle. Placing it on the dashboard immediately in front of him, he said, "Be careful. It's loaded."

Tom sat in the back with the .22 rifle between his knees. After several miles, eyes were spotted with the headlights.

Bob explained, "Never use a flashlight on a main highway. They won't stop you if you use just headlights." In spite of his constant 23 miles per hour speed they passed the eyes. "Oh well, we'll turn around and try him again." Backing into a field road, Bob started back, sliding the 30-30 out the window. "Ah! There he is, a nice buck." The car slackened speed until almost even with the deer. Suddenly car lights danced behind them.

Tom shouted in panic, "That car's right on us, get out of here." At that Bob stepped on the accelerator the car jumping forward with a squeal of tires.

Hitting a dirt road, they careened south. The car did not follow. Passing several fields, they again used the flashlight. Several fields were checked via farm or logging roads. No deer were seen.

Nearing Exland, Bob sighed "Just one more field." Approaching the field, he shined the flashlight. Eyes were immediately illuminated in the darkness. Handing the flashlight to Harry, he said, "You shine the field and Tom you be ready with the 30-30." Swinging it over the seat carelessly the muzzle pushed into Harry's neck making his hackles rise. *My God, what an operation. Someone's going to get killed.*

Bob shut off the lights and drove into the field completely black. He stopped in a position where the deer should have been in good range. "Try him now Harry." Harry turned on the light. The deer were in the back corner of the field. Angrily Bob snorted, "Too damn far. The hell with it. There's always another night. Besides we thought we would take you spearing yet tonight. If it's okay with you?"

"Sure, I'll try anything once."

While Bob was heading for home, he explained to Harry, "Maybe you noticed the guns we're using. The .22 has a broken bolt and the 30-30 has no clip for it. We do this so if we get stopped we can always tell them we are on the way to a gunsmith to repair them. Another thing is we are very careful hunting main roads. It's too easy for wardens to set up and run you down out there. You know the wardens don't have trucks so they can't get off the road much. Their cars will go like hell though."

Upon returning to the trailer they immediately began gathering their equipment for the spearing expedition. The underwater light was broken. Searching around they found an old car sealed beam that worked and hooked it onto the old frame. Loading the aluminum boat on top of the station wagon, Bob grumbled, "Everybody uses my equipment and brings it back broken. Oh well, Harry we're going to try the Weigore."

Reaching the creek, Tom jumped out and opened a farm fence. Bob quickly drove through hiding the car behind some tall weeds. "You guys unload the equipment and I'll unhook the car battery." In a few moments everything was in the boat already bobbing in the water. Bob hurried over with the car battery, snapping the aligator clamps on the battery poles he whispered, "Harry, you get in the back and handle the light. Tom you take the spear." They pushed off with Bob directing the boat with the oars. They worked downstream stern first. Harry, kneeling on the back seat aimed the underwater light. Fish were easily spotted and speared by Tom who stood alongside of him.

After a few northern and walleyes were in the boat, Bob said, "Harry you take the spear for a while."

Harry hesitated worrying about entrapment in the courts and trying to explain the illegal spearing of fish by a warden to the district attorney. "Okay but I've never done this before."

Bob chuckled, "Nothing to it. You'll learn."

Harry deliberately missed several fish, *I'll have to be more convincing than this,* he thought. He drove the spear at what he thought would be a very near miss of a northern pike. *Damn now I did it.* One tine caught the fish and crippled it. Half on its side the fish darted for cover.

Bob directed the boat. "We'll get him, watch where he goes." Bob pushed the boat expertly over the fish. "Now Harry, take him."

Harry thought. *There's no way I can legitimately miss it. I will just have to explain to the D.A.* The jab was swift and sure and the northern came into the boat squirming and pounding. The atmosphere immediately changed. Harry could feel their careful acceptance turn to open companionship. They were completely convinced he was one of them. Harry speared a couple of suckers on the way back to the car thinking, "At least they are not game fish."

On the return trip, Bob laughingly carried on a conversation of constant chatter about the fishing trip. "Beats hook and line fishing all to hell. You get more fish and you never get your line tangled up. Ha. Ha! You thought that was fun, Harry, I'm going to show you more fish yet tonight. I know of a private pond where a guy raises fish." At that he wheeled into an old sand road. "Tom take the flashlight and check the pond."

After flashing the light around for about five minutes, he returned, "The pond is real muddy. Can't see a thing, we'll have to try this another night."

"Aren't you taking a big chance taking someone's private stock?"

Bob shrugged, "Oh well, they will never know the difference. Besides he has money to spare."

Harry said, "I have to get to Radisson. If the tavern is closed, I won't be able to get my motel key. It's after 10 o'clock now and the bar closes at 12 o'clock."

Bob agreed. "Guess we've had enough for tonight anyway. Come on over again tomorrow. This is almost a nightly occurence. We didn't get any meat today, but tomorrow will be different."

"I thought I would hunt ducks tomorrow."

"Why don't you try the Weigore where I showed you before. You may pick up some woodcock and partridge too. The partridge season isn't open yet but the woodcock season is. No one will notice the shots." As soon as dropped off, Harry left for Radisson.

On the first and second of October, Harry hunted with Tom and Bob with varied luck. They picked up a few ducks while scouting a stream for spearing.

Then on the 3rd of October, about midmorning, Harry arrived at the Glasco trailer to find Bob asleep.

After dressing he began doling out corn to his animals. He had become much more open toward Harry. "You know Harry, I'm seriously considering planting some corn. All this corn I've been feeding the animals mysteriously appears in my yard. Ha! You know the neighbors have plenty to spare. Beisdes I give all of them venison. If they don't give me something in return, I just even the score in the night time. In fact, Joe's going to give me some corn soon, as I'm about out. He just doesn't know it."

Bob began naming the many persons he had given venison. "Lots of times I take them the deer. They dress it out and cut it up for half. That way we don't have to do the cutting." He continued to babble.

Harry's mind was in a jumble trying to remember all the people's

188   *The Hit*

names mentioned. "My God, the whole neighborhood is eating illegal venison." Walking behind a building on the pretense of urinating, Harry hurriedly wrote down some of the names.

"Come on Harry. Let's go hunting. Mindy is going into Bruce today to tell them at the sawmill that I've been sick."

They drove several miles from home after picking up Tom and parked near Spring Creek and the old railroad grade.

Bob chortled, "Let's see who can get the most game. We'll each go in different directions. Remember squirrels, rabbits, partridge, etc. count. Only things you can eat. No chickadees, skunks or foxes, Harry."

Harry said, "I'll follow the old grade so I don't get lost."

In good cheer all three started hunting away from each other. Harry noticed Tom tied a piece of binder twine into a sling to carry the old broken .22 rifle, yelling, "We'll meet back here at two."

Harry leisurely hunted the three hours and arrived back at the car as planned just as Tom came noiselessly out of the woods. They were tied at three squirrels a piece. About a half hour later, Bob came struggling out of the woods under the weight of a full packsack.

"Well, looks like I'm the winner." He laughed.

Shocked, Harry asked, "What in God's name do you have in there?"

"Well, let's see now. I believe the grand total is four squirrels, one brook trout and a nice buck. I walked right on top of him and knocked him down with one shot to the neck. Wouldn't you know, I forgot my knife at home. I made out though. Found an old mason jar in the woods, broke it and used it for a knife. Worked pretty good. Skinned and boned him out and here I am."

Confusedly, Harry said, "How did you get the trout? You didn't have any fishing equipment."

"Oh, I saw him in the creek and shot close to him. Turned him up. I really like trout." Bob still chattered excitedly as they reached the car. He lifted the rear tailgate and the cover over the spare tire well. It was empty. Carefully stuffing everything into it, Bob exhorted, "Never carry a spare. Good place to hide things. Been stopped a lot by the wardens and Harry they've never looked here yet."

"You mean you operate like this all the time and you've never been caught?"

"Oh, I was caught once for spearing fish on Knutson Creek. Made a fool of the wardens though. When they were booking me at the jail I walked right out. Ha. Ha. They picked me up several days later, but I really pulled one on them. You know they impounded my car thinking I would come forward. Hell, the car wasn't worth anything, let them look for me."

"You've really had an interesting life."

"Wouldn't trade it for anything. Come let's get home. It's time for supper."

Arriving at the Glasco trailer, Harry wondered how he could document the new evidence. *I believe Bob really trusts me. I'm going for the camera.* Walking to his truck, he picked the camera off the dashboard. "Bob you're the champ. Mind if I take a picture of the proof?"

Bob chuckled pleasantly, jutting his chest out. "Go ahead. The pictures will be proof forever. They will be worth their weight in gold."

Harry photographed the game along with Bob and Tom. "I'll get copies of these pictures for you fellows. Harry chuckled to himself thinking, *The district attorney will have the originals.*

Bob yelled, "Come on you guys, supper is ready. In fact, we have apple pie from those apples you brought yesterday, Harry. Smells delicious."

After the meal, the meat was put in the freezer.

Bob was anxious. "Come on, Tom and I want to canoe the Weigore and see if we can get another deer yet today. You can meet us later. Two in a canoe is enough."

Harry helped load the canoe and other sundry equipment. "Don't you use life preservers? You know I can't swim and I wouldn't go on the water without them. Besides the law requires them."

"Hell, they can't drown me, he chorted out his logic why worry about breaking a boating law when you're violating anyway?"

Harry laughed heartily, "Guess you're right there. See you later."

Meeting the Glasco boys later that evening, Harry asked, "How did you do?"

Disgustedly, Bob answered, "Only saw one buck and he was too far to shoot."

Tom interrupted, "Really found a good crossing though. We'll sure get deer there yet this fall. Harry, you don't have to help us load. I know you have a long drive back to Bloomington. You go ahead."

To which Harry said, "Yeah, about 300 miles. See you fellows next month."

On November 12, Harry tried a new approach by hunting before contacting Bob. He shot several squirrels along the old railroad grade thinking, "I'll have an excuse to get into Bob's freezer again." As luck would have it, as he approached his truck, an old car came wheeling down the logging road.

It was Tom. "What are you doing in here Harry?"

"I just shot a couple of squirrels and then was going to stop and see you guys."

"Bob's working right here. Hear that chainsaw? He's logging now and should be out in a few minutes. I'm here to pick him up. Wait here. I'll be right back."

When they returned Harry was cleaning the squirrels. "How's things going, Bob?"

"Great. I've been thinking of you. The huntings been so good we've got everyone filled up. Had you stopped in I could have given you some. I believe we've killed at least 18 deer this year. Come on over to the house."

Upon arrival, Bob unlocked the door and all entered a very icy trailer. "We don't have heat or lights yet. Damn pipes are all froze too. Guess it don't make much difference. We finally drove a well but don't have any electricity to run the pump. We've just been too busy hunting."

Mindy arrived and the rattling of dishes promised supper.

Bob pointed at the three dogs milling around, "I thought we were going to get rid of at least one of these dumb dogs. They are eating us out of house and home. Tom, why don't you take that one out and shoot it right now?"

"Okay." Picking up a piece of rope hanging on the wall he unceremoniously tied it around the dog's neck and dragged him to the door nonchalantly lifting the .22 rifle off the nails above the door. With the slamming of the door the dog was dragged toward the woods.

"Good riddance," snorted Bob.

"Guess I should bring you up to date Harry. We've been busy butchering. Killed everything except Floozy, our heifer. We've been butchering deer too." He began naming names and places where they had delivered deer. "We have three in a deep freeze in Ladysmith. My folk's freezer is full as well as Tim's and mine. Gave my neighbor lady a deer. She carried that damn deer a half at a time home across the fields. I also got two for Sam Berger."

Harry's mind was racing, trying desperately to remember.

Mindy brought on the supper featuring canned venison. After the sumputious meal, Bob was in an unusually cheerful mood as he leaned his chair back and said, "I'm going to tell you something I have told very few others. I found a cave in the Blue Hills a few years ago. Damndest thing you ever saw. My father knew where it was and told me how to get there. It's miles back in the woods. I wandered around that country for several days before I finally found it. You just would not believe. There are five Indian bodies in there. Well, Indians or some other ancient men. They're sealed in beeswax or something like it. Four of them are laying in a row with the fifth laying across the others. Sam Berger and I broke through the beeswax and took some artifacts. There were some gold figurines in the head area. Between the bodies were some spears and knives with copper heads, and some shields. The shields are rotted and crumble at the touch. You can see their outline though."

Harry interjected, "My God, you've got the find of a life time. You're not putting me on?"

"Honest Harry, everything I'm telling you is the gospel. Sam and I checked with an expert in Minneapolis who said the artifacts are valuable. In fact, we sold him some. He's an attorney. Has lot's of money. Gave me $7,000 for 17 pieces. I'm going to use the money to build a house. Harry, it's the damndest thing I've ever laid eyes too."

"How big is this cave?"

"The opening is small, about five feet high and three feet wide. It's really deep though. At first it goes down hill and then levels off. I explored it once laying a fish line as I went in so I couldn't get lost. It's 681 feet deep. The bodies are located about 160 feet deep from the entrance. They are laying on a sort of raised area in the soil. It's very strange. I've never seen any animal tracks in the soil. It's been about four years since I first found it and you can still see my tracks from then. Gives you a very scary feeling to be in there. I'm afraid to return. Some artificats are still encrusted around the bodies that Sam and I couldn't get loose. I don't think I'll go back. Anyway I have the $7,000 in a lock box in the Ladysmith bank. That way they can't check on me and make me pay taxes."

Tom came stomping into the house. Bob did not mention the cave further.

"Well, your dog has been taken care of. How many deer do you think we actually killed this fall?"

Bob picked up a pencil stub and an old envelope and began a tally. "It won't be hard to figure out." Together they counted by recounting the place and circumstances of each kill. Bob finally reached a final tally. "It was exactly 21 and it took us 37 shots to get them. Three were fawns, the rest adults. We only wounded three. Would say two of them lived, but that one died for sure."

Tom calculated that they had gotten at least 1,200 pounds of meat and concluded it cost approximately $6 per trip whether successful or not. "You know Harry, we only killed one near home. We're true conservationists. Ha! Sure had some sleepless nights. But a lot of fun, hey Bob."

"Really a successful fall. We should keep the overhead down though. I think next fall when someone wants a deer we sould collect $6 and the cost of shells in advance. You should have been with us, Harry."

"Well, I suppose you are done hunting for the fall."

"Hell no. I have an order for 2 more bucks for Henry Papinske, he won't be able to hunt much during the gun season. I don't know if I can afford to hunt. Let's see, figuring a license and rental of a gun for Mindy plus a license for me and at least $5 for gas. I will need about $28. Maybe I could borrow the $5 for gas and kill a buck to sell during deer season."

Harry jumped at the opportunity. "You know, my buddy, Paul Woodman would be happy to buy one from you."

"Yeah, he's the guy you had here once. Can't hunt much as I recall. Can't walk."

"Yeah, he has a lung problem."

Mindy interrupted. "Bob, go down to dad's place and pick up some meat for tomorrow."

Harry accompanied Bob and when the freezer door was opened it was obviously packed full to the point of falling out.

Bob gloated. "All venison Harry. Quite a fall." Harry told Bob he was going to hunt partridge and squirrels the following day and would stop and see him at his woods job.

As Harry was leaving, he heard the group planning a picnic where they were to steal some traps at Missionary Point on Lake Namekagon. They knew where the traps were hanging in an old building. The traps were to be sold to finance the hunting season.

The following afternoon Harry walked into the logging job and met Bob busily sawing up some trees. Seeing Harry, he immediately shut the chainsaw down and sat down on the tree trunk to talk.

Harry led right off. "Are you going hunting tonight? You mentioned selling a deer. My boss still wants one. If you plan on hunting, I will wait over an extra night. Otherwise I'm heading out for Bloomington right now."

Bob thought briefly, "I'm pretty tired, but we'll bring you a deer tonight. Where will you be staying?"

"I will be at the Ranch Motel in Ladysmith. If you get one, bring it right down there, room four. How much is the deer going to cost?"

"How about $20?"

"Okay. That's reasonable. Remember Paul wants one for deer season too."

"Yeah, shouldn't have any trouble getting him one. I've still got five nights to hunt. Want to come over for supper? I'm sure Mindy will have it on when I get home. I'm calling it a day now."

"No thanks, I'm tired and want to get back to the motel, take a shower and relax."

As he left, Bob waved, "We'll be knocking on your door tonight."

Harry returned to the motel thankful to get some sleep. Shortly after midnight, there was a loud pounding on the door, shaking Harry out of a deep sleep. Stumbling around and finally reaching the light and the door, Harry opened it to find Bob and Tom standing in the darkness.

Bob stepped into the room. "We've got a deer for you. Come get dressed; we'll put it right in your truck."

Harry slipped on some clothing and stepped into the bitter cold night with them. Smiling Bob opened the car trunk exposing the deer, a freshly killed large doe with the steam billowing out of her carcass into the cold November air. Tom snatched the deer out of the rear of Bob's car and slid it onto a canvas in Harry's camper. Returning to the room, Bob helped himself to some food Harry had left on the table. "Been thinking about the price. Guess $20 will be enough." Upon accepting the money, he commented, "That's actually $2 too much. I will buy you a drink some day."

"Will you still get a deer for Paul?"

"No problem. We've still got five nights to hunt. We will pin its eyeballs shut with a clothes pin. That keeps the eyeballs from sinking back. Them damn wardens always look at that. They can tell if a deer is killed before the season. They just can't prove it. Tim gouges the eyeballs out and puts in glass ones. They really look natural. When will you pick up the deer?"

"Paul and I will stop the Friday evening before the season."

After washing their hands in the bathroom, the Glasco boys waved Harry good-by. "See you Friday."

As soon as they were gone, Harry drove to Rice Lake and turned the deer over to Warden Owen Anderson, and drove the 200 miles home to Lodi thankful for a couple of days rest.

As promised, Paul and Harry stopped at Bob's place again on Friday evening.

Mindy swung the door wide. "Come on in Harry. Who's your friend?"

"This is my brother-in-law, Paul Woodman."

"Oh yes, Bob mentioned him."

"Where's Bob?"

"He's still working - still cutting logs."

Knowing that identification of all the people Bob had mentioned was vital, Harry questioned her about them. Mindy was very cooperative and finally Harry had all the names straight in his mind along with where they lived. "Did you do any good this week?"

"Yeah. We got a buck last night. It's out in Floozy's stall right now. Tom and Bob are going out again tonight."

"Where did they get the buck?"

"Up on GG near Mellen. You know where they got those other two. By the way did you ever meet Bill Brickson? He got a beautiful 10 point buck today. You know he's the fellow Bob worked with on the survey crew."

"I never met him but believe Bob mentioned his name. He started the season a little early too."

Mindy lapsed into a spell of complaining about how Bob's friends and relatives took advantage of him. "He furnishes everyone in this country venison and whenever they get a chance they beat him on every deal he gets involved in. Bob is too guillible. I kicked George Rensis out the other night. He was trying to talk Bob into going back up into that old cave to get some of those artifacts. We got what we wanted. The less known about it the better. It's a serious offense to rob Indian graves. I believe the only Indians that wrapped their dead in wax were the Aztecs and they were not supposed to be this far north."

"Have you ever seen the cave?"

"No, but I saw the artifacts."

"What do you think is keeping Bob?"

"He's probably over at his mother's BS-ing. Why don't you walk over and see?"

Harry and Paul walked through the fall darkness, crawling under the fence separating the two places. Noticing a light in the barn they entered to the mellow sound of milk squirting into the foamy liquid in a bucket, as Tom milked one of their two cows.

"Hey Tom, looks like you're earning your keep."

"Yeah, this is hard work. You should see what's in Floozy's stall."

"Mindy told us. We'll take a look."

"Go ahead." The stall contained a slick buck, his seven point rack tied with binder twine to the ceiling joist.

"Really a nice deer Tom. We're waiting for Bob. Leaving the barn they heard Bob's old car rattle into his driveway so they returned.

"Hi Harry, good to see you, got a deer for Paul."

"Just took a look at it. It's a nice buck. Let's get it, we're in kind of hurry."

Following Bob as he led the way to the barn, Harry's mind wandered to the meeting at the armory in Hayward earlier today. Area Warden Supervisor Larry Miller handed out assignments among the twenty-two apprehensive,

eager wardens gathered. Omar Stavlo - Ladysmith, Lynn Thompson - Winter, Milt Dieckman - Hayward, Max Harter-Grantsburg, Owen Anderson-Rice Lake, Jerry Wagner-Amery, Ken Larkin- Chippewa Falls, Jim Flanigan - Webster, Glenn Chaffee- Luck, Art Schoeder - Eau Claire, Ed Nelson - Minong, George Phillips - Drummond, Tom White - Solon Springs, Area Warden Joe Pelikan - Eau Claire, District Wardens Bill Barton - Eau Claire, and Earle Gingles - Spooner, Safety Specialists, Larry Keith - Eau Claire and Bill Hoyt - Spooner and Special Warden Rex Schultz. "We have a number of search

194

warrants to serve. Twelve in Rusk, Sawyer and Bayfield counties to be exact and of course an arrest warrant for Bob." As Larry allotted the warrants, Harry assisted in the instructions, advising the layout of each search area.

Larry continued, "We'd like to hit these people simultaneously to insure no communication between them. Owen and I will take the arrest warrant. Milt and Max can team up, Ken you take Art with you" and so the assignments continued. "Harry, is it my understanding Paul and you will return to Madison?"

"Yeah, soon as we get the last deer. See you tonight. Good luck."

Noticing his pacing Bob jolted Harry back to reality. "Come on Tom give us a hand,

Harry is in a hurry." Tom joined them near the stall. Bob, opened his jackknife and cut the deer down. Each took two legs and carried it toward Harry's truck. As they neared the truck a car starled them, bumping laboriously into Glasco's drive. Bob yelled, "Quick throw it in the truck" The deer was hustled into the truck with Tom quickly slamming the door. The neighbor Henry Papinske waved to Bob, "Hi, what's going on?"

"Man, you scared the hell out of us. We have a deer in Harry's truck. Come take a look." The door was opened and all admired the deer. Impatient, Harry said, "Pay the man Paul and let's get going."

"How much do I owe you?"

Tom fidgeted with his feet for some time. "How about $30. Is that too much?"

"No that's all right." Paul put the money into Bob's nervously outstretched hand. Looking embarrassed he did not mention the extra $10 asked. quickly stuffing it into his pocket. "Thanks, sure you fellows don't want to join us for supper?"

Harry answered, No thanks, not tonight. We'll see you soon though, thinking, *yeah, in court.*

They drove swiftly to the gravel pit where the wardens were meeting. The deer was marked and turned over to Owen Anderson.

The team immediately moved out through the inky blackness to serve the warrants. Every search, but one, was successful with hundreds of pounds of illegal venison seized and arrests made.

Jerry Wagner mistakenly stopped at one residence. Before he realized his mistake, the man present produced illegal venison. Later he was to say. "Never look a gift horse in the mouth. We took him."

Bob and Tom immediately arrested, plead not guilty to all charges. People in the area were shaken at the magnitude of the raid and numbers of deer killed.

All twelve persons charged beyond Bob and Tom Glasco immediately posted bond or pleaded guilty to a multitute of charges. Large penalities were levied. A very good conclusion to a long hard and unusual effort covering a year of investigative work.

Bob Glasco was livid with rage at what had happened to him and the sneaky way Harry had approached him in his home. Mindy further frustrated him picking this time to leave. Rumors circulated that Bob was out to get Harry. Everyone including Harry took the threats with a grain of salt. Many wardens have been threatened thoughout the years. Very seldom do people follow through with such threats.

Meanwhile Harry made contacts with the Madison headquarters and told the intriguing story of the cave. The Department of Natural Resources felt it would be worth an attempt to locate the cave as it may be an important archaeological find. A decision was made to try for information from Bob while charges were still pending against him.

Warden Omar Stavlo contacted the Rusk County District Attorney at Ladysmith who agreed to cooperate in the endeavor. The two Glasco's had agreed to change their pleas to guilty. A meeting was arranged at the courthouse in Ladysmith on the day of their court appearance. Attending were Harry, Omar Stavlo, Lynn Thompson, the warden from Winter, and Bob's attorney.

The District Attorney, James Perry, led off by telling Bob they would like to have his cooperation in finding the cave.

"What's in it for me? I know where it's located."

The D.A. proceeded cautiously. "Tell me about the cave, what it looks like, and what's in it."

"The opening is about five feet in height and three feet wide. When you enter you go down a ways and then it levels off. The furthest I've been in was 681 feet, I measured it with a fish line. We found some Indian bodies encased in beeswax."

At that James interrupted. "You said we. Then there was someone with you?"

"Yeah, Sam Berger and I went in together. The bodies were located on a sort of raised area in the cave. We took some artifacts. Some of them were made of gold. I sold them to an attorney in Minneapolis."

James droppd the bait. "Bob, we are in a position to offer you amnesty on any crimes that were committed in an around that cave, providing you cooperate in leading the authorities to the cave."

"I don't want to get other people involved."

"We will offer amnesty to anyone else involved as well." Bob's attorney encouraged him to make a clean breast of things and clear the air once and for all.

Bob sighed thoughtfully, "It will take me a few days to clean some things out of the cave before I will take anyone in." Under repeated questioning, he said, "I have some things in there that I don't want anyone to see."

Perry countered, "If it's something illegal as I've told you before we are prepared to offer you and anyone else involved amnesty. I have also personally talked to the federal attorney's office and they also have agreed to offer amnesty should any federal crimes be uncovered."

"Okay. I have some munitions in the cave. There are several cases of dynamite, some plastic explosives, detonators, fuses, two M-14 rifles and at least 1,000 rounds of ammunition. If you give me amnesty on this, I will take you out to it."

"You can be assured we will grant amnesty for all crimes, federal and state. Now, you have nothing to lose. However, it's court time. Let's go."

In the court proceedings, both Bob and Tom changed their pleas on all counts to no contest and were found guilty by the court. A presentence investigation was ordered with sentencing to follow.

Plans were quickly made to grab a sandwich at a local cafe and go look for the cave before Bob changed his mind.

In the restaurant, Bob came to Harry. "Could I make a telephone call?"

""We don't have time."

Bob became very agitated. "It's very important I make this call. Important for you, Harry."

"What do you mean Bob? Tell me the nature of the call and perhaps I will let you make it."

Hesitantly, Bob began. "If someone asks you if you want a job done for you and you say yes, I want the job done and then that person changes his mind and doesn't want the job to come off. Well, if he can't use the phone to call if off, it will come off right?"

This alarmed Harry. "Are you trying to tell us that you have arranged for something to happen to someone, me for instance?"

"I'm not saying any more Harry, but let me make the call."

After a hurried conference, it was decided they would let him make the call. Wardens Stavlo and Thompson took Bob to a pay phone. Not having change, Lynn gave him his state credit card to make the call, thinking the call would be easier to trace.

Bob dialed and with Lynn and Omar within earshot said, "Let me speak to the alcoholic." A pause, "I've changed my mind. I don't want to go through with the plans we talked about - You know the deal down near Madison. Call it off. Okay!" And hung up.

Omar immediately reported to Harry. "It appears the hit is called off. It also seems that is just what he had planned too. I believe they call Chuck Dodge, the alcoholic."

One of the Rusk County Deputy Sheriffs volunteered information that he knew Dodge who is Bob's brother-in-law. "He was in prison for murder and he killed a fellow with a crowbar while in stir. Very dangerous. He's out on parole now."

Meanwhile Omar continued to question Bob in the squad car. "Why are you so interested in getting even with Harry? After all he was just doing his job."

He babbled in fury, "Harry is a sneaky S.O.B. Don't believe what he did to me is right. He violated with me. He came right into my home and we welcomed him like part of the family. Mindy even left me because of Harry. He hurt me and damn it, I'm going to hurt back. They're others around here that caused me a lot of problems too. I'm going to get even with every damn one of them."

Omar querried, "What did the others do to you?"

"They turned me in. That's how Harry knew what I was doing. That's why I put those munitions in the cave. I'll get even, Omar, you wait and see."

"Where did you get the guns and explosives?"

"Oh, up at the Indian reservation, from some Indians."

"You mean La Court Oreilles?"

"Yeah. They're pretty well armed you know. Anyway I don't have anything to live for any more. I'll get even. I'll terrorize the western half of Rusk and Sawyer counties. I'll burn, bomb, cut timbers on railroad trestles, and dump trains in rivers. They will all be sorry for what they did to me." He was very agitated his voice trembling with emotion.

Omar directed the conservation while he had Bob talking so well. "How was this hit to come off?"

Bob shrugged, "Hell, might as well tell. You know most of it anyway. A friend of mine has some contacts in Chicago. He made arrangements with these people to do a job on Harry. At first I wanted Harry killed but my friend talked me out of it. He said there are worse things than death. Those guys are experts. He said we'll have them go to Harry's house and beat him with baseball bats. Break his knees and elbows. Hurt him a long time for what he did. So I agreed."

"You must have offered to pay for Harry's hit. The people you describe don't do things like that for nothing."

"Yeah, I gave them $5,000 of the money I had in the safe deposit box in the Ladysmith bank. It's part of the $7,000 I got for the artifacts. I've no other use for the money now anyway."

When asked who was involved, Bob immediately clammed up. Omar suggested, "You better tell Harry everything and make it as easy as possible for yourself." After his rage had passed, he repeated what he had said to Harry.

A quick disucssion was held. Is he telling the truth? Such an outlandish story is difficult to believe. Finally Harry approached Bob again, "Would you be agreeable to taking a lie detector test?"

There was no hesitation. "Sure, I'm telling you the truth.

Harry called the Madison Headquarters and talked to the Deputy Chief of Enforcement, Harold Hettrick. Harold agreed a lie detector test should be given and agreed to make arrangements with the Eau Claire Police Department for the test. Harry, concerned with his home and family, was not convinced the hit had been called off. The Lodi Police and the Columbia County Sheriff were called. An around the clock watch was placed on their house after the house was searched by wardens Larry Miller and Jim Chizek. Mrs. Borner (Arlene) had earlier left to stay at a friend's house that evening. The police intercepted Harry's daughter who was enroute to Lodi and diverted her.

At about 4 p.m., Harry, Omar and Lynn left with Bob for Eau Claire. Harry, still concerned, questioned Bob further about the hit.

He was very quiet and thoughtful, finally he ventured. "You know Harry the people we're talking about are very dangerous and I'm afraid to talk about it. One of them has already killed a couple of guys and I may be next if he finds out I'm talking to you like this." Through the conversation it became apparent without a straightforward admission that the person Bob had called was indeed Chuck Dodge. Bob admitted people called him the alcoholic.

After two hours of driving they reached the Eau Claire police department where polygraph operator David Backstrom was waiting. Harry told the operator they were principally interested in knowing whether there had been a hit planned, if so had it been called off and was Bob telling the truth about the cave.

During the course of the polygraph testing, the operator had Bob make a phone call to ascertain if the hit had been called off. Bob dialed and Harry listened as he said, "Hello. Is this Irene? (Chuck Dodge is married to Bob's sister Irene.) I want to talk to Chuck." After a pause, he said, "Chuck, were you able to call it off?"" a pause. Sure glad to hear that. I pled guilty on all counts, might as well get it out of the way. Are you sure you could call it off? I've even taken a lie detector test. They know all about it. I'm sure am glad you got it called off."

After the call, Harry being satisfied the hit had been called off, called Harold who cancelled the police watch.

Later while talking to Backstrom, the polygraph operator, Harry was assured that Bob was a very good subject for the lie test and everything he said was true about the hit and that it had been called off. When questioned about the cave, Backstrom said Bob had also told the truth about it.

Subsequently many attempts to locate the cave were made. Bob failed to cooperate. After serving a long jail sentence, he left Wisconsin for the east coast. Other persons supposedly having information about the cave were contacted without success. Many unsuccessful attempts were made to find it. Without Bob's help, the cave could not be located and the location remains a mystery.

In 1978, at the age of 49, Harry passed away in his home at Lodi, Wisconsin.

Chapter 21

So Ended the Lives of Two Persons

This report was written by Game Warden Ed Apel, new deceased, recalling and describing an incident near Marinette, WI.

Ed became a warden in 1917 and retired in 1937.

On May 22, 1923 while Apel was returning from the bayshore at Marinette the sheriff, Oscar Dahl, overtook Apel and asked him. "Have you got a gun with you?" Apel replied "No"; Dahl says to Apel, "Get in my car I will take you home so you can get one." Apel replied, "O.K. but what's wrong?" to which the sheriff replied. "John Holt just killed the Undersheriff, I want you to get John Holt". The sheriff drove Apel to his home which was near by.

Apel took his 30-30 rifle and Lugar. The sheriff than drove with Apel to the scene of the shooting.

A large crowd had gathered by this time but all had taken refuge behind buildings waiting and watching for what might happen next. The fire department had been called. They attempted to take Holt with water but Holt opened fire with his .22 rifle. One bullet striking the hose near the hand of the fireman that was holding it, upon which the chief fireman recalled his men stating "he was not going to have any of his men killed that way."

Holt was barricaded in his home, a one story L shaped tar paper shack and continued to fire in the general direction of the crowd, until he discovered Apel in the road in front of the house. When he directed his fire toward Apel shooting by guess and by God as there were no windows on that side of the house that faced the road. By this time the sheriff had become impatient and called to Apel from a distance, "Start shooting and get Holt". However, Apel replied, "Give him a chance, perhaps he will surrender." Apel than called to a neighbor of Holts and told him to call Holt to come out and surrender or be shot. "We will wait five minutes." However, this request was greeted by more rifle fire from Holt. When the five minutes were up the sheriff called again, "Start shooting, the five minutes are up." Several times little clouds of dust in the road not to far from Apel showed where some of Holts bullet were hitting. His by guess shooting at times was not bad. By this time Apel had begun shooting, shooting through the higher part of the house hoping that Holt would realize that further resistance was hopeless and it would be better to come out and surrender. But do doubt Holt had decided not to be taken alive as he continued to fire. The sheriff for the third time called to Apel to open fire and get Holt. Where upon Apel opened fire, starting on one end of the building shooting into the building about eighteen inches from the floor at about fifteen inch intervals, across the side of building; than raising eighteen inches higher and again covering nearly the entire side of the house, when the police captain came rushing up to Apel saying, "I think you got him as there is no more shooting from the house," so Apel and the captain circled the building reaching the door which was bolted but which they crashed and entered.

Holt was sitting on the floor dead, still holding his .22 rifle in his hands. One rifle bullet of Apel's 30-30 had entered his body just below the right arm passing through his heart and body. The body of Emmet Butts lay outside just beneath the window. In front of Holt was a small bench on which Holt had piled his ammunition, six hundred .22 shells, on the floor were fifty six empty .22 shells which he had fired.

The trouble started when the undersheriff attempted to serve a warrant on Holt, who saw the undersheriff coming, entered the house and bolted the door. When the undersheriff rapped at the door Holt shot him from the window, than came out of the house, stood over the undersheriff and shot him three times more.

So ended the lives of two persons on a Monday morning.

Signed / Ed Apel

ORDER FORM

Game Warden Centurion

Sold To: _____

_____

_____

Number of Books _____ @ $12.95 (Tax Included) = _____

Shipping & Handling _____$3.45_____

Total in U.S. Funds _____

Send Orders To: **Flambeau River Publishing**
W10298 Wells Road
Lodi, Wisconsin 53555
or
Call (608) 592-3752